SILENCE and DEMOCRACY

SILENCE and DEMOCRACY

Athenian Politics in Thucydides' *History*

JOHN ZUMBRUNNEN

The Pennsylvania State University Press
University Park, Pennsylvania

Library of Congress
Cataloging-in-Publication Data

Zumbrunnen, John.
Silence and democracy : Athenian politics in Thucydides' history / John Zumbrunnen.
           p.   cm.
Includes bibliographical references and index.
ISBN 978-0-271-03358-7 (pbk : alk. paper)
1. Democracy—Greece—Athens—History—To 1500.
2. Political participation—Greece—Athens—History—To 1500.
3. Thucydides. History of the Peloponnesian War.
4. Athens (Greece)—Politics and government.
I. Title.

JC75.D36Z86 2008
320.938'5—dc22
2007043310

Copyright © 2008
The Pennsylvania State University
All rights reserved
Printed in the United States of America
Published by The Pennsylvania State University Press,
University Park, PA 16802-1003

The Pennsylvania State University Press
is a member of the
Association of American University Presses.

It is the policy of
The Pennsylvania State University Press to use
acid-free paper. This book is printed on stock that
meets the minimum requirements
American National Standard for Information
Sciences—Permanence of Paper for Printed Library Material,
ANSI Z39.48–1992.

CONTENTS

ACKNOWLEDGMENTS vii
INTRODUCTION 1

1 Athenian *Stasis* and the Quiet of the Mob 27

2 The Silence of *Hoi Athenaioi*:
Two Modes of Athenian Action in the *History* 45

3 Deliberative Action and Athenian "Character" 71

4 The Silence of the Demos and the Challenges of Political Judgment: On the "Decline" of Athenian Politics 95

5 Justice and Empire: Athenian Silence and the Representation of Athens Abroad 125

6 Athenian Silence and the Fate of Plataea 157

Conclusion: Thucydides for Democrats? 181

BIBLIOGRAPHY 192
INDEX 198

ACKNOWLEDGMENTS

This book has its deepest roots in a short paper I wrote for Mary Dietz's seminar in ancient political thought at the University of Minnesota. Something of the spirit of that paper, which I titled "In Defense of Nicias," still survives in these pages. And so I first thank Mary for nurturing my interest in Thucydides and for sharing her wisdom for many years now. Thanks, too, to others at Minnesota who offered feedback on my work. They include Jim Farr, Terence Ball, Sandra Peterson, Norman Bowie, Andrew Seligsohn, Laura Janara, Rob Geroux, Paul Soper, and Catherine Guisan-Dickinson. Special thanks to John Transue, Dan Hope, Sam Chambers, John Bies, and Ryan Fortson for their friendship.

Union College has provided a wonderful setting in which to work; I am grateful for Union's ample research support and generous junior sabbatical policy. My colleagues in the Political Science Department have provided help in all sorts of ways. From their example I have learned that it is possible to be a scholar while being a teacher. Thanks in particular to Zoe Oxley, Lori Marso, and Richard Fox for their friendship and encouragement. And thanks, too, to my students, on whom I depend for periodic renewals of intellectual curiosity and energy.

I could not have hoped for a better editor than Sandy Thatcher of Penn State Press. Sandy has patiently and thoughtfully seen this book through some quite substantial revisions. I am grateful to him for staying with the project and with me. Thanks also to Peter Euben for offering especially helpful suggestions at a crucial moment.

My parents and siblings have been a constant source of support throughout my life. They have cheered my successes, helped me over the inevitable rough patches, and only occasionally wondered how someone could be so fascinated by Thucydides. As I turn the page on this project, it seems fitting to make special mention of my father, who saw me off to graduate school but did not live to see me finish. He remains a presence in my life and in my heart. I like to think that he knows, somehow, that I am in fact okay.

Special thanks to my youngest collaborators. Abby joined the book project in its earlier stages. Charlie came on at a pivotal moment, ready to oversee submission of the original manuscript. Beyond their many contributions to my writing, I have come to rely on the two of them for beautiful artwork, obscure knock-knock jokes, and the occasional, mostly friendly critique. Ben and Maggie arrived as a team only days before I submitted the final draft and just in time to help with last-minute editing. As I write these words they are sleeping, for which I am especially grateful.

My deepest thanks come last. Amy Gangl started out as a tennis partner and became my partner in everything, for life. She is also my very best friend. More than anyone else, and in many ways, she has made this work possible. As we continue on our amazing and sometimes crazy journey together, she makes my life infinitely richer and makes me a better person in many, many ways.

An earlier version of Chapter 3 appeared as "Democratic Politics and the 'Character' of the City in Thucydides" in *History of Political Thought* 23 (Winter 2002). I am grateful to the editor and publisher for permission to reprint parts of that article here.

Introduction

I. THE SILENCE OF THE DEMOS AND THE MEANING OF DEMOCRACY

Reflecting on the life and career of the great Athenian politician Pericles, Thucydides tells us that during his ascendancy in Athens, "what was in name a democracy [*logō men dēmokratia*] became in actuality rule by the first man [*tou tropou andros archē*]" (2.65).[1] How ought we to understand the political transformation suggested here? As his accounts of *stasis*, especially at Corcyra and Athens, make clear, moments of revolutionary political change hold considerable interest for Thucydides. But those moments as they appear in the *History* involve attempts to change the form of government or, more precisely, attempts to bring about institutional changes that warrant an accompanying change in name. At both Corcyra and Athens, the revolutionaries thus move more or less openly to replace democracy with oligarchy. By comparison, the transformation of Athenian politics under Pericles appears considerably more subtle, one might even say insidious. Here the institutional structure of the city's politics remains the same. The people still hold ultimate political power, exercised most visibly by making decisions in the assembly about what the city will do. Athens remains a democracy not only in name but also in its institutional form. Somehow, though, Pericles has come to exercise a kind of rule or *arche* that Hobbes, Thucydides' first English translator, describes as "monarchical."[2] How might that have come to pass?

Living in a time when nearly everyone claims to be a democrat and nearly every regime claims to be democratic, we are all too familiar with

---

1. Throughout, I cite Thucydides by book, chapter, and (where appropriate) line number. Unless otherwise noted, I draw translations from Lattimore's translation of Thucydides, *The Peloponnesian War*. As the notes indicate, I have made frequent use of Smith's *History of the Peloponnesian War*. I have also relied on the Greek text provided in the Loeb (i.e., Smith) edition.
2. Hobbes, "On the Life and History of Thucydides."

the tendency of democracy to become merely nominal. In America in the early years of the twenty-first century, mass politics seems particularly susceptible to the subtly developing dominance of a centralized elite that, somewhat like Pericles, renders the meaning of democracy suspect precisely as it claims to be protecting democracy at home and democracy's interests abroad. We are no doubt more likely to be troubled by this sort of undermining of democracy than the author of the *History*. At least on a theoretical level, contemporary democrats will likely not share Thucydides' apparent approval of the Periclean transformation of Athenian politics. Elsewhere in the passage with which I began—the so-called "eulogy of Pericles"—Thucydides clearly rates the dominance of a single elite more highly than the struggle for power that he says followed Pericles' death. We are unlikely to agree with that judgment, even if we recognize the pathologies of Athenian democratic politics that perhaps help account for the disasters the city later suffers. We are even less likely to share Thucydides' admiration for the moderate oligarchy of the five thousand, which briefly replaces Athenian democracy in both name and form late in the war. In the end, though, these disagreements with Thucydides' own political judgments ought not to obscure the possibility that he may have something to teach us about democracy. As Arlene Saxonhouse has it, we must set about "learning about democracy from Thucydides rather than just portraying him as antidemocratic."[3] Most immediately here, whatever its author's political commitments, the *History* may have something to contribute to a central critical task of contemporary democratic theory: determining when—and how—democracy comes to exist in name alone and, by extension, what mass democracy that is more than merely nominal might look like. In this book I aim to recover the *History* as a resource for exploring these questions. As the title I have chosen suggests, doing so will require grappling with the role of silence in Thucydides' account of Athenian politics.

The idea of a political transformation amounting to a move away from democracy absent overt institutional changes resonates not only with contemporary political experience, but also with contemporary arguments that we ought not to understand democracy as a form of government at all. Sheldon Wolin's claims along these lines have been especially influential. Wolin describes democracy not as a particular sort of political constitution that might (or might not) endure through time, but rather as an "experience" that unsettles all forms of government and that calls into

---

3. Saxonhouse, *Athenian Democracy*, 152n1.

question political "boundaries" that aim to "domesticate." He insists that democracy is in this way a "rebellious moment," one that is intimately connected to revolution understood as "the wholesale transgression of inherited forms." "Revolutions," he writes, "activate the demos and destroy boundaries that bar access to political experience."[4] Wolin in fact describes the development of Athenian politics in the fifth century BCE as a series of revolutionary moments in which the demos gradually asserted its full power. Surveying these claims and similar arguments by Jacques Rancière and others, Pachen Markell describes them all as focusing on "the uncomfortable fit between democracy and rule" or *arche*.[5] That is, from this perspective, the imposition of any form of rule marks a diminution of the formless experience of democracy. Conversely, the mere presence of a particular type of constitution or a particular set of institutions may not in fact indicate the presence of democracy.

We might well draw on this notion of democracy as a political moment independent of and likely in tension with any institutional form for a preliminary understanding of what happens when Pericles comes to dominate politics in Thucydides' Athens. According to the eulogy, Pericles apparently managed to impose a kind of rule or *arche* on Athenian politics that co-opted the potential activation of the demos otherwise allowed by existing Athenian institutions. Athenian politics thus became something other than democracy, though its outward form and its name remained the same. Thucydides' explicit analysis of Pericles' "rule by the first man" adds credence to this reading. According to Thucydides, Pericles exercised a "free control" over the Athenians and so was able to lead them instead of being led (2.65). Rather than "speak to please in order to acquire power," Pericles stood before the assembled demos and confronted its worst political inclinations. When they were "arrogantly confident," he "shocked them into a state of fear." When they were "unreasonably afraid," he "restored them to confidence." Using Wolin's terms, we might say that Pericles, on Thucydides' telling, was able at various points to "domesticate" the rebellious instincts of the demos.[6] Driven by a desire for power,

---

4. Wolin, "Fugitive Democracy," 38. See also Wolin's "Norm and Form"; and the responses to Wolin's view of democracy collected in Botwinick and Connolly, *Democracy and Vision*.

5. Markell, "The Rule of the People." See in particular Rancière's "Ten Theses on Politics" and *On the Shores of Politics*. In chapter 6 of the latter work, Rancière draws on Thucydides' summary comment on Pericles' *arche* in a way that bears some similarity to my use of the passage here. See also Hardt and Negri, *Multitiude*.

6. In the *Gorgias*, 515d–516d, Plato has Socrates offer a much harsher view of Pericles' influence on the Athenians, saying he was "not a good statesman" because he "made his charges

Pericles' would-be successors did not—dared not, one supposes—"contradict" the Athenians as Pericles could and did. Athenian politics descended into a struggle for influence among contentious elites. Where Thucydides laments the consequent "handing over [of] affairs to the people's pleasure" (2.65), we might well see a potentially democratic if perhaps still modest [re]activation of the demos. On Pericles' death, neither the form nor the appellation of Athenian politics changed; but democracy again became something more than merely nominal as the actual relationship between demos and elites changed.[7]

Thucydides' narrative at times complicates the seemingly unambiguous conclusions he offers in the sort of authorial comment I have been examining so far. At various points in later chapters, I will in fact argue that Pericles' relationship with the Athenians is not as exceptional as Thucydides' eulogy of him suggests. Indeed, read in a certain way, aspects of the eulogy itself call into question the idea of Pericles' exceptionality. Still, if we turn—as we almost inevitably do—to the moments in which he speaks before the Athenian assembly, we find seeming support for the idea that Periclean politics involved a sort of de facto deactivation of Athenian democracy. That support comes in the form of two sorts of silence, one relatively familiar and straightforward, the other more complex, harder to grasp, and so—ultimately—more interesting.

First, whenever Thucydides records Pericles' words in the *History*, he records *only* Pericles' words, rendering silent the voices of any other would-be speakers. In the case of two of the three Periclean speeches he includes in the *History*, Thucydides suggests that all the Athenians except Pericles remained silent. In introducing Pericles' famous Funeral Oration, he thus tells us that the Athenians, in accordance with ancestral custom, chose Pericles as the one speaker they would hear (2.34). As for Pericles' final appearance, Thucydides says that Pericles himself called an assembly to respond to the Athenians' growing unease about the war and their

---

fiercer than when he took them on" and that as a result the Athenians became "more vicious and less good." This assessment, though, rests on an understanding of Pericles' relationship with the demos similar to Thucydides' notion of "free control." Socrates thus compares Pericles to those "in charge of asses or horses or cattle," saying that Pericles was "in charge of men."

7. A note is in order here regarding my use of the term demos. In Greek usage, the term can refer to the people as a whole or, more specifically, to the common people or the poor. As my reading of Thucydides will make clear, I use the term in a similarly complex way. At times (as in the present paragraph) the demos stands as the mass of ordinary citizens juxtaposed to the vocal political elite whose speeches Thucydides records. At other times—when Thucydides records no speeches—the demos in a sense expands to include all Athenians. As I suggest in Chapter 2, Thucydides uses the term *hoi Athenaioi* in a similarly complex way.

anger at him; so far as we can tell from the *History*, no one else was given the opportunity to speak at this assembly. On the other hand, when Pericles first speaks in the *History*—late in book 1, where he lays out his strategy for the impending war—the absence of other voices seems clearly the product of an authorial decision. Describing the Athenian assembly called to respond to Sparta's ultimate demand that Athens "let the Hellenes be independent" or face war, Thucydides writes that "there were many speakers who came forward and gave their support to one side or the other." But, again, he records only the words of Pericles, "the first man of his time at Athens" (1.139). For the reader, the result is the effective if not the literal silencing of voices other than that of Pericles.[8]

The actual silence or textual silencing of other voices when Pericles speaks stands in contrast to Thucydides' reliance elsewhere in the *History* on paired speeches by contending speakers. When the Athenians consider how to deal with their rebellious imperial subjects in the city of Mitylene, Thucydides allows into his work the words of both Cleon and Diodotus; in describing the assembly at which the Athenians make the ultimately disastrous decision to sail for Sicily, he records the arguments of both Nicias and Alcibiades. Whatever else the presence of contending speakers may tell us about Athenian politics in these moments, it throws into sharp relief Pericles' repeated solo appearances in the *History*. One can hardly avoid concluding that Thucydides crafts the silence of potential opponents as a way to emphasize Pericles' temporary political dominance and the consequent reduction of democracy to a hollow name for Athenian institutions.[9]

In short, what I will here call the *silence of contending voices* does indeed seem to distinguish the time of Pericles' ascendancy from other moments of Athenian politics. It is worth noting that Thucydides actually has Pericles offer what we might read as an explanation for the singularity of his own voice in Athenian politics. Describing Athenian political practice in the Funeral Oration, Pericles claims that "wherever each man has earned recognition he is singled out for public service in accordance with the

---

8. We might also note that Thucydides in effect treats the assembly as the only site of democratic politics in the city of Athens. He does not, that is, take us to the other places where the demos might appear more vocal and active: the law courts, the *deme* assemblies, the agora. This privileging of the assembly and of a small number of speeches made therein only heightens the sense of the silence of the demos.

9. Monoson and Loriaux, "The Illusion of Power," 286, similarly note that the fact that Pericles is "the only speaker of the *History* whose words are never disputed by those of an adversary" has led many readers to elevate him above other Athenian leaders.

claims of distinction" (2.37). He adds that "it is within the capacity of some of us to manage private right along with public business." In short, those who are able to guide the affairs of the city will, in Athens, be recognized and "singled out for public service." By extension, Pericles has so been "singled out," quite literally. As we will see in Chapter 3, Pericles makes this point explicitly in his final speech in the *History*, when he explains to the Athenians in no uncertain terms why they have chosen to follow him. In this sense, the silence of contending voices amounts to a recognition of the merit of the single remaining voice. Along these lines, it is also worth noting that Pericles, before offering his understanding of how the meritorious rise to prominence in Athens, says that "by name [Athens] is called a democracy" (2.37). Here, perhaps, he is hinting obliquely at the conclusion that Thucydides will later draw regarding the true nature of Athenian politics during Pericles' reign.

In any event, beyond Thucydides' emphasis on Periclean control or "rule by the first man," we can readily find abundant contemporary theoretical resources for understanding why the silence of contending voices might render democracy merely nominal. It is surely a basic tenet of democratic faith that silence is inherently undemocratic insofar as it embodies and reflects the exclusion and thus the fundamental political inequality of those who might speak but cannot. What is more, in calling for the reinvigoration of political participation[10] or for the expansion of democratic decision making to the economic realm,[11] important strands of contemporary democratic theory surely emphasize the importance of enabling all citizens to exercise their political voice in a meaningful way. From this perspective, and setting aside the obvious exclusion of women, slaves, and non–Athenian born residents, Thucydides' portrayal of Athenian politics points to the unequal political standing of most of those actually admitted to citizenship.

Beyond this basic denial of a political voice to particular individuals or groups, we might also view the silence of contending voices as reflecting a kind of procedural pathology. For example, the Periclean monologue must seem undemocratic to those who place deliberation at the core of democracy.[12] The unchallenged control over the demos with which Thucydides

10. Here I have in mind, for example, Barber's emphasis on "democratic talk" in *Strong Democracy*.

11. As in Pateman, *Participation and Democracy*. More recently, see Hahnel, *Economic Justice and Democracy*. See also Dahl, *A Preface to Economic Democracy*.

12. As, for example, Fishkin, *Democracy and Deliberation*; Gutmann and Thompson, *Democracy and Disagreement;* and Habermas in (among many other works) "Three Normative Models of Democracy."

credits Pericles—especially given its seemingly emotional foundation—hardly leads to the sort of rational deliberative consensus among diverse and well-articulated points of view that democrats might seek. Yet even if we eschew the idea that democracy demands a particular set of institutions or procedures, the presence of contending voices seems a baseline measure of democratic experience. Thus consider the "agonal" democrats—including Wolin—who have recently challenged the deliberative vision.[13] There seemingly can be no democratic agon—over resources or matters of culture or identity or anything else—when one actor so dominates as Thucydides' Pericles does.

Given that various strands of contemporary democratic theory are appropriately wary of the silence of contending voices, the *History* perhaps has relatively little to add on this score. Thucydides certainly shows no real interest in the apparent lack of actual political voice among the vast majority of individual Athenians. But consider, too, a second sort of silence that seems at first glance to buttress Thucydides' analysis of Periclean dominance. I will refer to this as the *silent presence of the demos*. Most basically, I have in mind the seemingly simple fact that when Pericles speaks, the mass of Athenians remain *collectively* silent. We know that he speaks before mass gatherings of his fellow Athenians, but those assembled as the demos remain utterly silent while he does. Indeed, at the end of each of Pericles' speeches in the *History*, Thucydides either indicates that the assembled Athenians silently decide what to do (as at 1.145 and 2.65) or else simply omits any mention of them and turns to narrate other events (2.47). Because the collective silence of the assembled Athenians at such moments stands as a central puzzle for the remainder of this book, let me at the outset consider three seemingly straightforward yet ultimately unsatisfactory explanations for the collective silence of the demos in such moments.

First, we might well consider the assembled Athenians as a group of individuals each of whom, as a citizen of Athens, might speak but does not. In that sense, their silence amounts to nothing more than the cumulative silencing of many contending voices. Yet even when there are contending voices—as when Cleon clashes with Diodotus or Nicias with Alcibiades—the silent presence of the demos remains. More generally, we might say that Thucydides' practice of reporting some speeches in direct discourse inevitably depicts democratic politics as involving one or more speakers

---

13. Besides Wolin's view of "fugitive democracy" as the periodic activation of the *demos* against elite domination and institutionalized repression, I have in mind here in particular Connolly's description of "agonal" democracy in *Identity/Difference*.

appearing before those who do not speak. Thucydides, that is, depicts Athenian politics (at least in those moments when he records speeches—as I emphasize later, most often Thucydides in recording Athenian actions reports only the silent presence of the Athenians as a whole) as the interaction of a vocal political elite with a silent and largely undifferentiated mass audience. This manner of recording speeches draws our attention to only a few voices. In the case of Pericles' speeches, it draws our attention to a single voice, thus reinforcing the sense of Pericles' special prominence. We tend in turn to neglect the rest of the Athenians. Instead of treating the demos simply as a collection of those who might speak but do not—as those who are part of the mass of ordinary citizens simply because they are not members of the vocal elite—I mean to examine the character and significance of their collective silence on its own terms. Since the demos maintains its silence both when Pericles appears alone and when contending voices sound in the assembly, we must also eventually ask whether and how the significance of that collective silence varies from one moment to the next.

Beyond thinking of the silent presence of the demos as simply embodying the absence of many voices, we might understand it as indicative of a kind of attentive collective listening in preparation for exercising the power of the demos to decide. The mass of citizens, that is, might remain silent as they attend to what those who do speak have to say. Indeed, some theorists have recently stressed the importance of listening as a kind of democratic virtue. Susan Bickford argues that "listening—as part of adversarial communication—is a crucial political activity that enables us to give democratic shape to our being together in the world."[14] However important it may be for some visions of democracy, it seems unlikely that the silent presence of the demos can be explained as this kind of listening. Democratic listening takes place among political equals and stands as part of a respectful give and take. I listen both to deepen my understanding of another's perspective and so that I may be listened to with similar care. There is simply no indication of this sort of mutuality in Thucydides' Athenian politics. In that politics, again, a handful of citizens speak while many others consistently remain silent.

More generally, it is worth emphasizing that silence and listening are not coextensive. Indeed, alongside her careful exploration of the democratic

---

14. Bickford, *The Dissonance of Democracy*, 19. See also Villa's discussion of agonal democracy in *Politics, Philosophy, Terror*; Mouffe, "Democracy, Power, and the Political"; and Honig, *Political Theory and the Displacement of Politics*.

possibilities of listening, Bickford emphasizes that silence "has multiple meanings," some of which stand opposed to listening. Silence may, for example, "reveal an unwillingness to debate, a reluctance to take up another's words."[15] By the same token, one can surely listen without being silent. As Silvia Montiglio has shown, the logocentric culture of the Greeks in particular did not view listening as a silent activity. From the descriptions of gatherings of heroes in the Homeric epics to the fourth-century orators' references to the properly vocal character of their audiences, the Greeks seem to have seen silence as, in Montiglio's words, an "embarrassment" to both speaker and audience rather than as a sign of listeners being "absorbed" in a speaker's words.[16] It is, of course, possible that Thucydides simply had an understanding of listening different from that of most other Greeks and more akin to the idea of listening in rapt silence that Montiglio finds in Roman sources. And I can provide no textual evidence that suggests that the Athenians did not listen to, say, Pericles or Cleon or Nicias. But it seems more likely that Thucydides' way of rendering moments of political speech reflects an understanding of the relationship between the words of elite speakers and the collective silence of the always present demos that cannot be fully captured by the idea of listening. The demos may well listen to speeches, but Thucydides' presentation of it in the *History* as consistently and utterly silent would seem to carry some other, or at least some additional, meaning.

If the collective silence of the demos does not simply indicate an active, engaged listening, does it, then, suggest passivity and hence a kind of irrelevance? The temptation here is to see the silence of the mass of ordinary citizens as evidence of the reduction of democratic politics to the interaction of elites (or with Pericles, again, to the dominance of a single elite actor). We can find theoretical resources for thinking about this way of reading silence, too. Most generally, the notion of "tacit consent"—a central issue for liberal theory since Locke—suggests the possibility of taking mass silence as an indication of support for or at least acquiescence to political decisions or settlements negotiated by elites or imposed by the state.[17]

15. Bickford, *The Dissonance of Democracy*, 154.
16. Montiglio, *Silence in the Land of Logos*, 151–52.
17. Locke's discussion of tacit consent In Chapter VIII itself resonates with the silence of the liberal subject. He thus asks, "How far any one shall be looked on to have consented, and thereby submitted to any form of government, where he has made *no expressions of it at all*" (§119, emphasis added); and he concludes, in part, that simply "living quietly" in a country binds one to obey its laws, though it "makes not a man a member of that society" (§120). Locke, *Second Treatise of Government*.

As a more particular example, debates between the twentieth-century pluralists and their critics rested in part on differing explanations for the "nonparticipation" of nonelites. In his influential study of Appalachian coal-mining communities, John Gaventa thus argued that pluralist accounts of political power assume that all potential grievances are "recognized and acted upon," so that nonparticipation by nonelites reflects either a rational calculation of the costs and benefits of acting or an unspoken consensus on basic values. Gaventa challenged this view with his own reading of the silence of ordinary citizens, concluding that the "quiescence" of Appalachian coal miners flowed from an abiding sense of "powerlessness" brought on by persistent political, economic, and social defeat.[18]

Making no specific reference to tacit consent, underlying consensus, or learned powerlessness, the literature on Thucydides focuses largely on interpreting the words and deeds of the speakers in the *History*, and it does so without much attention to the role of the mass of ordinary citizens. Recent work on the nature of ancient democracy, though, warns us against taking the silence of ordinary citizens as a sign of their disempowerment or irrelevance. Both M. I. Finley and Josiah Ober have argued that the ancient demos was a political force to be reckoned with despite the appearance of elite dominance of ancient politics. Finley sees in the polis a basic problem of political stability. Why should the demos have accepted—as the mass of Thucydides' Athenians seem to have accepted—the prevalence of "spokesmen in the Assembly" drawn solely from the elite group of the politically active?[19] Finley insists that we cannot attribute this apparent acquiescence to powerlessness or apathy; the demos held ultimate political power and was ready to use it. Finley argues that politics remained stable only because and so long as prevailing political arrangements furthered the ends of the demos, for politics are "wholly instrumental: the objectives are what matter in the end."[20] For Finley, the objectives of the demos were largely economic; thus stability depended on "subsistence crisis insurance" in the form of public works, liturgies, and trierarchies. Such material concessions do not simply suggest elite co-optation of the masses. They reflect the ultimate power of the demos

---

18. Gaventa, *Power and Powerlessness*, 6–8. In critiquing the pluralist position, Gaventa in particular has in mind Dahl, *Who Governs?* and Polsby, *Community Power and Political Theory*. In advancing his own view, Gaventa cites Friere's analysis of the "culture of silence" in *Cultural Freedom for Action*. For an assessment of this debate in the context of more recent thinking about the nature of power, see Hayward, *De-Facing Power*, chap. 2.

19. Finley, *Politics in the Ancient World*, 27.

20. Ibid., 97.

over its advisers, a power quite real even though it had rarely been employed directly or overtly.

We find in the pages of Thucydides no evidence of elite responsiveness to the material needs of the demos. Finley, however, also points to an "ideological aspect" of ancient politics. Political stability flowed as well from "a whole complex of beliefs and attitudes" that suggested the suitability of elite dominance.[21] Ober's work emphasizes a similar role for ideology in elite/mass relations. He finds, mainly in the fourth-century Athenian orators, a host of rhetorical tropes the purpose of which was to affirm elite claims to dominance while acknowledging the power of the demos. That speakers turned to these tropes suggests the very real power exercised by the demos over the advisers it chose to follow, something Ober terms "the ideological hegemony of the masses."[22] Because would-be leaders had to win the approval of the demos and because the demos ultimately decided which leader to follow, the masses influenced the arguments advanced by elite speakers seeking support. Democratic politics as rhetorical interaction thus allowed ongoing elite influence while reflecting mass power.

The work of Finley and especially Ober suggests an ancient demos that may have been silent but that nonetheless was active in a way that went beyond merely listening and deciding. This provides a response to any suggestion that the collective silence of the demos indicated disempowerment or passive acquiescence or tacit consent in the liberal sense.[23] Again, the mass of ordinary citizens had political power over the elites and were willing to make active use of it. Ober's work in particular points toward one way of understanding the relationship between mass silence and elite rhetoric in the *History*: we ought to read that rhetoric as shaped by the silent presence and silent power of the demos. But this, ultimately, only complicates the puzzle. For in the *History*, the particular meaning of the silent presence of the demos in any given moment ultimately cannot be resolved in the manner, say, of contemporary public opinion polling. Thucydides does not, for the most part, let us know in any detail what the

---

21. Ibid., 9.
22. Ober, *Mass and Elite in Democratic Athens*. See also his argument that the origins of Athenian democracy are to be found not in elite-driven reforms but in a spontaneous uprising by ordinary Athenian citizens. Ober, *The Athenian Revolution*.
23. Ironically (in the context of my dependence on their work), both Finley and Ober echo the common assessment of Thucydides as an aristocratic critic of democracy. Ober, *Mass and Elite in Democratic Athens*, thus describes Thucydides as a member of an "Athenian critical community" of elites wary of democracy (41).

mass of Athenians think about a particular issue or decision in advance. So we cannot say with any certainty that the silent power of the demos has been exercised in the shaping of any particular words spoken in the assembly. My ultimate argument will be that the collective silence of ordinary citizens renders the demos unknowable; thus the presence of the demos threatens to destabilize any apparent "ideological" nexus between elite rhetoric and mass opinion.[24]

In the end, the silence of the demos cannot be fully explained as the denial of voice or the attentive listening of those who will ultimately decide; nor can it be dismissed as the disengagement of satisfied, disempowered, or disinterested citizens. To understand democracy in the *History* we must grapple with the presence of an abiding and meaningful collective silence—a silence that Thucydides locates at the core of Athenian democratic politics. And for us to understand the nominalization of democracy under Pericles we must assess the changing relationship between the collective silence of the demos and the Athenian political elite. More generally, to grasp Thucydides' perspective on mass democracy we must work through the complex relations among speech, action, and silence. Having recognized the thematic significance of silence to Thucydides, we will find indications of that significance not only in those moments when he makes us witness to the play of politics in the Athenian assembly but also throughout the *History*'s account of Athenian action in the world.

II. SPEECH, ACTION, AND SILENCE: "REALIST" AND "CONSTRUCTIVIST" READINGS OF THE *HISTORY*

In exploring the relationship between silence and democracy in Thucydides' Athens, I intend to contribute to the growing body of work that takes Thucydides seriously as a theorist of democracy.[25] This includes most notably the work of Peter Euben, Cynthia Farrar, Sara Monoson, and Arlene Saxonhouse. As will become clear, I often disagree with particular aspects

---

24. In this context, see Wolin's analysis of Ober's approval of the "institutionalization" of Athenian democracy in the fourth century BCE. Wolin concludes that "the twentieth-century image of the 'constitutional democracy' of the 4th century bears a striking resemblance to Madisonian democracy," with its emphasis on limits on the *demos* aimed at producing stability." Wolin, "Norm and Form," 43–44.

25. Again here, I emphasize that one can read Thucydides as a theorist of democracy without taking him to be a democratic theorist in the contemporary sense—that is, one who begins with the presumption that democracy is, in principle, a political value to be celebrated or defended.

of the readings offered by these scholars, and emphasizing those disagreements will at times prove useful when it comes to situating my own reading of the *History*. That said, my own approach to Thucydides owes much to their work, and in general I mean to advance the basic goal reflected in it: namely, to learn about democracy from Thucydides.

Learning about democracy from Thucydides requires us to engage with what has in the past been a fairly common idea about the *History*: that Thucydides' interest focuses on relations *between* cities rather than on politics *within* cities. As Clifford Orwin has written, "Thucydides is little known as a theorist of domestic politics," democratic or otherwise.[26] This idea has been especially prominent in readings of Thucydides by realist students of international relations, who view politics in the *History* as centering on the power struggles of city-states out to promote their own interests. In recent years, much of the vast secondary literature on Thucydides has reflected the emergence of self-proclaimed "constructivist" readings. Constructivists tend to position themselves as critics of realist readings; they insist on the importance of speech among citizens and within cities and on the relevance of communicatively constructed norms as well as calculations of interest to the behavior of Thucydides' actors. As will be clear in what follows, I find much to admire in constructivist readings of the *History*; and I see certain aspects of my arguments about the relationship between speech and silence as offering new insights into the constructivist approach. This does not, however, mean that I reject realist approaches altogether; for in the realists' assertion that domestic politics are irrelevant in the *History* there lies an important complication for the questions of silence that interest me. In the end, my reading of democracy in Thucydides draws on both realist and constructivist insights while emphasizing the undertheorized way in which both depend on the silences that I find thematic in the *History*.

Realists have long claimed Thucydides as one of the founding figures of their school of thought. Robert Keohane summarizes well the realist approach, arguing that the *History* evinces agreement with "three key assumptions" of realism: "(1) states (or city-states) are the key units of action; (2) they seek power, either as an end in itself or as a means to other ends; and (3) they behave in ways that are, by and large, rational, and therefore comprehensible to outsiders in rational terms."[27] Keohane's

26. Orwin, *The Humanity of Thucydides*, 172.
27. Keohane, "Realism and the Study of Politics," 7. There exist a wide variety of definitions of realism. Donnelly provides a useful summary of several prominent definitions of realism,

assumptions 2 and 3 define action as essentially instrumental. In the rational means–end calculation that, consciously or not, drives state behavior, action is a means to gain power. A state may pursue power as an instrument that can be used to further other ends—one supposes security or glory, perhaps even justice as it sees justice—but this does not change the fact that action itself is always taken as a means to an end.

This basic account of the character of action fits some parts of the *History* better than others. It seems a particularly good description of those actions Thucydides reports in his narrative of events—a narrative that in fact constitutes most of the *History*. For vast stretches of the work, Thucydides describes the actions of the Athenians (and everyone else) but records no speeches. In the terminology I have been developing here, we might say that so far as Thucydides tells us, in such moments all contending voices are silent. Disagreements between elite speakers disappear, and so does the very distinction between elite speaker and ordinary citizen. Put differently, the silent presence of the demos spreads to include all Athenians, who appear to act with no vocal disagreement. All of this does fit with the realist notion of the Athenians as a unit of action, instrumentally pursuing agreed upon ends with no apparent need for any discussion of those ends or, for that matter, of the means to pursue them. But such a conclusion has as its largely unacknowledged and unexamined foundation a particular understanding of the meaning of the Athenian silences as crafted by Thucydides. A key task of Chapters 2 and 6 will be to explore more carefully the nature of Athenian action taken in this fully silent mode.

If moments of utter Athenian silence lend themselves to realist interpretations, the speeches interspersed in the narrative pose problems for each of the three realist assumptions Keohane finds in the *History*. Against assumption 2, one can argue that Thucydides' actors do indeed weigh the demands of justice or nobility in addition to those of rank expediency, as the speeches make clear. Against assumption 3, one can draw from the speeches to argue that passions often overwhelm rationality in determining the actions of city-states in Thucydides.[28] Given my concern with

---

as well as a typology of "realisms" based on those definitions, in *Realism and International Relations*, 6–7. Doyle, in "Thucydidean Realism," also provides a typology. While the variety of definitions means, of course, that no single definition is authoritative, the three realist assumptions Keohane identifies and locates in the *History* are common.

28. Besides making similar critiques of the realist reading of Thucydides, Ahrensdorf, in "Thucydides' Realistic Critique of Realism," offers an up-to-date listing both of works that appropriate Thucydides as a realist and of works questioning that appropriation (see esp.

Thucydides as a theorist of *democratic* speech and action, I want to focus on assumption 1. How does the breaking of Athenian silence bear upon the realist idea of the city as a *unit* of action? Put more sharply, why should the arch-realist Thucydides concern himself with noisy domestic political squabbles that are, again, irrelevant given that the action of the city is determined by its situation within Greek affairs? In this very strict sense, Thucydides hardly seems to see cities as "units of action."

A less strident realist appropriation of the *History*—one more attendant to the significance of speech and plurality within the city—would have Thucydides advancing not a deterministic theory of unitary state action but, rather, a theory of statesmanship.[29] Thucydides presents a realist course of action by cities not as inevitable, but as the best course and as the result of sound leadership. We can easily enough raise questions about whether Thucydides really presents a self-interested eschewal of justice and morality as good policy: the supposedly harshly realistic Athenians, after all, ultimately meet defeat.[30] But the notion that Thucydides envisions the molding of the city-state as unitary actor pursuing its interests to be the primary task of the statesman has had appeal stretching beyond the realists. Here internal politics *do* matter, but as a source of problems for the statesman to solve, of threats to the rational pursuit of power in the interest of the city. Not surprisingly, the mighty Pericles almost inevitably emerges as the statesman par excellence. Thus for Peter Pouncey, Thucydides shows Pericles as "the "guardian of Athens's true destiny, protecting her against her enemies, shaping her policies, and defining her ideals."[31] And according to Charles Cochrane, the period of Pericles' predominance was for Thucydides a time marked by "wisdom, strength, and incorruptibility on

---

232n2). Along similar lines, see Johnson, *Thucydides, Hobbes, and the Interpretation of Realism*; and Gustafson, "Thucydides and Pluralism," 174–79.

29. The less strident realism I have in mind here would be something like the "strong realism" identified by Donnelly in *Realism and International Relations*, 12, which allows "modest space for politically salient 'non-realist' concerns" and tends "to present realism as a positive theory of (international) politics or statesmanship." Donnelly describes Hans Morgenthau and Kenneth Waltz as "exemplary strong realists" and compares them to those "radical realists" who see little room for choice or statesmanship because of their "extreme versions of the three realist premises of anarchy, egoism and power politics." Donnelly suggests that the Athenians of Thucydides' Melian Dialogue (which I discuss in Chapter 4) are among the very few consistent "radical realists." Thucydides himself, on the other hand, Donnelly describes as at most a "hedged realist," though he suggests that "the hedges are more important than the alleged realist 'core'" (24; see also the entirety of Donnelly's chapter 6). Along similar lines, Doyle, "Thucydidean Realism," argues that Thucydides' realism is "at least minimalist" but neither "fundamentalist" nor "structuralist."

30. Along these lines, see chapter 4 of Lebow, *The Tragic Vision of Politics*.

31. Pouncey, *The Necessities of War*, 19.

the part of leaders, self-restraint and a disposition to follow sound counsel on the part of those who were led."[32]

Insofar as it allows for a stronger focus on internal politics, this statesman-centered reading readmits the speeches in the *History* as a worthwhile object of study. From this perspective, speech, like action, has a basically instrumental character. Words serve as the tools with which the statesman might manage the demos by teaching it enough about its true interests, thus unifying the city around the best course of action for achieving its ends. Here again, though, we can note some underlying assumptions about the meaning of silence in the *History*. On this reading, Thucydides' juxtaposition of the silent presence of the demos and the speeches of the Athenian political elite signals the relationship between statesmen or would-be statesmen and their potentially unruly charges. The only question is whether the silent demos will listen to the true statesman or follow one rogue or another. Meanwhile, the silence of contending voices that accompanies Pericles' appearances in the *History* stands as clear evidence of his statesmanship. That is, the silence of contending voices comes to mean that he and he alone manages to tame the demos.

My point here, again, is not simply to reject realist readings outright. The realists' insistence on the city's status as a unit of action resonates throughout my reading, always challenging the idea of Athenian democracy as the flourishing of plurality expressed through speech. More immediately, as we have just seen, this insistence draws our attention to moments of seeming complete silence in Thucydides' Athens. I mean here chiefly to emphasize that realist readings make undertheorized assumptions about the meaning of various sorts of silence in the *History*. But the realists' chief critics, the constructivists, make analogous assumptions themselves.

Only recently have some scholars begun to label their readings of the *History* "constructivist." But these readings have precursors in earlier

---

32. Cochrane, *Thucydides and the Science of History*, 95. Clifford Orwin, *The Humanity of Thucydides*, 28, suggests that Thucydides sees Pericles as the exception rather than as the standard which we should expect and from which Athens declines. But whether we read the *History* as pessimistic or optimistic about the possibility of great statesmen like Pericles, the reading of Pericles' relationship with the Athenian demos remains the same. And again, such a reading is common. See, for example, Cornford, *Thucydides Mythhistoricus*, 49–50; J. H. Finley, *Thucydides*, 156–57; Jones, *Athenian Democracy*, 62; Proctor, *The Experience of Thucydides*; and Woodhead, *Thucydides on the Nature of Power*, 49f. With admittedly interesting variations, all accept some version of the masterful Periclean skill in controlling or managing the demos, to the exclusion of any in-depth consideration of the complexities of democratic politics in Thucydides' Athens.

challenges to the dominant realist approach—challenges that emphasize the importance of speech and language in the *History*. In particular, James Boyd White's arguments have been influential. In a chapter on the *History* in *When Words Lose Their Meanings*, White argues that Thucydides traces the decline of a "culture of argument" that existed in Athens and throughout Greece at the beginning of the war.[33] In its healthy form, this culture allowed for talk of justice and thus for both moral argument and moral agreement. As this culture declined, White argues, it became less possible for speakers to introduce justice into considerations of what must be done. Collective political judgment faltered, and many suffered as a result. More recently, constructivist students of international relations have begun to concern themselves with the collective identities of the Greeks and of particular city-states in Thucydides. Thus Per Jansson, for example, considers how Athenian "identity" is "maintained" or "expressed" in the *History*. In this context Pericles' Funeral Oration stands as "largely an act of self-identification" for the Athenians.[34]

As the following chapters will make clear, I find much to admire in such arguments, for they correctly and usefully complicate the overdrawn realist notion of the city or state as a package of interests. Political actors—be they individual or collective—find themselves embedded in a culture of norms that shape what can and cannot be said and thus what can and cannot be done. We ought to direct our attention not simply toward action as the instrumentally rational pursuit of interests but also toward speech, which, rational or not, constitutes and reveals who we are and thus gives meaning to what we do. Yet existing constructivist readings seem to me both incomplete and undertheorized. Because of their focus on speech, these readings risk overlooking the vast stretches of the *History* in which Thucydides records *no* speeches; as I have suggested, the challenge of understanding Athenian democracy in the *History* involves grappling with those moments when Thucydides renders the Athenians silent. Moreover, in considering the meaning of speech in general and of particular speeches, constructivist readings tend (like realist readings) to make unacknowledged assumptions about the meaning of silence. Thus the assertion that Thucydides traces a "culture of argument" in the words of speakers leaves

---

33. White, *When Words Lose Their Meaning*. Lebow, in *The Tragic Vision of Politics*, follows White in finding such "constructivist" arguments in Thucydides, but also aims to situate Thucydides' "constructivist" conclusions as part of the tradition of "classical realism."

34. Jansson, "Identity-Defining Practices in Thucydides' *History of the Peloponnesian War*," 159.

unexamined the question of whether and, if so, how this culture of argument extended to and was understood or accepted by those present who remained silent—the ordinary citizens of the demos. And, as with the realist reading of Pericles as the ultimate statesman, the idea that the Funeral Oration serves as an "act of self-identification" for the Athenians rests on a particular way of reading the silence of contending speakers; it assumes that because Pericles alone seems to be describing Athenian identity, his account of that identity must in some way be authoritative.

Where the realist reading quite usefully centers our attention on the dynamics of unity and action, the constructivist reading emphasizes the revelation of identity through words and deeds. In doing so, it also calls for us to think about how norms shape and are shaped by words and deeds, and thus brings back deep issues of justice and responsibility that realist readings tend to eschew. Yet insofar as existing constructivist readings lack a full appreciation of the complex relationship between speech and silence, they tend to underestimate the complexity of these deeper issues as well. In the end, an understanding of democracy in the *History* requires both realist and constructivist insights. But it also requires careful attention to the silences that Thucydides weaves into his text.

III. READING SILENCE

Arguments from or even about silence are notoriously risky. In a treatment of the role of silence as thematic in Thucydides' account of Athenian politics, two particular dangers stand out. First, such an approach risks reading too much into the *History's* silences, with the result that one finds there precisely the preconceived ideas one brings to the text. Second, and conversely, emphasizing silence risks underemphasizing what we *do* find in the text. In the particular case of the *History*, the danger here lies in giving too little play to Thucydides' own explicit authorial comments and analysis or to the ways in which his narrative pulls the reader toward particular conclusions. In the face of such risks, there is some comfort in the fact that other readers of the *History* have grappled with similar issues of interpretation. Let me mention two especially prominent ones here.

I have already drawn from "On the Life and History of Thucydides," the essay that Thomas Hobbes appended to his translation of the *History*. In describing Thucydides' "disposition or method," Hobbes notes that Thucydides "never useth" what he calls "digressions for instruction's cause" and concludes that "the narration doth secretly instruct the reader."[35] "Secret instruction" here contrasts with what Hobbes calls the "open conveyance of precepts." Hobbes thus goes beyond Thucydides' evaluation of the success or failure of particular actions, in the sense that he finds Thucydides openly offering such evaluations "where there is just occasion." The reader is apparently meant to find Thucydides' deepest conclusions by reflecting on the "grounds and motives of every action," which Hobbes says Thucydides "setteth down before the action itself, either narratively, or else contriveth them into the form of *deliberative orations* in the persons of such as from time to time bare sway in the commonwealth." This sort of indirect view of the springs of action would seem to feed into Hobbes's claim that Thucydides has "clearly set before men's eyes the ways and events of good and evil counsels."

The secret instruction that Hobbes finds in the *History* ultimately leads the reader, by reflection upon the connections among motives, deliberation, action, and results, to a hard-earned understanding of "good and evil counsels." Hobbes is quite forthright about his reliance on both Thucydides' explicit claims and his silences. His idea of secret instruction rests in part on a reading of the *History* whereunder Thucydides offers ample evidence of the motives of the actions of the Athenians and others, both when he records speeches and when he allows silence to reign. As regards Athenian democracy in particular, Hobbes would seem to be pointing toward what I have called the silent presence of the demos in the face of elite rhetoric as a Thucydidean method of portraying a sort of civic deliberation in which those who "bare sway in the commonwealth" reveal why the city acts as it does. Along these lines, the silence of contending voices no doubt further suggests that Pericles bore more "sway" than any other Athenian. Hence Hobbes's view of Pericles' dominance as "monarchical." Indeed, one of the more fundamental precepts the *History* reveals—both explicitly and through its subtle, silent instruction—seems for Hobbes to be captured in the idea that Thucydides "least of all liked democracy."

Like Hobbes, Nietzsche sees the *History* as indirectly revealing its deepest truths. In *Twilight of the Idols,* Nietzsche describes Thucydides as his "recreation" from Platonism. He is gesturing in part here to the contrast between Plato's cowardly idealism and Thucydides' "courage in the face of reality." But he also preferred Thucydides' style; so the actual process of reading Thucydides would have been, for him, rather more enjoyable

---

35. Hobbes, "On the Life and History of Thucydides," 577.

than reading Plato. The *History* for Nietzsche required deep and careful textual engagement: "One must turn [Thucydides] over line by line and read his hidden thoughts as clearly as his words; there are few thinkers so rich in hidden thoughts."[36] I have elsewhere argued in greater detail that perhaps the foremost hidden thought Nietzsche finds in the *History* concerns what he calls the "terrible" reality that emerges in the infamous Melian Dialogue.[37] On my reading, Nietzsche here foreshadows the constructivist vision of reality as the creation of rhetoric. In particular, Nietzsche sees Thucydides as understanding that the meaning of justice is merely the product of rhetorical negotiation between equally powerful parties.

If I am right about Nietzsche's reading of Thucydides, then he finds in the *History* rather different "hidden thoughts" than does Hobbes. Where Hobbes sees Thucydides as silently (as well as, at times, openly) instructing readers about "good and evil counsel," Nietzsche draws on the *History* for support for his attempt to move "beyond good and evil."[38] Here I am less interested in whether Hobbes or Nietzsche has the better reading than in the emphasis both place on Thucydides' use of silence. That they find different meanings in that silence points back to the first risk I identified earlier: that of reading one's own preconceived ideas into the *History*. But Hobbes and Nietzsche also point toward what I take to be the best way of dealing with that risk. If the *History* does "secretly instruct" through its "hidden thoughts," we as readers will inevitably make something of its silences. It will, then, be best to make the role of silence explicit, as Hobbes and Nietzsche both do. Some will find in this approach an invitation to subjectivity; I, however, ultimately see the *History*'s thematization of silence as yielding an interpretive flexibility that in the end can only add to its power to spur our own thought.[39]

This is not to say that Thucydides, because he allows his text to reflect the significant role of silence in action and politics, licenses just any interpretation. The *History* is not *that* flexible. As per the second risk I mentioned

---

36. Nietzsche, *Twilight of the Idols*, 118.
37. See Zumbrunnen, "Courage in the Face of Reality."
38. Along these lines, and in the context of what I take to be Nietzsche's anticipation of constructivist approaches to the *History*, it is worth noting that Hobbes, with Thucydides, is often considered a central figure in the realist tradition. In the rather schematic reading I have offered here, Hobbes's appears to fall in line with the statesman-centered realist approach discussed in the previous section. For a more complex reading of Hobbes's and Thucydides' relationship with realism, see Johnson, *Thucydides, Hobbes*.
39. See Connor's insightful discussion of changing perceptions of the particular relevance of the *History* in the mid-twentieth century, first in the Cold War and later during Vietnam, in Connor, *Thucydides*, 3–8.

above, Thucydides' relatively rare authorial interventions demand attention; and no reader can ignore the potential significance of the broad narrative structure of the *History*. These aspects of the text provide the context for approaching the matter of silence, and I have tried to remain attentive to them throughout. In the end, I find that the relationship between text and textual silence evades any simple account. At times, I see the language or structure of the *History* as providing more or less explicit support for my reading of silence, as in my discussions of "quiet" in Chapter 1 and of the "sudden" mode of Athenian action in Chapter 2. At other points, I find the silences that Thucydides embeds in the *History* standing in tension with his explicit authorial analyses; in dealing with the matter of Athenian character in Chapter 3, I discuss this tension in terms of the difference between Thucydides' perspective as historian and the perspective of the political actor, which the *History* also presents.

Still elsewhere, including in Chapters 4, 5, and 6, I find that attention to the role of silence complicates common readings of various narrative arcs in the *History*, including most notably the supposed decline of Athenian politics and the increasing harshness of Athenian ideas and actions. The structure of my own argument in some sense stacks the deck in favor of such a conclusion. I here offer a thematic rather than a sequential reading of the *History*.[40] This sort of approach serves well to emphasize the role of silence in various contexts throughout the *History*; but it perhaps risks downplaying the ways in which events in the text relate to one another as part of broader stories of historical continuity and change that Thucydides means to tell. Here, then, let me emphasize that I never mean to treat the narrative arc or arcs of the *History* as imagined or nonexistent. I mean rather to suggest that Thucydides is always prompting us to question any sense of historical certainty we might develop in thinking about such matters. His work always encourages us to consider the perspective of the political actor, where little if anything is certain, in large part due to the persistent role of silence in politics.

At various points in the following chapters, I thus emphasize the presence of textual silence in the *History* to highlight what I find to be the speculative nature of certain familiar readings. That is, I find many existing interpretations to rest on unacknowledged assumptions about the silence of contending voices and the silent presence of the demos. But my own

---

40. See ibid., 18–19. See also Orwin, *The Humanity of Thucydides*, 12–13, for thoughtful discussions of the merits of reading the *History* sequentially as opposed to more thematically, as I do here.

readings of the *History* are themselves speculative at various points. At times, a reading of silence only takes us so far, and I have tried to identify those moments where the *History* leaves us with more questions than answers and where it invites us to do our own thinking. At another level, as I have tried to acknowledge here, my own approach to the *History* of course rests on assumptions of its own. Most obviously, I begin with the idea—supported by Finley, Ober, and others—that the Athenian demos had real power and actively exercised it. In the end, I see in the *History* evidence that Thucydides held a similar view. To the extent that this latter conclusion follows from my own reading of the significant silences I find in the text, it is itself speculative, both in its general form and in the particular instances in which I see the silent power of the demos at work and interpret its effects. In the end, I think the *History*, by its sheer complexity and by its enigmatic theoretical power, calls us to such speculative thinking. More broadly, I hope the reading of silence I offer here can in some small measure spur our thinking about how the largely silent mass of ordinary citizens might yet hold and exercise meaningful power in the nominally democratic politics of the contemporary world.

IV. PLAN OF THE BOOK

My focus throughout this book remains on Thucydides' Athenians and their words, deeds, and silences. I aim to offer a reading of democratic politics and action that may provide fresh angles of approach to the peculiarities of mass democracy, both ancient and contemporary. I begin near the end of the *History*, focusing in Chapter 1 on Thucydides' account of the oligarchic coup that toppled Athenian democracy near the end of the Peloponnesian War. I set my argument against the backdrop of Thucydides' account of the revolution at Corcyra. Political theorists—and constructivists in particular—are often drawn to this latter account, in which Thucydides famously states that as Corcyra came apart "words lost their meaning," with revolutionary rhetoric turning traditional values upside down. Corcyra, in short, experiences political disintegration as a chaotic cacophony of political speech. By contrast, I draw attention to Thucydides' emphasis on the role of what he calls the "quiet" of the Athenian "mob" as democracy falls in Athens. The quiet of the mob ultimately amounts to a sort of acquiescence to the imposition of oligarchy. It thus contrasts with what I have here called the collective silence of the demos. Put differently, my argument in Chapter 1 suggests that the silence of the demos that prevails in Thucydides' account of democracy does not amount to bowing before the rule of a small corps of elites. The silent demos, that is, is not simply a quieted mob.

Chapter 2 begins more directly to address the place of silence in Athenian democracy in the *History*, focusing in particular on the Athenians' response to the affair of Mitylene. Going beyond the common focus on the denouement of this affair in the famous Mitylene Debate, I identify two modes of Athenian action toward Mitylene. Thucydides records political speeches in the Athenian assembly to mark what I refer to as moments of "deliberative action." Much more often, though, he shows the Athenians as a unit engaging in what I term "sudden action"; he records no speeches and simply reports the actions taken. I situate my discussion of these two modes of action—and the complex role of silence in each—against the backdrop of Aristotle's discussion of deliberation and voluntary action and Hannah Arendt's concern with the disastrous potential of instrumental thinking. These theoretical resources help us begin to reframe the deep questions of justice and responsibility that arise from Thucydides' account of Athenian democratic politics.

In Chapter 3, I challenge existing readings of the collective "character" of Thucydides' Athenians. This character has most often been described as a set of underlying traits—most notably boldness and daring—that distinguish Athens from other Greek cities, in particular its chief adversary, Sparta. According to the common argument, these traits explain Athens's imperial success, but they also explain the city's eventual defeat. Against this reading, I argue that Thucydides and his Greeks discuss character not as a set of traits but as a characteristic way of acting. What is more, this "Athenian way" does not stand as a constant explanatory background for Athenian action; rather, it appears as a malleable subject of deliberation, something that speakers claim to define authoritatively as they try during moments of deliberative action to persuade the silent demos. In making this argument, I pay special attention to Pericles' Funeral Oration, which we must understand as a moment of deliberation and democratic politics. Beyond exploring the dynamics and inherent changeability of the Athenian character, my aim here is to explore the interactions among elite arguments that claim to reveal the collective character of Athens. I do so with reference to the silence of the mass of Athenian citizens as those arguments are made.

Chapter 4 continues the exploration of the deliberative mode of Athenian action and deepens the questions of responsibility raised in Chapters 2 and 3. Some locate the causes of Athens's fate in the nature of the Athenian character; others point to a supposed decline of Athenian democratic politics from the lofty heights of Periclean leadership to the petty squabbles of his successors. In Chapter 4, I explore this notion of decline by considering the descriptions that Athenian speakers themselves offer of the workings of Athenian democracy. In offering these descriptions, the speakers contribute to what appears to be an ongoing and in a sense unresolvable debate over a particular aspect of the Athenian way. Here I explore the challenges of political judgment faced by the speakers as they attempt to describe the Athenian way. and faced as well by the silent demos as it sorts through what the speakers have to say. I conclude that, precisely because of the collective silence of the demos, we cannot easily construct a narrative of Athenian political decline. Nor can we instantly locate responsibility for Athens's fall in such a decline.

Chapter 5 marks the transition from consideration of the "deliberative mode" to the "sudden mode" of Athenian action. I focus here chiefly on the Melian Dialogue, the infamous exchange in which anonymous Athenian envoys, demanding the surrender of the small island of Melos, reject all appeals to justice. The Athenian envoys' arguments have often been taken as evidence of the realism of both Thucydides and his Athenians. This view, however, requires us to view the envoys as representative of Athens and the Athenians. I raise questions about the sense in which the envoys are in fact Athenian representatives, arguing that we must in the end approach them—and any supposed "spokesmen" for Athens—as political actors in their own right, engaged in their own rhetorical strategies. Meanwhile, Thucydides depicts the Athenians at home as utterly silent about Melos; in this way, they pose difficult challenges of political judgment for both the Athenian envoys and, more important, for the Melians.

In Chapter 6, I consider the fate of Plataea, a small city in central Greece allied with Athens that falls to Sparta early in the war. The affair of Plataea reveals much about how the Spartans deal with the smaller Greek cities (just as the affairs of Mitylene and Melos reveal much about Athens). I focus my attention, though, on the persistently silent role of Athens in the affair, as this provides a paradigmatic instance of the sudden mode of Athenian action and reminds us that, whatever their limitations, realist readings that take the city as a unit of action do resonate at certain points in the *History*. On my reading, the Athenian failure to deliberate about how to respond to the Spartan siege of Plataea renders Athenian action and inaction indecipherable—not just to Thucydides' readers but, most important, to the Plataeans (and, one suspects, to the Athenians themselves). My aim here is to continue to explore the implications of action taken without deliberation and the ways in which we can and cannot assess responsibility for those implications.

In the Conclusion, I return to the fundamental questions about the nature of democracy raised at the outset of this Introduction, focusing in particular on how mass politics may, in the context of particular manifestations of silence, become only nominally democratic. Here I bring to the fore a basic tension between the project of contemporary democratic theory and the concerns of the *History*. It is worth reminding ourselves here that Thucydides certainly did not set out to write a defense of democracy or an exploration of its possibilities. He prided himself instead on having "recorded the war between the Peloponnesians and the Athenians" (1.1) and having produced a work that might be "judged useful" by those observing human affairs "at some future time." I proceed in that spirit of contemporary usefulness, aiming to draw out the implications for our own concerns of Thucydides' understanding of democracy—and, in particular, the central and paradoxical role of silence in democratic politics.

1

Athenian *Stasis* and the Quiet of the Mob

I. INTRODUCTION

Before turning more directly to democratic politics in Thucydides' Athens, I consider in this opening chapter Thucydides' accounts of *stasis*, first at Corcyra and then at Athens. As I noted in the Introduction, Thucydides in both cases deploys the language of *stasis* to describe oligarchic movements against established democracies.[1] In this sense, his understanding of revolutionary politics apparently stands opposed to contemporary work— most notably that of Sheldon Wolin—that sees democracy itself as the revolutionary overturning of existing forms. In the case of Athens in particular, Thucydides' different understanding of the phenomenon to which *stasis* properly refers in turn reflects a different understanding of the role of the mass of ordinary citizens in *stasis*. Where Wolin and others see *stasis* as the activation of the demos, Thucydides in describing the oligarchic revolution at Athens in book 8 of the *History* leaves us a complex account of the "quiet" of the "mob." In this chapter I explore the way in which the mass of Athenians keep quiet during *stasis*. My purpose here is twofold. First, I mean to show that quiet and silence work at a thematic level in the *History*. That is, Thucydides makes it clear in book 8 that he finds quiet and inaction as important as speech and action. Second, I mean here to set up the quiet of the mob in the face of oligarchic plotting as a comparison point for the silent role of the mass of ordinary Athenians in moments of democratic politics.

At a basic level, silence sets book 8 as a whole off from the rest of the *History*, for here Thucydides records no speeches in direct discourse. Where many have found here evidence of the unfinished state of the *History's*

---

1. As Proctor, *Experience of Thucydides*, 53, notes, "revolution, in [Thucydides'] eyes, was generally an oligarchical, not a left-wing, activity." This is certainly the case at both Corcyra and Athens.

concluding book, others have suggested that Thucydides' omission of speeches reflects his sense of the decline of deliberation or the disintegration of civic unity in the face of the trials of war.[2] In arguments to follow in later chapters, I find such arguments about decline and disintegration problematic. Still, I too begin from the idea that the silences of book 8 reflect changes in Thucydides' perception of the war and its impact on politics. The absence of speeches in book 8 and especially Thucydides' emphasis on the quiet inaction of the Athenian people suggest a shift in his ongoing thematic concern with the tension between plurality and unity in the city and with the interplay of speech and silence as a way of grappling with that tension. Put differently, an understanding of the quiet mob's interaction with the oligarchic conspirators of book 8 can provide us with a backdrop for understanding the interaction of elite speakers and silent demos that Thucydides calls democracy. Before turning to the oligarchic revolution at Athens, though, I set the stage by considering Thucydides' account of *stasis* at Corcyra, which, perhaps because it is noisier, has drawn more attention.

II. REVOLUTION AT CORCYRA

And in self-justification men inverted the usual verbal evaluations of words.

(III.82)

Thucydides' description of the *stasis* or "revolution" at Corcyra marks one of the longest and most directly analytical authorial interventions in the flow of his narrative. The struggle between oligarchs and democrats in Corcyra was facilitated and abetted by Corcyra's situation during the war between Sparta and Athens. The revolution started when the Corinthians

---

2. Cogan, *The Human Thing*, thus argues that "the absence of speeches from book 8 of the history—usually attributed to its unfinished state—might well be deliberate rather than accidental." In particular, Cogan thinks that Thucydides' decision not to record speeches may reflect his sense that, because the war had rendered political positions between and within cities "rigid," the deliberation reflected in earlier speeches had disappeared (165). In a similar vein, Connor, *Thucydides*, sees in the general roughness of book 8 a "disintegration of the units and techniques" Thucydides has employed before. More than simply a consequence of Thucydides' failure because of his untimely death to edit and polish the book, this disintegration is the "literary analogue" to the political disintegration of Greece, including the disintegration of internal harmony in Athens. "The reader," Connor concludes, "can no longer assume civic unity" (215). See also Proctor, *Experience of Thucydides*, 52: "in the earlier books of the *History* Thucydides had generally treated the nations as collective entities."

returned Corcyreans whom they had taken captive after earlier sea battles. These captives, Thucydides says, "had been bribed to bring Corcyra over to the Corinthian side" (3.70). The dispute thus begun over whether Corcyra would remain allied with Athens or turn to an alliance with the Peloponnesians soon enough became as well a battle between the imposition of oligarchy favored by the newly returned captives and the maintenance of Corcyrean democracy. Thucydides makes it clear that he sees Corcyra as a model for what later happened throughout Greece: "And during the civil wars the cities suffered many cruelties that occur and will always occur as long as men have the same nature, sometimes more terribly and sometimes less, varying in their forms as each change of fortune dictates" (3.82). In addition to much violence, the "cruelties" of the Corcyrean *stasis* included the alteration of language, to which Thucydides points in the quotation that heads this section and which has drawn much attention and inspired much controversy.

In his long-influential translation, Crawley has the passage at hand reading that "words had to change their ordinary meanings." Together with the vivid examples Thucydides offers—"irrational recklessness was now considered commitment . . . moderation was a cover for lack of manhood . . . senseless anger helped to define a true man"—this passage has led some to see linguistic decay as a—or even *the*—central aspect of *stasis*. Here is James Boyd White: "When Thucydides wishes to express his sense of the internal chaos brought upon the cities of Greece by the civil wars that arose during the time of the Peloponnesian War, he tells us, among other things that words themselves lost their meaning."[3] Euben follows White, emphasizing that the corruption of language "as words lose stable meaning" marks the most fundamental sort of *political* corruption: "For language and speech are constitutive of public life, not external to it . . . political corruption and linguistic corruption imply each other."[4] Thucydides' description of the revolutionary use of language in Corcyra stands as a central piece of evidence as well in more recent, explicitly constructivist readings of the *History*.[5]

This emphasis on linguistic change as in a sense constitutive of *stasis* can be challenged at various levels. The most basic challenge concerns the proper translation of the passage at hand, which contains some of Thucydides' most difficult Greek. Some have argued that Thucydides' phrasing

---

3. White, *When Words Lose Their Meanings*, 3.
4. Euben, *The Tragedy of Political Theory*, 189.
5. See Lebow, "Thucydides the Constructivist," 554–55.

and the examples that follow suggest not a loss of meaning but, rather, a change in the application of words whose meanings remained constant.[6] That is, the revolutionaries at Corcyra did not suddenly alter the evaluative force of, say, "commitment"—they simply applied it to different sets of actions than before. Along these lines, Orwin argues that the fundamental dynamic at Corcyra works not at the level of communicatively constituted convention but instead at the level of human nature. The essence of *stasis* is not the collapse of collective identity through the loss of shared meaning; rather, it is the overwhelming of convention by human nature—something marked in part but not exclusively by the misapplication of ethical terms.[7]

As part of his broader argument that Thucydides understood the Peloponnesian War as a sort of *stasis* within Greece as a whole, Jonathan Price stakes out something of a middle ground between those who like Orwin find in the *History* indications of a constant, guiding human nature and those who see Thucydides as some sort of a constructivist. Thucydides, on Price's reading, sees human nature as "mute and devoid of independent will and character." Both "such characteristics as greed, aggression and megalomania" *and* the manipulation and misuse of language "are functions of the forces acting on human nature in disturbed times like *stasis*."[8] Drawing on the long-noticed affinity of Thucydides for Hippocratic medicine, Price argues that Thucydides saw *stasis* as a disease that, in acting on an essentially neutral human nature, led to the exhibition of symptoms that the careful observer could recognize in both the deeds and the words of revolutionaries. Thus Corcyra provides the basis for a "pathology" of *stasis*,[9] though as Thucydides indicates in the passage from 3.82 quoted above, the precise unfolding of *stasis* and its symptoms will vary from one case to the next.

Whether or not Price is correct regarding Thucydides' view of human nature or the centrality of medical analogy to Thucydides' thought, his notion of "pathology" suggests that we consider the dynamics of the course of a given case of *stasis*. Largely because of poor leadership, the intervention

---

6. See Proctor, *The Experience of Thucydides*, 81, who makes this argument after reviewing the controversy over the translation of 3.82.4.

7. Orwin, *The Humanity of Thucydides*, 177–78, esp. n. 11.

8. Price, *Thucydides and Internal War*, 28. Price agrees with Proctor, Orwin, and others on the proper translation of 3.82.4: Thucydides means that during *stasis* words retain their agreed-on meanings but the value assigned to them—that is, how their meanings are enacted in society—changes (41).

9. Price, *Thucydides and Internal War*, 39.

of the Peloponnesians and Spartans, and the "fanaticism" that followed "once men were committed to the power struggle," the Corcyrean revolution came to a fully "savage" stage (3.82) that included "every form of death" (3.81) and a "revolution in thinking" as well as the perverted use of shared language. As Connor has it, by this stage "language has ... become an agent of violence, intensifying rather than alleviating the *kinesis* and the destruction."[10] Price notes that the disease took a different course in Athens, where the emergence of the Government of the 5000 "brought the city nearer to the end of *stasis* before the city reached the extreme stage witnessed in Corcyra and elsewhere."[11] In part, this meant that the Athenians were able to avoid the extent of bloodshed suffered at Corcyra, as well as the linguistic corruption that marked the dissolution of Corcyrean politics. A key question remains: How did they succeed in doing so? How, that is, did the course of Athenian *stasis* lead toward a sort of uneasy moderation rather than to the full savagery—in words and deeds—of Corcyra? One key to the answer lies in the Athenians' ability to "keep quiet" at key moments.

III. The Quiet of the Mob

The mob [ochlos], whatever anger it felt for the moment over these arrangements, kept quiet [hesychazen].

(8.48.3)

As Price argues, the precise moment when healthy politics yields to the diseased condition of *stasis* can be obscure.[12] On the one hand, Thucydides clearly marks the beginning of his explicit account of the *stasis* at Athens, announcing at the beginning of 8.48 that the "movement [*ekinesthe*]" to overthrow the Athenian democracy began in the Athenian camp on the island of Samos "and subsequently moved from there to the city." The original conspirators, who were among the leaders of Athenian forces on Samos, sought to create an Athenian oligarchy in part for their own benefit and in part as a way to ensure the return of the exiled Alcibiades, who

---

10. Connor, *Thucydides*, 101. Connor suggests that the failure of language at Corcyra fits into a basic theme of book 3 of the *History*: "language, as we have come to expect in this book, is unable to impede violence" (98).
11. Price, *Thucydides and Internal War*, 321.
12. On this point, see Price, *Thucydides and Internal War*, 305.

might bring with him help from the Persian Tissaphernes. On the other hand, Thucydides' eulogy of Pericles hints that certain signs of *stasis* can be seen much earlier. In 2.65, Thucydides indicates "the abundance of resources at Pericles' disposal" when he marvels at the remarkable resiliency of the Athenians after their disastrous defeat in Sicily. The final fall of Athens to Sparta came in spite of those resources, with the Athenians "coming to grief through individual disputes" (2.65). But those individual disputes emerged at least as early as the expedition to Sicily, which Thucydides says the Athenians failed fully to support because Athenian politics came to be dominated by "personal attacks over the leading position among the common people" (2.65). If such individual disputes and personal attacks are part of the dynamics of *stasis*, then we might well, from the vantage point of history, see the first hints or symptoms of *stasis* as early as the Mitylene Debate.[13]

Thucydides indicates that healthy politics and *stasis* are clearly distinguishable as conditions of the city (particularly when *stasis* reaches the extremes of Corcyra). But he also suggests that the distinction between the two is neither simple nor complete. Key aspects of *stasis*—personal attacks, individual disputes, the manipulation of language—may appear in moments of relatively healthy politics as well. Of more immediate interest for my purposes here, Thucydides brings to his consideration of Athenian *stasis* two thematic concerns that, I will argue, resonate throughout his portrayal of Athenian politics. Those concerns include, first, the tension between unity and plurality in the city and, second, the interplay of speech, silence, and action. The passage that heads this section, though, reflects a shift in the way Thucydides grapples with these themes, indicated by his deployment of a particular set of terms to understand Athenian *stasis* that he does not use in discussing Athenian democracy. He writes that in its earliest stages the oligarchic movement benefited from the fact that "the mob [*ochlos*]" of Athenians on Samos "kept quiet [*hesychazen*]." Here and at other points in his account of the oligarchic revolution, Thucydides uses *ochlos* as a way of describing one part of *hoi Athenaioi*—as a way, that is, of understanding Athenian plurality; similarly, he uses forms of *hesychia* to describe a sort of quiet or *in*action that plays a crucial role in the unfolding of events in Athens. In the next section I consider this usage of *ochlos* and *hesychia* in the context of Athenian *stasis*. First, though, I want to explore how Thucydides has used these terms earlier in the *History*.

---

13. Ibid., 305, suggests precisely this.

In most cases throughout the *History, ochlos* appears in military contexts. At times it suggests an unruly or undisciplined or unskilled mob in general. In exhorting his forces before battle, Brasidas thus paints the barbarians whom they face as "rabble [*ochloi*]" (4.126.6); similarly, Alcibiades dismisses the people of Sicily as a "mob [*ochlois*]" unlikely to "go into action in a common cause" (6.17.2). When applied to Greek forces, *ochlos* generally serves to distinguish light-armed infantry and sailors from the more elite hoplites and cavalry. In the aftermath of the Athenian victory at Pylos, Thucydides tells of a single Spartan garrison that stood firm in the face of Athenian attacks on the Peloponnesian coast. These Spartans, he says, "terrified the unorganized mob [*ochlon*] of light-armed by charging them but faced with hoplites they drew back again" (4.56.1). He puts this same distinction to work in describing the casualties of the second outbreak of the plague in Athens, with *ochlos* now representing not simply light-armed infantry but seemingly anyone who was not a hoplite or a member of the cavalry: "No fewer than four thousand four hundred from the hoplite ranks and three hundred cavalrymen died, and an untold number of the general population [*ochlou*]" (3.87.3).[14]

This broader application of *ochlos* connects to a handful of appearances of the term in more directly political contexts prior to the outbreak of *stasis* in Athens. Several of these—at 1.80, 6.31, and 6.57—refer to the Athenian populace as a whole or to the general public or to a crowd of Athenians in a public place. Others suggest a sharper sense of political stratification in Athens; here *ochlos* more obviously carries its pejorative sense of a "mob." At 4.28, Thucydides describes Cleon's attempt to back out of his boasts about what he could accomplish at Pylos. The Athenians, Thucydides says, "shouted at Cleon to sail," growing more excited by the moment "as a crowd [*ochlos*] is apt to do." At 6.89, he records Alcibiades' complaint—in a speech to the Spartans—that whereas his family had always been "leaders of the whole" in Athens, there were others "who steered the crowd [*ochlon*] in evil directions." And, finally, at 7.8 Nicias, facing insurmountable difficulties in Sicily, sends messengers home to Athens but then worries that they "would not report the facts," instead "speaking to please the crowd [*ochloi*]." Thucydides thus only rarely uses the term *ochlos* to describe the mass of ordinary Athenian citizens in their political role; typically he uses simply *hoi Athenaioi*, "the Athenians," to remind us of their silent presence.

---

14. For other uses of *ochlos* in military contexts, see 1.49.3, 2.88.2, 2.109.2, 6.20.4, 6.63.2, 6.64.1, 7.62.1, 7.75.2, 7.78.2, 7.85.2, and 8.25.4.

As we will see in the following section, the role of the "mob" or "crowd" in the *kinesis* of Athenian *stasis* often involves keeping quiet. Beyond its importance in Thucydides' understanding of *stasis*,[15] the juxtaposition of *kinesis* with "quiet" or *hesychia* runs at various levels throughout the work; indeed, as L. B. Carter has shown, the thematic dichotomy of *kinesis–hesychia* played an important role in Athenian culture generally.[16] At the broadest level, Thucydides contrasts the movement or upheaval of war with the quiet of peace. The *History* opens with the declaration that the "war between the Peloponnesians and the Athenians" was "certainly the greatest disturbance [*kinesis*] to effect the Hellenes" (1.1). By contrast, Thucydides and his Greeks frequently use *hesychia* and its cognates to describe conditions of peace. Thucydides tells us, for example, that in the wake of the Trojan War and "after a long period of difficulty, Hellas was securely pacified [*hesychasasa*]" (1.12.4). Similarly, during the one-year truce leading to the Peace of Nicias, "on account of the armistice, matters were quiet [*hesychaze*]" (4.134.1).[17] During the time of the Peace of Nicias itself, the Eleans protest that the Spartans had attacked them in violation of the truce and by surprise, since they themselves, in accordance with the truce, "were in a tranquil [*hesychazontōn*] and unsuspecting state" (5.49.3).[18]

Alongside this idea of the quiet of peace as the counterpart to the *kinesis* of war, Thucydides and his Greeks use *hesychia* to describe actors and actions during war. At the broadest level, the contrast between *kinesis* and *hesychia*, between action or movement and inaction or quiet, is reflected in descriptions of the Athenian and Spartan characters or ways of life. Here we need only recall the Corinthians' description of the Athenians as "definitely innovators and quick to form their plans and carry out whatever action they resolve" (1.70). In this context of the supposed Athenian bent for kinetic activity, Alcibiades, when arguing in favor of sailing for Sicily, warns the Athenians that if they "stay inactive [*hesychazoien*]" they will be placing in danger the "very existence" of their empire (6.18.2) and that "the city, like anything else, will cause its own deterioration if left idle

---

15. Price, *Internal War*, argues that the notion of *kinesis* provides for Thucydides the conceptual link between the localized *staseis* he describes in the *History* and the Peloponnesian War as a kinetic *stasis* among all of Greece.

16. Carter, *The Quiet Athenian*.

17. Here I use the Loeb translation. Lattimore does not directly translate *hesychaze* in this passage, offering "there was little or no Athenian or Lacedaemonian activity because of the armistice."

18. See also Nicias' warning to the Athenians that, should they give up their inactivity by sailing to Sicily, they can expect the Peloponnesians to attack them, truce or no truce (6.10.2).

[*hesychazei*]" (6.18.6). As for the Spartans, Thucydides himself notes that they "remained inactive [*hesychazon*] most of the time" between the Persian Wars and the Peloponnesian War (1.118.2). Again, it is the Corinthians who use the notion of quiet in the context of character, saying that the Athenians "were born to have no peace [*hesychian*] themselves and allow it to no one else" (1.70). Beyond these uses of *hesychia* to contrast Athens and Sparta, the term often simply denotes the precarious neutrality of smaller states caught between the two powers. The doomed Melians, for example, had before the war "been unwilling to submit to Athens, at first taking neither side and staying inactive [*hesychazon*]" (5.84.2).[19]

These thematic uses of *hesychia* are relatively rare. Most often, Thucydides uses the term at a tactical level, as a way of describing the military (in)action of particular forces. The tactic of "keeping quiet" appears in a variety of contexts. At times, Thucydides uses the term to describe the calm before battle, as one or both sides deliberately remain quiet, waiting to see what will happen. As the naval battle of Naupactus unfolded, for example, "the Corinthians stayed inactive [*hesychazon*] at first, then, when the signal was raised at what seemed the right moment, they sailed at the Athenians and began the battle" (7.34).[20] At other times, "keeping quiet" amounts to a tactical pause during an attack or a tactical withdrawal after an attack. Early in their revolt, for example, the Mitylenians attacked the Athenian camp and, "despite an advantage in the fighting," withdrew and "kept quiet" (*hesychazon*), waiting for help from Sparta (3.5.2).[21] Then, too, a force may keep quiet less from choice than from necessity—either fleeing to a place of safety or declining to fight altogether. When, for example, the Thebans attacked Plataea and took the city "in an instant," the Plataeans, instead of fighting, "came to an agreement and accepted the proposals [of the Thebans] without opposition [*hesychazon*]" (2.3.1).[22] Finally, sudden and unforeseen developments—negative or positive—on the battlefield

---

19. See, too, 3.68.1, where Thucydides says that the Spartan judges at the trial of the Plataeans noted that Sparta had "requested" that the Plataeans "stay inactive [*hesychzein*]." And see 2.7.2, where the Spartans, at the outbreak of war, tell some of their allies to prepare for war but to continue to receive Athenian ships and to otherwise "remain at peace [*hesuchazontas*]."

20. See similar uses at 1.52.2, 3.107.3, 4.56.1, 4.73.1, 4.111.1, 4.122.6, 5.6.2, 5.7.1 5.54.4, 5.56.3, 6.44.3, 6.97.2, and 7.3.3.

21. See similar uses at 1.49.3, 2.81.8, 3.102.7, 4.33.2, 4.71.1, 4.90.4, 4.127.2, 4.129.1, 5.115.4, and 7.38.2.

22. In a related and especially poignant usage, Thucydides describes Nicias and the Athenian force he leads "watching for the quiet [*hesuchazon*] part of the night" in attempting (and failing) to escape from their Syracusan besiegers (7.93.4). See also 3.94.2, 4.44.1, 4.57.2, 4.124.3, and 7.11.3.

may make for a kind of quiet confusion. In the wake of a sudden withdrawal of Spartan forces by Agis, the Argives, Thucydides tells us, "did not know what to think" and so "they themselves were keeping still [*hesychazon*] and not pursuing" (5.65.3).[23]

Once again, these frequent references to "quiet" as either a thematic contrast to war or a tactic during battle contrast with Thucydides' very infrequent usage of *hesychia* in political matters. He thus does not use *hesychia*, for example, to describe either of the two types of silence that I identified in the Introduction. He does not, that is, use the term in describing the mass of Athenians who remain silent while elites speak in the assembly. Nor does he use it to describe the silence of contending voices when Pericles appears alone in the *History*. This suggests that his use of the term in describing Athenian *stasis* marks a new wrinkle in his thematization of speech, silence, and action. As the military examples above indicate, the "keeping quiet" that *hesychia* marks in fact does not amount to simple silence. It is more properly understood as a mode of action through inaction, one that often appears on the battlefield, either through the designs of commanders or through the force of circumstances. While working within the same broad thematics that drive his portrayal of Athenian democratic politics, Thucydides uses *hesychia* to mark a new sort of inaction in Athens, one that appears only with the simultaneous appearance of the new sort of plurality marked by his use of *ochlos*. Again, he imports these two terms, which he has heretofore used chiefly in military contexts, to describe aspects of the dynamics of revolutionary politics in Athens. I turn in the following section to consider more closely the role played in those dynamics by the quiet of the mob.

IV. KEEPING QUIET DURING *STASIS*

H. D. Westlake detects in the second half of the *History* a changed Thucydidean attitude toward prominent individuals. In books 5 through 8, he argues, Thucydides "devotes more attention . . . to examining the personality of such individuals and their relations with others . . . because he is more convinced that their general qualities constitute a vital factor in

---

23. Similarly, Thucydides describes the "general inactivity [*hesychazen*]" among the Athenians on Pylos in the wake of the rejection of Demosthenes' initial plan (4.4.1). See also 4.13.4 and 4.104.3.

determining the course of history."[24] This argument seems most convincing as regards book 8, dominated as it is by the account of Athenians *stasis*. The machinations of the various instigators of the oligarchic coup that leads to the Government of the 400 at Athens, together with the dealings of the Spartan leaders, the Persians, and the wily Alcibiades, nearly overwhelm the reader in their complexity and provide a fascinating portrait of political intrigue. The temptation in this context is to focus on the actions of those who led the "movement [*ekinēthē*]" (8.48) against democracy. As I have suggested, though, such an approach misses a key aspect of the new sort of plurality and division that engulfs Athens in book 8. Thucydides' account juxtaposes the actions of the oligarchs with the quiet inaction of the "mob." Instead of tracing the intricacies of the coup itself, I here focus on the pivotal role played by the mob's inaction at key moments in the unfolding of the revolutionary situation.

As we have already seen, Thucydides locates the beginnings of Athenian *stasis* in the actions of "influential men" (8.47) among the Athenian forces that have gathered on the island of Samos. These men make contact with the exiled Alcibiades as part of a plan to replace Athenian democracy with oligarchy and gain the support of the Persians. Thucydides first refers to the quiet of the crowd in recording its response to these initial stirrings of the oligarchic movement (8.48). "The crowd" here consists of Athenian sailors and soldiers on Samos. Its "keeping quiet" does not follow, as one might suspect, from ignorance of or support for the plot, for Thucydides refers to the "anger it felt for the moment" about these developments. The material self-interest of the sailors and soldiers apparently tempered their dissatisfaction. The plotters promised to bring not only the exiled Alcibiades but also the Persian king to the Athenian side. With the latter would come financial support and hence, for the sailors, "the expectation that ... pay ... would be easy to get" for all in the ranks (8.48). In short, Thucydides attributes the early survival of the oligarchic coup to the success of the oligarchs in buying the momentary acquiescence of the crowd.[25]

---

24. Westlake, *Individuals In Thucydides*, 308. More precisely, Westlake describes 1.1 through 5.24 as the "first half" of the *History* and 5.25 to 9.109 as the "second half" (1). See also Connor, *Thucydides*, 214.

25. It is worth emphasizing that this momentary acquiescence, in which material incentives trump anger and dissatisfaction, fits well with the general idea that silence—or here, "quiet"—need not be passive. What I refer to as "acquiescence" thus differs from "consent" (tacit or express) or from disempowerment or disengagement. Though it allows the oligarchic plot to go forward, the Athenian "crowd" on Samos retains its power to influence events. See my brief discussion of consent, powerlessness, and silence in the Introduction.

More generally, this first episode points to one way in which quietness plays into Athenian *stasis*, particularly in its earliest stages. Here and elsewhere *hesychia* serves to allow *stasis* to proceed; the inaction of the mob abets the actions of the conspirators. After complicated wrangling among themselves and fitful and ultimately unsuccessful negotiations with Alcibiades, representatives of the conspirators on Samos—led by Peisander—arrive at Athens (8.66). They find, Thucydides tells us, that their oligarchic compatriots have already begun the work of overthrowing the Athenian democracy. And, as on Samos, that work has benefited from the inaction of common citizens. Using the less pejorative *demos,* Thucydides notes that "the populace kept quiet [*hesychian*]" (8.66).[26] Quiet here follows not, as on Samos, from greed but rather from fear. If anyone opposed the oligarchs "suddenly and in some convenient way he was dead," and so among "the populace," "anyone who suffered no violence, even if he had kept silent, considered it a gain" (8.66). The assembly was subsequently dissolved and the 400 established in the chamber of the *boule,* itself ruling and holding the power, which it would never use, to "convene the five thousand whenever they saw fit" (8.67). All this, Thucydides says, occurred "with no voices in opposition" (8.69); the "citizens offered no challenge but remained quiet [*hesychazon*]" (8.70).

The early stages of *stasis* in Athens are marked, then, not by noisy confrontation but by silent and at times deadly action by the oligarchs, in the face of which "the crowd," though "dissatisfied," remained "quiet."[27] In what emerges as a relatively distinct, intermediate stage of *stasis* in Athens, the role of *hesychia* changes, as the mob or crowd reacts to a new round of moves by the oligarchs. Having by their bold actions apparently taken firm control in Athens, the 400 made peace overtures to the Spartan king Agis, who occupied nearby Deceleia. Agis, though, remained uncertain of the status of affairs in Athens. In particular, Thucydides says, he worried that if the Athenian people "saw a sizable army of Lacedaemonians they would not stay inactive [*hesychazein*]" (8.71). Agis thus rebuffed the overtures from the 400, though he did send Spartan forces deeper into Attica. Thucydides' description of Agis' thinking has the effect of suggesting that

---

26. Here I use the Loeb Classical Library translation. Lattimore here has "remained immobilized." While such a translation perhaps captures the connotations of *hesychian* in this context, I use Smith's translation to maintain the language of "quiet."

27. The plotters themselves make use of their own "keeping quiet" as well. See 8.69, where Thucydides uses *hesychia* to describe the quiet planning for the seizure of the *boule* chamber. Again, "keeping quiet" is not strictly speaking passive; it marks an active stance toward events.

the quiet of "the crowd" in Athens is not absolute and final. Though rendered inactive by fear in the initial stages of *stasis*, the *ochlos*, given the right circumstances, might well take action, moving against the 400.

We soon learn that the pay-inspired quiet on Samos has begun to give way, too. In 8.72, Thucydides tells us that the 400 sent ten of their number to Samos, concerned that "a mob [*ochlos*] of sailors would in itself be unwilling to stay under an oligarchic system." And in 8.73, he makes clear that those fears were well founded, as on Samos "a reaction had already set in against the oligarchic movement." Holding an assembly in which they deposed those of their leaders associated with the movement, the sailors and soldiers on Samos vowed to live "as citizens of a democratic government" (8.73). Soon Thrasyboulos, who had been opposed to the oligarchic conspiracy, "persuaded the majority of the soldiers" to recall Alcibiades, promising him immunity from prosecution. Alcibiades thus sailed to Samos and, making exaggerated promises of his ability to bring along Persian help from Tissaphernes (8.81) was soon elected general.

When the envoys from the 400 later arrived on Samos, they thus faced a hostile reception from the soldiers, who were "clamoring instead for killing those who were overthrowing the democracy" (8.86). There follows a critical moment. Thucydides says that the sailors did hear out the envoys from Athens, but only after "they managed to quiet down [*hesychasantes*]." The envoys' words apparently had little effect, for the sailors remained furious and were inclined to board their ships and sail to Athens. Here Alcibiades stepped in and "restrain[ed] the crowd [*ochlon*]" (8.86). Thucydides claims that only Alcibiades could have quieted the sailors in this way and that in doing so he "did the state a service, one that was unsurpassed." Had the sailors made for Athens, beyond the violence and turmoil in the home city itself, the Peloponnesians would surely have seized Ionia and the Hellespont. Where the quiet of the crowd at both Samos and Athens had initially facilitated the oligarchic coup, in this middle stage the crowd's keeping quiet, its continued inaction, prevents *stasis* from escalating and saves Athens from disaster in the eastern Aegean.

From initially permitting *stasis* to checking its worst possibilities, *hesychia* emerges in the final stages of the oligarchic revolution at Athens as a key prerequisite for the return of social harmony and the emergence of the Government of the 5000. Following the return to democracy on Samos, matters come to a head in Athens as well. Buoyed in particular by the recall of Alcibiades, dissenters within the ranks of the 400 began to "talk in small groups and criticize the government" (8.89). In response, the more hard-core among the 400 redoubled their efforts to secure terms with Sparta and to finish a fort at Etioneia, which would control the entrance to the Piraeus. The opponents of the 400, led by Thermanes, saw the fort for what it was: a way to secure the entry of Spartan forces into the Athenian port and hand the city to the enemy (80.90–91).

Spurred on by "many rebellious speeches," the hoplites working on the fort turned on the 400, arresting one of their number and bringing the city to the brink of violent strife (8.92). Only the intervention of "older men" and of Thucydides, the Pharsalian *proxenos*, prevented renewed violence, as the Athenians "managed to quiet down [*hesychasan*]" (8.92). In the wake of this pivotal moment, "the crowd [*ochlon*]"—a term now applied to hoplites as well as citizens from the lower ranks—turned to tearing down the controversial fort, with the cry that "whoever wanted the Five Thousand to Rule instead of the Four Hundred should get to work" (8.92.11). This work done, the hoplites in the Piraeus started the next day to move against the 400. Seeing this, the 400 sent a group to urge them to "to keep quiet [*hesychazein*]" and "be reasonable," and promising that the 400 would publish the names of the 5000 and that that group would now have true power to choose the guiding group of 400. With the passions of both sides cooling, an assembly was soon held at which the 400 were formally deposed and the Government of the 5000 was firmly established (8.97).

At the end of Section II, we were left with the question of why Athens' political strife did not come to the fully savage stage reached at Corcyra. As I have tried to suggest, the answer must focus on the quiet inaction of the Athenian mob. This inaction, in part, is a matter of restraint in the face of provocation. If we read the Corcyrean disaster as a matter of human nature bursting the bounds of convention in favor of revolutionary action, then we can find a sharp contrast in, for example, the Athenian sailors' willingness to remain inactive when they most wanted to sail to Athens to confront the oligarchy. If we focus on the decline of language as a way of binding the community together, on the communal incoherence that seizes Corcyra, then we can see in the crowd at Athens, instead, a willingness to respond to calming words with quiet rather than with revolutionary action of its own. None of which is to say that the quiet of the mob is to be admired without qualification. For, again, the mob's acquiescence at the outset allowed the oligarchic movement to gain a foothold when a more active response might have squelched it; *hesychia* here is as much a matter of disengagement or submission as restraint. The point is simply that the course of *stasis* at Athens turns as much on the quiet of the crowd as on the actions of the oligarchs.[28]

V. CONCLUSION

After describing its emergence from Athenian *stasis,* Thucydides expresses considerable admiration for the Government of the 5000: "And during the first phase, the Athenians clearly had their best government, at least in my lifetime; for a moderate [*metria*] blending [*xynkrasis*] of the few [*oligous*] and the many [*pollous*] came about, and it was this which first lifted the city out of the terrible current condition of its affairs" (8.97). Thucydides goes on to qualify this judgment in two ways that leave its overall significance open to question. First, he carefully limits his comments on Athenian forms of government to his own lifetime. The passage above consequently will not support any general claim about Thucydides' ultimate judgment on regimes. The most that can be said is that, based on his observation and experience, the Government of the 5000 appeared superior to either the narrow oligarchy of the 400 or the radical democracy that preceded it. This does mean, of course, that Thucydides seems to have preferred the rule of the 5000 even to the kind of nominal democracy that prevailed in Athens under Pericles; but we can hardly draw any further conclusion about what form of government Thucydides thought best, either for Athens or in general. Beyond this qualification, Thucydides firmly situates his praise in the specific context of Athenian *stasis*. The Government of the 5000, he says, brought Athens out of political turmoil, allowing the city to respond to immediate external threats brought on by the 400's interest in an immediate peace with Sparta, seemingly at whatever the cost.

Our understanding of the Government of the 5000 is further complicated by the fact that Thucydides gives us little detail on its precise makeup or functioning. That power was placed in the hands of the 5000 rather than in the hands of the entire citizenry suggests a moderate oligarchy. On the other hand, Thucydides says that with the advent of the 5000 "the oligarchy and strife ended" in Athens (8.98), and he indicates that the grant of power to the 5000 took place in a meeting of the full assembly

---

28. Here, compare Ober's analysis of the "Athenian revolution" of 508–7 as turning not on the reforms imposed by Cleisthenes but rather on a spontaneous riot of ordinary Athenians. Ober, *The Athenian Revolution*.

(8.97)—suggesting perhaps not the establishment of an oligarchy but in Proctor's words "a voluntary act of the restored democracy" temporarily limiting its own power.[29] In the face of Thucydides' refusal to attach a particular label to the 5000, Connor concludes that the *History* here "point[s] to a state of political analysis beyond the partisan claims for democracy or oligarchy."[30] Orwin, similarly, argues that the 5000 "functions less as a model than as a heuristic," which calls attention to the excesses and deficiencies of both oligarchy and democracy.[31]

If we thus move away from attempting to find the correct name for the form taken by the Government of the 5000, we are left chiefly with wondering about the nature of its "moderate blending of the few and the many" and how this, in Thucydides' eyes, compares to pre-*stasis* Athenian democracy. The "moderate" character of this blending no doubt has to do most basically with the fact that it leans neither too much toward oligarchy nor too much toward democracy. Thucydides, after all, admires the Government of the 5000 precisely because it brought an end to factional struggle in the city. But I would suggest, too, that we can see this moderation in the context of the particular dynamics of action and inaction that mark Thucydides' account of Athenian *stasis*. In a sense, the quiet inaction that emerges in that account must characterize the Government of the 5000, too. Part of the civil blending that follows *stasis* must be the willingness of both the few and the many to remain quiet, the agreement by each to forgo revolutionary action against the other. In this context, the reader senses in Thucydides' praise for the 5000 an appreciation for the momentary break, the brief moment of rest, it provided from both democracy and oligarchy. This is not, of course, to say that the Athenians become inactive as a city. Thucydides reports that *hoi Athenaioi* began immediately to take actions—including recalling Alcibiades—that "lifted the city out of the terrible condition of its affairs" (463). These actions, though, depended on the inaction of the factions within it, on both the few and the many remaining quiet so that the city could recover.

By contrast, democracy—nominal or otherwise—in Thucydides' Athens involves the neither the quiet of the few nor the quiet of the many. More

---

29. Proctor, *The Experience of Thucydides*, 49. Proctor here follows Ste. Croix, "The Constitution of the Five Thousand," and provides an excellent overview of the dispute over the nature of the 5000. Gomme, Dover, and Andrewes in *Historical Commentary on Thucydides* argue that the Government of the 5000 was essentially oligarchy.
30. Connor, *Thucydides*, 229.
31. Orwin, *The Humanity of Thucydides*, 192.

precisely, and as I have already indicated, the very categories of "the few" and "the many" are absent from Thucydides' account of democratic politics. In that account, elite speakers and the mass of ordinary citizens interact, but not as factions engaged in conflict with one another or agreed upon a "moderate blending" that follows from an agreement by both to remain quiet. Thucydides, that is, at first glance portrays democratic politics not as factional conflict or coexistence, but rather as the interaction through political rhetoric of elite speakers with the silent mass of ordinary citizens. Just as the rhetorical ploys of elite speakers here do not seem to amount to the revolutionary actions of oligarchs, so the silence of the demos does not seem to amount simply to the quiet of the mob. With this in mind, I turn in the next chapter to a fuller exploration of the role of silence in Athenian action while the city remains democratic, at least in name.

2

The Silence of *Hoi Athenaioi*: Two Modes of Athenian Action in the *History*

I. INTRODUCTION

Many times before now, I have felt that a democracy is incapable of ruling others, and more than ever during your present change of heart on the Mitylenians.

—Cleon (3.37)

So Cleon, according to Thucydides the "most violent" but also the most influential Athenian in the years after the death of the great Pericles, launches his "volcanic tirade against the democratic practice of full discussion."[1] Much is at stake in the debate that Cleon thus joins. Most immediately, hanging in the balance is the fate of those captured upon the fall of the city of Mitylene, which is part of the vast Athenian empire. Only a day before, the Athenians have decreed death or slavery for their rebellious eastern Aegean subjects; now a night of remorse and regret has somehow moved them "to deliberate (*bouleusasthai*)" anew on this "savage and extreme" sentence (3.36). On this day, they reconvene to face questions of life and death, freedom and slavery for the conquered.

Cleon's opening salvo suggests the depth and importance of the question at hand, not just for the Mitylenians, but for the imperial city itself and for its identity and politics. Caught up in the midst of a war precipitated on Thucydides' account by the complexities and complications of alliance,[2] priding themselves as Pericles has suggested they should on the

---

1. J. H. Finley, *Thucydides*, 171.
2. Thus Epidamnus and Plataea, the two cities around which arose the "reasons publicly alleged [*aitia*]" (1.22) for the outbreak of the war, are both entangled in complicated relationships of colonization and alliance with Sparta and Athens. Just what Thucydides has in mind as the relation between these *aitia* and what he calls the "truest explanation [*prophasin*]"— Spartan fear of Athenian expansion—has, of course, been a matter of considerable dispute. Among the better-known readings of Thucydides as a "scientist" concerned with causation

present power and future glory of their empire, the Athenians cannot but concern themselves with how to rule others. The wrangling of Cleon and the otherwise unknown Diodotus, who rises at this assembly to speak against him, makes clear the difficulties the Athenians face on this score. There are arguments from both justice and expediency, and arguments about the meaning of each, to be considered. And, of course, there is the question of whether the consideration of such arguments is at all necessary or at all desirable in a city that would govern others. Cleon's suggestion that continuing deliberation, a readiness to revoke decisions and change plans, and a willingness to hear speakers on all sides are inconsistent with the possession of empire strikes at the heart of the vision of Athenian democracy offered by Pericles in the Funeral Oration.

Cleon's demagogic attack on speech and speakers and his argument for silent perseverance are, strictly speaking, self-defeating. To stand before the assembled demos and warn of the dangers posed by speakers in the assembly requires not only the brashness that Cleon constantly exhibits but also more than a little of the "cleverness" he himself decries in others.[3] To offer in a political speech an attack on political speech is to invite precisely the sort of retort that Diodotus soon offers: "As for speeches, whoever maintains that they do not teach practicality is either stupid or has some personal bias." We will not find, Diodotus suggests, "some other way [in which] the future and its uncertainty can be considered" (3.42). In warning of the ill effects of Athens's noisy politics, Cleon must himself add to the cacophony; he must become what he says he deplores.

From a broader perspective, Cleon's dismissal of deliberation runs afoul of another sort of difficulty. Thucydides has Cleon lamenting the Athenians' desire to keep talking about Mitylene, but in the entire affair Cleon himself is the first Athenian we hear speak. His harsh words shatter the silence that has prevailed in Thucydides' Athenian assembly since Pericles' third and final speech (2.60–64). By the time Cleon rises to speak, the revolt of Mitylene is more than a year old. The Athenians have more than once acted in response to events on Lesbos, but Thucydides records no earlier Athenian discussion of the matter. His rendering of the Athenian reaction to the first reports of revolt is typical in this regard:

---

are Cochrane, *Thucydides and the Science of History,* and Bluhm, "Causal Theory in Thucydides' Peloponnesian War." For a brief critique of this reading, see Ball, "When Words Lose Their Meaning."

3. As Ober, *Political Dissent in Democratic Athens,* has it, "Cleon's clever speech is embedded in a clever speech" (98).

Worn out both by the plague and by the war that had broken out recently and was at its height, the Athenians [*hoi Athenaioi*] considered it a great hardship to fight against Lesbos as well, which had a fleet and intact resources, and at first did not credit the accusations, giving priority to wishing them untrue; when they were unable, however, to persuade the Mitylenians to abandon either the unification or their preparations, they became alarmed and were willing to strike first. They suddenly sent out forty ships. (3.3)

In this and several similar moments over the course of his account of the Athenians' engagement with Mitylene, Thucydides reports Athenian deeds, but no Athenian words. It seems at least mildly ironic for Cleon to fault the Athenians for their tendency to talk too much. His argument surely loses force insofar as they have not to this point talked about Mitylene at all.

Or have they? Given what we know of Athenian politics it seems impossible that the talkative Athenians would have been so silent about Mitylene. In his Funeral Oration, Pericles, as we have seen, praises the Athenians precisely for their penchant for deliberating prior to acting. Beyond Thucydides, our sources often enough portray the Athenians as talking to the point of excess about political matters. Thus Plato (in, for example, the *Gorgias*) depicts both the sophists and all Athenian politicians—Pericles included—as speechifying demagogues and the Athenians as a willing, even fawning, audience. Aristophanes, in *Knights* and elsewhere, offers a similar portrait. As for more mundane institutional matters, we know from other historical evidence that the Athenian assembly met regularly, roughly every twenty days, and that it could be called to meet on extraordinary occasions.[4] In this context, it seems highly unlikely that the *ecclesia* did not meet during the lengthy span of time for which Thucydides records no speeches.

If the assembly did meet, it seems equally unlikely that the Athenians—or at least some Athenian speaker—did not bring up the revolt of Mitylene. The *ecclesia*, after all, had final authority to make such a decision, and its

---

4. See Stockton, *The Classical Athenian Democracy*, chap. 3, for a discussion of the evidence regarding meetings of the *ecclesia*. See also Sinclair, *Democracy and Participation in Athens*. We might also note here that the *History* focuses our attention on the assembly as the site of deliberation in Athens, though of course various other possible sites of deliberation existed in Athens in the fifth century (the law courts, the *boule*, the local demes, the agora). From the point of view of my argument here, the fact that Thucydides presents deliberation occurring only periodically and only in the assembly further highlights the (again, effective if not literal) silence that he suggest more often exists in the city.

agenda was open to the raising of any issue. What is more, the Athenians could hardly have been apathetic on the matter. Many perhaps would have reacted with anger, some with fear; others would have felt a degree of sympathy for the Mitylenians or concern about the consequences of sending a sizable Athenian fleet across the Aegean. It would not have been difficult to see that their response would carry implications for their broader conflict with the Spartans. The Athenians surely must have discussed matters, must have heard arguments made by the more politically active and ambitious among them. But Thucydides tells us nothing of such arguments; he neither records nor even mentions a meeting of the assembly.

Why should this be so? Why does Thucydides, who insists on the "accuracy" (*akribeia*) of his account of the war, not record political speeches when, as we should like to think, we know that speeches must have been given? What can be the meaning of the silence he seems to impose on the Athenians? One possible answer draws on Thucydides' much-discussed claim to accuracy itself. The "methodological preface" at 1.22, where Thucydides describes how he arrived at his account of the war, seems clearly to draw a distinction between his recording of speeches and his reporting of the deeds of the war. The accuracy of the narrative, he there tells us, he "tried by the most severe and detailed tests possible," checking his own account against those of others, never trusting his own "impressions."[5] As to the speeches, on the other hand, Thucydides suggests that he ultimately did in a sense trust his own impressions. It proved "difficult" to remember actual speeches "word for word," and so, he says, "my habit has been to make the speakers say what was in my opinion demanded of them by the various occasions, of course adhering as closely as possible to the general sense of what was really said" (1.22). From these passages, Clifford Orwin, to take but one recent example, concludes that "for the deeds Thucydides claims accuracy; for the speeches, accuracy to a point."[6]

From this point of view, speeches and narrative appear to differ largely in terms of Thucydides' aims and practices as an historian. There follow various essentially methodological possibilities as to why Thucydides might have recorded no Athenian speeches on Mitylene prior to those of Cleon and Diodotus. Perhaps he had particular or particularly detailed knowledge

---

5. I draw "impressions" from Crawley's translation. Where Crawley offers "impressions," Smith has "as seemed to me probable."

6. Orwin, *The Humanity of Thucydides*, 207. Hornblower, *Thucydides*, 43, is more troubled by the apparent discrepancy, finding in the difference between the accuracy of speeches and narrative evidence a broader "fluctuation . . . between extreme subjectivity and extreme objectivity."

of the final assembly meeting that made the recording of speeches possible—knowledge that he lacked regarding earlier debates about the revolt. Perhaps he wished to record only one set of speeches in order to keep the role of his "impressions" to a minimum. Perhaps, that is, he wished his report of the earlier stages of the revolt to reflect that seemingly higher standard of accuracy that he claims for his narrative of events.

Reflection on such possibilities can lead back to old questions about the composition of the *History* or, alternatively, toward important and interesting issues of the status of Thucydides' work as history.[7] For now, though, I want to bracket such questions about Thucydides' methodological practices and epistemological commitments. I am instead interested in exploring the understanding of Athenian action and speech suggested to the reader by the text as we have it.[8] In this context, our chief question will not concern how Thucydides came to offer the particular account of events embodied in the *History*. Rather, we will want to ask what this account of events—as a sort of surrogate political experience—suggests to us about, among other things, speech and action in democracy.

Marc Cogan has taken a similar tack, insisting that we appreciate what he terms the "historicity" of the speeches in the *History*. The speeches do not stand as exhibitions of Thucydides' methodology or of his own political principles. Rather, they are to be read as political moments, as attempts by speakers in particular circumstances to persuade their listeners to take a particular course of action. Together, the speeches contribute toward the subtle portrayal of a Thucydidean understanding of action: "We can reasonably assert that Thucydides provides us, *throughout the History* with that evidence necessary for our understanding of the war as an event under the *continuously deliberate direction* of the participants. Speeches are

---

7. For example, in *Political Dissent in Democratic Athens*, Ober draws on the distinction between words (*logos*) and deeds (*ergon*) to argue that Thucydides establishes a distinction between "democratic knowledge" and "historical knowledge."

8. I have in mind something similar to the approach suggested by Connor, who emphasizes "the responses [the *History*] evokes from its readership." That emphasis follows from his recognition of Thucydides' "implicit strategy," in which "readers [are] led to re-experience the war, to live through it again, seeing it fully, without averting their eyes from the most unpleasant or revealing episodes." Connor, *Thucydides*, 16. In this sense, learning from the *History* depends less on the literal "accuracy" of Thucydides' accounts of words or deeds than from a kind of dramatic "truth" that emerges from "re-experienc[ing] the war." Insofar as this re-experiencing involves "seeing [the war] fully," it incorporates a different kind of accuracy. Connor's analysis of Thucydides' "implicit strategy" echoes Hobbes's on the "secret instruction" of the *History* and Nietzsche on Thucydides' "hidden thoughts." See my discussion of this point in the Introduction.

recorded to make clear that deliberation occurred to direct the war."[9] For Cogan, Thucydides has carefully selected the particular speeches found in the *History* as "the most vital *representatives*" of such deliberation. The reader thus witnesses or experiences deliberation informing action in a few instances and can conclude that deliberation *continually* preceded action. Now Cogan is obviously correct that the presence of the speeches points to some Thucydidean thinking about deliberation and its role in collective action. But, again, what of the absence of speeches earlier in the affair of Mitylene? What are we to make of the silence of the Athenians in such moments?

The answer implied by Cogan's claim (though not explicitly developed by Cogan himself) is that the speeches we do find in the history are in some sense representative of other, unrecorded speeches. The recorded speeches stand as exemplary moments in the "continuously deliberate direction" of the war by those who speak and those who listen and decide. We can thus assume the occurrence of deliberation even in the face of the apparent silence of the Athenians when Thucydides records no speeches. In this chapter, I call this sort of assumption into question by approaching the absence of Athenian speeches in the early stages of the matter of Mitylene as something more than a methodological or stylistic choice on Thucydides' part. The absence of speeches at some points in the *History*, that is, carries as much meaning for our understanding of the character and relation of speech and action as the presence of speeches at other points. To grasp the full complexity of Thucydides' understanding of action in democracy, we must take silence seriously.

I argue here that Thucydides' account of the Athenian reaction to the revolt of Mitylene in fact presents to the reader what we can think of as two modes of Athenian action: one preceded by the sort of debate in which Cleon and Diodotus engage and to which Thucydides attaches the term deliberation, another in which such deliberation does not take place. At first glance the distinction between what I will call "deliberative action" and what I will call "sudden action" seems to map straightforwardly onto a distinction between speech and silence in the Athenian assembly. In fact, silence plays a role in both modes. The intertwining of silence and speech in deliberative and sudden action thus provides an important part of the conceptual framework for the remaining chapters. In this chapter I explore these complex matters, drawing from the two types of silence

---

9. Cogan, *The Human Thing*, xv, emphasis added.

identified in the Introduction, and enlisting the help first of Aristotle and then of Arendt.

II. THE ATHENIAN RESPONSE TO THE REVOLT OF MITYLENE

and the actions we do on the spur of the moment [exaiphnês] are said to be voluntary but not to express decision [prohairesis]

We have found, then, that what we decide [proelointo] to do is whatever action among those up to us we deliberate [bouleutou] about and desire to do. Hence also decision will be deliberative desire to do an action that is up to us; for when we have judged [that it is right] as a result of deliberation, our desire to do it expresses our wish.

—Aristotle, *Nicomachean Ethics* (trans. Ross)

In book III of the *Ethics,* Aristotle takes up the nature of choice or decision—*prohairesis*—as part of his consideration of the nature of action and responsibility. We can, he says, attach responsibility and hence praise or blame to voluntary actions, but not to involuntary ones. The most obviously voluntary actions are those we choose, with choice depending on prior deliberation, as the second passage above suggests. The account of deliberation and "deliberative desire" or choice that Aristotle goes on to offer has recently been of considerable interest and debate, with scholars focusing in particular on the role of wish and the relative status of ends and means in it. By contrast, Aristotle does little to flesh out how he understands the sorts of actions described in the first passage, those taken "on the spur of the moment" or "suddenly." His refusal to attach to such actions his term for "decision," though, is suggestive. Since decision follows deliberation, it seems most likely that sudden actions lack deliberation and thus fall short of being truly and fully chosen.

Thucydides appears either not to have or at least not to deploy any developed conception of choice or decision parallel to Aristotle's *prohairesis.* At times, though, he uses the same term(s) as Aristotle for deliberation or consideration—forms of the Greek verb *bouleuō*. This is the case, for instance, in his introduction to the assembly meeting at which Cleon and Diodotus speak, an assembly called in response to the Athenians desire for another opportunity "to consider [*bouleusasthai*]" the punishment of the Mitylenians. On the other hand, as we saw in passing in the previous section, Thucydides describes the earliest Athenian response to the revolt of Mitylene as "sudden," marking it with the same Greek, a form of *exaiphnes*, that Aristotle uses in the first passage from the *Ethics* quoted above. What is more, Thucydides records this Athenian reaction—and in fact all Athenian actions toward Mitylene prior to the Mitylene Debate itself—without reporting speeches or deploying the language of deliberation that he will use to describe the exchange between Cleon and Diodotus. He thus suggests—as does Aristotle—a contrast between deliberative action and a more frequent sudden mode of Athenian action that we might think of as an analog to Aristotle's "actions taken on the spur of the moment." Though I cannot improve on the drama that Thucydides manages subtly to build as events on Lesbos unfold in the early chapters of book 3, I want in this section to trace the Athenians' actions in this sudden mode.

Mitylene comes to dominate the third book of the *History*, but it does so haltingly, by fits and starts. Thucydides begins book 3 at an almost leisurely pace. Chapter 1 rather blandly records military moves by the Spartans and their allies and by the Athenians. The former launched their annual invasion of Attica, proceeding to "ravage the land." As for the Athenians, their cavalry, as "usual [*eisthesan*]," struck where it could, harassing the enemy troops. When their provisions ran out, the Peloponnesians "withdrew and dispersed to their cities." By this point in the *History*, all of this has become the standard way in which each summer's warfare begins. Against this backdrop of the familiar and expected, Thucydides moves directly in Chapter 2 to the unfamiliar and unexpected turn of events on Lesbos. The Mitylenians have not appeared in the *History* to this point, and nothing has prepared us for their revolt. Thucydides does note that the revolt had been long simmering, but he begins the chapter in dramatic fashion: "Immediately after the Peloponnesian invasion, all the Lesbians except Methymna revolted from Athens" (3.2).[10]

In response, the Athenians sent forty ships to Lesbos. Again, Thucydides gives no indication that the Athenians engaged in deliberation prior to this action, and he says that they acted "suddenly [*exapinaiōs*]." The translation of *exapinaiōs* as "suddenly" suggests at first glance that the Athenian action, whatever else it may have been, was quick. From this point of view, the need for sudden action in response to unfolding events would seem in particular to rule out taking time for lengthy discussion in the

---

10. Thucydides similarly creates a sense of the unexpected in his account of the initial Theban attack on Plataea. As Connor, *Thucydides*, 53, puts it: "a sudden night attack at a place to which little attention has been paid encourages the reader to react like a contemporary with surprise." I discuss the Plataean surprise at length in Chapter 5.

assembly. In fact, though, Thucydides does not portray the Athenians as acting immediately or even particularly quickly at this point. Their initial reaction to the stirrings of revolt was instead some sort of willful disbelief. When friends on Lesbos brought news of the revolt, Thucydides says, the Athenians "at first would not credit the accusations, giving priority to wishing [to boulesthai] them untrue" (3.3). The Athenians then apparently sent envoys to Mitylene, though Thucydides tells us only of their return and of their failure to persuade the Mitylenians to stop their preparations. At this point, the Athenians "became alarmed and were willing [eboulonto]" to strike the Mitylenians; only then did they dispatch the above-mentioned naval force. On this account, the Athenians clearly had time to deliberate and then to act deliberately—but he offers no indication that they did. He instead leaves the impression that silence prevailed among the Athenians.

We are left to wonder what, other than simple speediness of response, might constitute the suddenness that Thucydides here attributes to Athenian action. Thucydides, though, gives the reader little time to ponder the nature of this initial Athenian response. Immediately after reporting the dispatch of the Athenian naval force, he shifts the focus of the narrative to Mitylene. Having been forewarned of the impending arrival of Athenian ships, the Mitylenians barricaded themselves inside their half-finished walls, dispatched envoys to both Athens and Sparta, and waited. After a series of initial skirmishes brought on by the arrival of the Athenians, a stalemate ensued, with the Athenians controlling the sea and the Mitylenians the land. "This," Thucydides says, "was how the war was going around Mitylene" (3.6).

Thucydides now turns to the first of several interludes that divide Athenian action toward Mitylene into a series of rather distinct episodes. This is not to say that either Athens or Mitylene disappear entirely from the narrative. Thucydides spends one chapter describing the exploits of the Athenian Asopius, who this same summer led a fleet around the Peloponnesus (3.7). He also records the speech given by the Mitylenian envoys sent to the Peloponnesians assembled at Olympus (3.8–15). Seeking Peloponnesian support for their city's struggle against Athens, these envoys present arguments both from "justice and honour" (3.10) and from expediency, telling the Peloponnesians that they have "an opportunity as never before" for striking a blow at the Athenians (3.13). This speech and the Peloponnesian response to it make clear that "the course of the war at Mitylene" remains fluid, but they simultaneously suggest the Athenians' detachment from developments. Thucydides tells us that the Mitylenians sent similar envoys to Athens. But he reports no speech from these latter envoys, noting only that they "came back from Athens unsuccessful" (3.5). The speech of the Mitylenians at Sparta, precisely with its calling on justice and expediency, no doubt calls to mind the later speeches of Cleon and Diodotus in Athens, where the justice and expediency of Athenian action become matters for "deliberation." But at this early stage, it is the Peloponnesians who, by hearing out the envoys, seem to be engaging in such deliberation.

This interlude complete, Thucydides returns us very briefly to Athens, presenting the Athenian response to the developing alliance between the Mitylenians and the Peloponnesians. These latter heed the arguments of the Mitylenian envoys and accept their proposals. They begin to prepare for an attack on Athens by land and sea (3.15), arousing the Athenians to new action: "The Athenians, aware [*aisthomenoi*] that that these preparations were based on contempt for their weakness, wished [*boulomenoi*] to show that this judgment was mistaken, and that without touching the fleet at Lesbos they were also able to defend themselves easily against the advance from the Peloponnesos, and they manned a hundred ships" (3.16). In describing this second round of Athenian action in the affair of Mitylene, Thucydides does not use the language of suddenness. In every other respect, though, the narrative here is similar to his account of the first Athenian response to the revolt. He uses precisely the same language to describe the Athenians perceiving (*aisthomenoi*) a challenge in their surroundings, wishing (*boulomenoi*) to achieve some effect, and acting accordingly. And he offers no hint of deliberation in the Athenian assembly, where, for the reader at least, silence continues to prevail.

Having reported this latest Athenian action, Thucydides devotes three more brief paragraphs to matters surrounding Mitylene before turning to other matters. As the Athenians and Peloponnesians make move and countermove around the Corinthian Isthmus, the Mitylenians launch a series of attacks. To this the Athenians respond by dispatching Paches, who, commanding a thousand hoplites, manages to invest Mitylene so that it is "cut off by both land and sea" (3.18). A siege and a new stalemate ensue. And the end of this episode in the affair of Mitylene is marked by another interlude. Thucydides turns to narrate in great detail the bold attempt by the Plataeans to escape from their city, besieged as it is by the Spartans (3.20–24). I discuss the significance of this bit of narration in Chapter 6. In the context of the developing situation on Mitylene, though, the siege of Plataea marks another diversion of the reader's and, perhaps, the Athenians' attention.

Thucydides once more returns to Mitylene, where siege and stalemate again give way abruptly, this time presenting the Athenians with a sudden and complete victory. When a promised Peloponnesian fleet under Alcidas fails to materialize at Lesbos, the Spartan Salethus determines to arm the Mitylenian commons. The latter quickly threaten to capitulate to the Athenians, but "the authorities" preempt such a move by "making an agreement" with Paches (3.28.1). The agreement amounts to an unconditional surrender; it allows Paches to enter Mitylene and allows the Athenians "to make whatever plans [*bouleusai*] they wished [*boulontai*] about the Mitylenians" (3.28.1). This provision, of course, paves the way for the initial harsh judgment passed on the Mitylenians and ultimately for the Mitylene Debate itself.

Before relating either, though, Thucydides offers a seven-chapter account of Paches' pursuit of Alcidas, who arrived, too late, with his fleet (3.29–35). At this point, the pursuit seems largely irrelevant to the course of events at either Mitylene or Athens. It serves as one final pause in Thucydides' developing account of the Mitylene affair. Together with those which precede it, this final interlude gives a particular and peculiar feel to Athenian action. The narrative of the Mitylene revolt is episodic, building to its climax through a series of disrupting developments followed by stalemate followed in turn by more disrupting developments.[11] When matters stabilize and Thucydides turns his and our attention elsewhere, the Athenians fade into the background. We are led to think that their attention has perhaps been diverted as well, to refocus on Mitylene only when something startling occurs. Instead of the continuous and deliberate Athenian action Cogan sees, Thucydides presents discontinuous Athenian responses to the actions of others, responses that flow seamlessly and silently from perception to wish to action, allowing the Athenians to turn to other matters.

The effect of all this is indeed to make Athenian action appear "sudden," though, again, not necessarily quick. In fact, the more colloquial "on the spur of the moment" perhaps better captures the nature of Athenian action in the early stages of the affair of Mitylene. As they act or, more properly, react, the Athenians indeed seem "spurred" by the events of "the

---

11. Connor, *Thucydides*, 149, and in appendix V, traces parallels in Thucydides' presentation of the "major siege narratives" of Plataea, Mitylene, and Melos. He notes, but does not explore, what he calls "intervals" in each of the three narratives. These intervals roughly parallel the "interludes" I here discuss.

moment": the initial report of rebellion, the Mytilenian alliance with Sparta, and the sudden fall of Mitylene. The Athenians are not, by contrast, "spurred" by careful thought or deliberation, or by disagreement among themselves. Put in the terms I used in the Introduction, we might say that moments of sudden action are marked both by the silent presence of the demos and by an absolute silence of contending voices. Alternatively, we might say that the silent presence of the demos expands to engulf all Athenians. Indeed, in moments of sudden action, the distinction between those few who speak and those who are silently present and decide vanishes. The silent presence of the demos becomes simply the silence of *hoi Athenaioi*.

Here we see again one reason why Thucydides enjoys such repute among realist students of international relations. In the sudden actions that dominate the narrative of the *History*, the Athenians (and, for that matter, other cities as well) appear as a unit of action. When the Athenians respond, suddenly, to happenings on Lesbos or to maneuverings by the Peloponnesians, they do so, at least so far as the reader can tell, as one. Whereas deliberative action entails debate about what is to be done, Thucydides in moments of sudden action offers no suggestion of disagreement. Only the plural subject—*hoi Athenaioi*—gives the barest hint of Athenian plurality; and its use, in the absence of any indication of actual disharmony, itself highlights the fact that noisy plurality has been subsumed by silent unity in the moment of acting.[12] A sharp reminder of Athenian plurality emerges, though, in the Mitylene Debate, which marks a turn to the deliberative mode of Athenian action.

III. DELIBERATION AND DELIBERATIVE ACTION: THE MITYLENE DEBATE

I noted above that Thucydides and Aristotle draw on the same language of deliberation or consideration (*bouleuō*); they also use the same terms

---

12. Thucydides in fact uses the plural subject to refer to other cities: hence "the Spartans," "the Corinthians," "the Corcyreans," and so on. In this way, though my focus throughout remains on Athens, much of what I have to say about his manner of recording Athenian action also holds for his manner of recording the actions of other cities. Put differently, in any city, action always gestures toward the simultaneity of plurality and unity. If Athens differs from other actors in the *History*, those differences depend on particular Athenian "characteristics" (something I take up in Chapter 3) and on the way in which the Athenians understand and practice democratic politics (which I focus on in Chapter 4).

for wishing—forms of the verb *boulomai*. As a way of approaching the deliberative mode of Athenian action as Thucydides presents it, let me begin this section by quickly highlighting two ways of understanding Aristotle's account of deliberation and the role of wish in each. On the simplest reading of the relevant section of the *Ethics*, wish and deliberation play separate and sequential roles in Aristotle's account of choice, roles based on the categories of ends and means: "the end, then, being what we wish (*boulêtou*) for, the means (*tōn pros to telos*) what we deliberate (*bouleutōn*) about and choose (*proairetōn*)."[13] Wishing an end is prior to deliberating upon and ultimately choosing means. We do not, in this sense, "choose" our ends: "for a doctor does not deliberate whether he shall heal, nor an orator whether he shall convince.... Having set the end, they consider how and by what means it is attained."[14] The wish to heal or to convince provides the end as a given. By itself such a wish may come to nothing; deliberation must find the best means to the end, if any exist. Indeed, we may wish for the impossible, but deliberation must deal with the possible: "if we come on an impossibility [in deliberation] we must give up the search."[15] On the other hand, when deliberation finds the appropriate means, wishing yields action. As Jean-Pierre Vernant, who offers a succinct summary of this reading of the *Ethics*, has it: "once the desire of *boulesis* has thus fixed upon the immediately realizable means, action follows and does so necessarily."[16] We come to wish the means that deliberation has determined will yield our already fixed end, and action follows inevitably.

If we accept this reading, then Aristotle seems to limit deliberation to a sort of truncated technical reasoning; concerned with means and not ends, it functions according to a simple "instrumental rationality."[17] A number of scholars have called this reading into question by problematizing its sharp rendering of the ends/means dichotomy in Aristotle's account of deliberation. This move is marked by an alternative translation of Aristotle's key claim that we deliberate not about ends, but rather about "means to an end" (*pros to telos*). Wiggins thus offers "what is toward the end," and argues that this surely involves considering what the end entails, what the

13. Aristotle, *Nicomachean Ethics*, trans. Ross, III.5/1113b.
14. Ibid., III.3/1112a.
15. Ibid., III.3/1112b.
16. Vernant, "Intimations of the Will in Greek Tragedy," in Vernant and Vidal-Naquet, *Myth and Tragedy in Ancient Greece*, 58.
17. Ruderman, "Aristotle and the Recovery of Political Judgment," 416. Ruderman, it should be noted, does not accept this reading of the *Ethics*.

end means in a given situation.[18] Similarly, Nussbaum suggests "what pertains to the end," and argues that deliberation can certainly include considerations concerning what achieving an end would involve.[19] Clearly here, the line between what counts as an end and what counts as a means blurs. Means and ends are both up for deliberation, and what appears as a guiding end may be recast at some point in the course of deliberation as a means to a more fundamental end.

We have, then, two readings of Aristotle on deliberation, the difference between the two hanging on the status of ends.[20] Now given the speeches he records, Thucydides seems to have in mind something like the second, more complex understanding of *bouleuō* when he introduces the Mitylene Debate as a moment of consideration or deliberation. Cleon and Diodotus certainly do argue about means—about what to do with the Mitylenian captives. But their speeches also revolve to a significant extent around the question of what we should like to call ends, of what is at stake in Mitylene, of what the Athenians "wish" to attain. Diodotus, counseling leniency, takes a particularly surprising tack, arguing that the Athenians ought to aim not at justice but at expediency: "we are not taking them to court to get justice but deliberating [*bouleuometha*] as to how they might be of use to us" (3.44). Some blame Diodotus for turning toward expediency; others suggest that he has little choice, given that Cleon has seized the rhetorical ground of justice. More accurately, Cleon has claimed that his course will yield both justice and expediency: "by following me, you will act both justly and expediently toward the Mitylenians" (3.40).[21] The broad point here, though, is that the Mitylene Debate, as a moment of deliberative action, involves a dispute over just what end the Athenians ought to be pursuing.

This more complex version of deliberation embodied in the Mitylene Debate, precisely because it admits deliberation on ends as well as means, raises theoretical and practical difficulties. Deliberating on ends involves

18. Wiggins, "Deliberation and Practical Reason."
19. Nussbaum, *The Fragility of Goodness*, 296–97.
20. Let me make clear that I by no means take these "two readings" to be an exhaustive typology of the literature on Aristotle. Those who read Aristotelian deliberation as involving something more than technical reasoning about ends take this argument in importantly different directions. Here I use an admittedly oversimplified characterization of readings of Aristotle to orient my own reading of Thucydides.
21. Here we still risk oversimplifying the arguments of both Cleon and Diodotus. Orwin, *Humanity*, chap. 7 (and earlier in "The Just and the Advantageous in Thucydides") argues that woven into the fabric of Diodotus' appeal to expediency is an argument from justice. As Orwin notes, Strauss, *The City and Man*, suggests a similar argument.

casting them as means to a still greater end, which in turn may prove deliberable as a means to a greater end—and so on. In practical terms, the problem, as Bickford has said, is that "not everything can be up for deliberation at the same time."[22] Aristotle himself recognizes this point, saying that "if we continue deliberating each point in turn, we shall have to go on to infinity" (*NE* III.3/1113a). This is perhaps what Cleon has in mind when he criticizes democracy's dithering: to constantly question one's ends (and their attendant means) through deliberation is tantamount to perpetual inaction; and inaction is deadly to empire. From this point of view, Aristotle's claim that we do not deliberate about ends amounts to the observation that deliberation must proceed against the backdrop of some assumed end about which we do not, strictly speaking, deliberate. Rather, we deliberate about what that end shall mean in the case at hand and about what will produce the end so specified. To take a familiar example, a doctor always aims at health, but this guiding end might be specified differently in different moments of deliberation. Health as an end is assumed but is in this sense deliberable as well.

There are, then, "assumed backgrounds to various instances of deliberation."[23] Precisely because it is assumed, the background to any particular instance of deliberation may prove difficult to identify, being either nonobvious or, in a sense, too obvious to notice. The arguments of Cleon and Diodotus draw our attention away from this agreed upon background and toward disputes over Athenian ends (justice or expediency?) and Athenian means (a harsh sentence or a more lenient one?). More generally, in such moments of deliberative action, Thucydides emphasizes the plurality of Athens—a plurality inherent in his consistent use of the plural *hoi Athenaioi*, but only made explicit when speakers contend with one another before the assembled demos. Thinking along Aristotelian lines, this plurality emerges against some sort of assumed background that brings the Athenians together. Most basically, this assumed background would seem to be the acceptance on the part of *hoi Athenaioi* that they are a "unit of action" and that they ought to pursue a course of action that is, in some sense, good for the city. Such an unspoken assumption stands behind Diodotus' call to the Athenians to understand that his "is the better course" (3.48) and Cleon's claim that he aims to "turn" or "steer" the Athenians away from their tendency to turn serious matters into rhetorical games.

---

22. Bickford, "Beyond Friendship," 401.
23. Ibid., 402.

Both speakers assume that *hoi Athenaioi* must seek the best course to follow.

At this point, then, we might say that Thucydides and Aristotle (on the more complex reading) share a focus on deliberation as the consideration of particular specifications of a backgrounding, guiding end and as the search for means to fulfill that end once it is specified. Thucydides links this activity of deliberation with the momentary eruption of plurality in Athenian political life, an eruption that disrupts apparent Athenian unity. In the following section I draw from Hannah Arendt for help in a preliminary exploration of the nature of that Athenian unity in moments of sudden action. And in the next chapter I find Arendt useful in thinking about the nature of Athenian plurality in the deliberative mode of action. Here, though, it is worth noting the different ways in which human plurality figures in Arendt and Thucydides. In *The Human Condition*, Arendt famously describes plurality as "the condition of human action." Plurality, Arendt writes, "has the twofold character of equality and distinction. If men were not equal, they could neither understand each other and those who came before them nor plan for the future and foresee the needs of those who will come after them. If men were not distinct . . . they would need neither speech nor action to make themselves understood."[24] Plurality provides the context in which human actors reveal their distinctiveness among those who are their equals, showing who they are by what they say and do.

As I argue in Chapter 3, Thucydides, too, shows an appreciation for the revelatory character of political speech. The deliberation that reveals plurality in Athens involves not only accounts of Athenian ends and means, but also claims about who the Athenians are, about what has often been termed the Athenian "character." But this simultaneous negotiation of both Athenian action and Athenian identity occurs, of course, at the collective level. The plurality that provides the context for the consideration of Athenian distinctiveness appears not between individuals but, more precisely, among *hoi Athenaioi*. Put differently, we must be careful not to reduce Athenian plurality in a moment like the Mitylene Debate to the interaction of two distinct and equal speakers. The temptation to focus on the words of Cleon and Diodotus as revealing something about both themselves and Athens risks overlooking the demos in its silent presence. To the more prevalent moments of Athenian unity, Thucydides juxtaposes

---

24. Arendt, *The Human Condition*, 7 and 176.

Athenian plurality not only as the emergence of distinct perspectives among those who speak but also as the emergence of a distinction between those who speak and those who do not. Borrowing Arendt's terms, we might say that this second aspect of "distinction" renders problematic the sort of "equality" that Arendt also locates in human plurality. If we are to avoid reducing the silent demos to a collection of spectators, so that they play an essentially derivative or subordinate role in deliberative action, we will need to continue to think through the role of the demos as Athenian plurality comes to the fore against the backdrop of Athenian unity.

In the Introduction I pointed to the work of M. I. Finley and Josiah Ober as insisting that we understand the demos as powerful even in its silence. Recent work by Jacques Rancière suggests a way more generally to situate the silent power of the demos in the dynamics of plurality and unity in the city. Like Sheldon Wolin and others, Rancière rejects the idea of democracy as a particular form of government. Democracy, rather, "is always beneath and beyond these forms,"[25] threatening—promising—to disrupt political forms through its power to divide: "this specific power of the demos, which exceeds all the dispositions of legislators, is in its simplest form the rallying-dividing power of the many, the power of the *Two of division*."[26] This power of the many or, more sharply, of the Two "refuses" not only "the One of a collectivity that assigns ranks and identities" but also "the pure abandonment of individual focuses of possession and terror."[27] Put in the language I have been using here, democracy erupts as (or stands as the potential for the eruption of) a basic plurality that divides any unity, whether that unity follows from constitutional dictate, elite imposition, or some unifying impulse of the people themselves, of the sort which Rancière calls the "frightening rallying of frightened men."[28]

The basic power of the demos to divide is reflected in the double meaning of *demos* as both the common people and the people as a whole.[29] This double meaning captures the tension between, on the one hand, the impulse of the people to be one and, on the other hand, the basic plurality of politics, located in the juxtaposition between the common people and those who would in some sense rule. We might see Thucydides as deploying

25. Rancière, *Hatred of Democracy*.
26. Rancière, *On The Shores of Politics*, 32.
27. Ibid.
28. Ibid. Rancière thus also describes democracy as "the power of the *demos* to divide the *ochlos*."
29. Along these lines, see Rancière's discussion of the people as "always more or less than they are supposed to be." Ibid., 94.

the term *hoi Athenaioi* in a similar way. Through the narrative of events, when Athenian action is sudden, *hoi Athenaioi* signifies the Athenians as a unity, as One. But within that One there always exists the potential for eruptions of plurality, of, in Rancière's words, the Two. But again, we ought not to reduce the Two to, for example, Cleon and Diodotus. Thucydides captures eruptions of Athenian plurality as the interaction between those who rise to speak and *hoi Athenaioi*, understood now not as a somehow unified Athens but as those Athenians who do not speak but who do decide. The appearance of *hoi Athenaioi* as the silent demos marks the emergence of Athenian plurality as much as does the appearance of contending speakers. Indeed, as we will see in subsequent chapters, the speakers themselves appear not so much as individual elements in Athenian plurality as advocates for particular visions of Athenian unity.

IV. THE NATURE OF SUDDEN ACTION

Here it is indeed true that the end justifies the means; it does more, it produces and organizes them.

—Arendt, *The Human Condition*

There remain important questions about the silent presence of the demos and its place in moments of plurality and deliberative action. How, for example, are we to understand the significance of its power to decide? What is the relationship of that silent power to the words spoken in deliberation? And why do particular Athenians speak? Why, that is, are other contending voices silent? I take up these questions about deliberative action in the next two chapters. Here, though, I return to the "sudden mode" to consider more carefully just what it means to say that the Athenians do not deliberate prior to their sudden actions. As I said above, we should be wary of saying that no deliberation in Athens means literally no interaction among the talkative Athenians. Even if Thucydides portrays *hoi Athenaioi* acting as one, even if he records no speeches, we cannot imagine that he means to indicate that nothing was said in Athens about, for example, dispatching the first forty ships to Lesbos. At the very least, the assembly would have to pass upon the proposal to do so. That Thucydides deals here with an at least formally democratic city demands the inevitability of this basic interaction. Can we really make sense of the idea that for much of the *History* democratic politics as the interaction of contending elite voices and the silent demos gives way to the sudden action and utter silence of *hoi Athenaioi* as all Athenians? Though I explore the sudden mode of Athenian action more fully in Chapters 4 and 5, I want in this section to offer some preliminary suggestions set against the backdrop of Arendt's notion of "the fundamental experience of instrumentality."

Arendt says of this experience that "here it is indeed true that the end justifies the means; it does more, it produces and organizes them." Let us first think about the types of ends that are at work in moments of sudden Athenian action. In considering the deliberative mode of Athenian action, I argued that even when the Athenians appear in their plurality to disagree over the relevant ends to be sought, there must remain in the background an assumed end that we might identify very broadly as the Athenians' wish to act in the Greek world as a city. In the speeches of Cleon and Diodotus, justice and expediency appear as, in Aristotle's language, *pros to telos*, as toward this background end or as particular proffered specifications of it. Now when *hoi Athenaioi* act in the absence of such deliberation, we might safely assume the presence of the same basic, background end. But if we look more carefully at Thucydides' use of the language of wishing as indicative of the ends of the Athenians, then we can see that in moments of sudden action, the Athenians share particular specifications of this general end as well. Consider again Thucydides' description of the Athenians' reaction to the budding Peloponnesian–Mitylenian alliance: "the Athenians, aware [*aisthomenoi*] that these preparations were based on contempt for their weakness, wished [*boulomenoi*] to show that this judgment was mistaken . . . and they manned a hundred ships" (3.16). Here, as elsewhere when they are acting suddenly, the Athenians, apparently as one, wish and are guided by a rather specific end: making a demonstration of their strength before their enemies. Let us investigate, first, how Thucydides depicts these ends as guiding Athenian action; and second, if we can, what he suggests about the origin of the Athenians' collective wishing.

Perhaps precisely because the Athenians' wishes, as Thucydides describes them, are for rather specific ends, the means to their fulfillment appear to follow closely and quickly. As Arendt suggests, the means are of a piece with the ends themselves. Thus in the passage just cited, the manning and dispatch of one hundred ships follows forthwith from the wish to correct misperceptions of "the enemy." So, too, with another case of sudden Athenian action. At 3.3, the Athenians "wished to forestall" the Mitylene revolt before it got fully underway and so "suddenly dispatched forty ships" to Lesbos. We could—perhaps even should—imagine the

Athenians' exercising a collective version of the truncated technical reasoning found in the simpler reading of Aristotle mentioned above. We could, that is, speculate that the Athenians in these instances held an assembly meeting at which some sort of reasoning from end to means, from wish to action, occurred. I would suggest that by not recording such an assembly Thucydides is pointing to the inevitability of the conclusions drawn at such a meeting and hence, in a sense, to the irrelevance of the activity of reasoning itself or, more generally, the irrelevance of political speech. Absent truly contending voices, there remains in effect, if not literally, only the silence of *hoi Athenaioi*. Again here we can see the affinity with the realist understanding of state or city-state action, which in its most strident form suggests the irrelevance of domestic politics to the state's pursuit of its perceived interests.

In considering this irrelevance, we might think of Thucydides' presentation of sudden and unified Athenian perceiving, wishing, and acting as merging Aristotle's "actions taken on the spur of the moment" with an instrumental reasoning strictly about means—reasoning that Aristotle, but not Thucydides, includes in the term deliberation. Thucydides' appreciation of such an amalgamation is possible precisely because of his grasp of the ever-present tension between unity and plurality in *hoi Athenaioi*. The Athenians as one can act "on the spur of the moment," in some sense without fully choosing what they do; at the same time, the Athenians as many must interact in a rudimentary way if they are to act at all. In this interaction, the Athenians do not so much deliberate on their actions as they—to borrow language from Arendt—collectively experience the instrumentality that must guide them. Their relatively specific end itself "produces" the means required for its fulfillment. So long as the Athenians wish as one, they need do no more than follow the consequences of the end they have wished. In moments of sudden action, Thucydides, I think, presents us with a version of the "fundamental experience of instrumentality," emphasizing the collective nature of this experience by choosing not to record speeches.

Now this way of understanding the sudden and silent mode of Athenian action leaves a host of questions for consideration. The Athenians as one wish a relatively specific end. But where does that end originate? In the Mitylene Debate, Cleon and Diodotus go on at some length about whether considering justice or expediency is most conducive to Athenian success. But in moments of sudden action, Thucydides reports no individual Athenian presenting accounts of the ends at stake; the Athenians as one simply wish an end. In the most straightforward cases, wishes follow from perception (marked by forms of *aisthonomai*). This is true at 3.16, where the Athenians perceive a certain attitude on the part of the Peloponnesians and Mitylenians. Perception here is marked by the same unity as wish. We have seen that Thucydides gives us no indication of how the Athenians come to wish a given end; he simply reports that that simultaneously singular and plural entity "the Athenians" do so wish. Similarly, he tells us nothing about the organ through which *hoi Athenaioi* come to a shared perception of their situation. Consider again the contrast with the Mitylene Debate. We might read Cleon and Diodotus as offering, in the context of their arguments about Athenian ends and means, different accounts of the situation at hand, different renderings of the proper way to perceive the revolt and surrender of the Mitylenians and the initial sentence passed on them. But in the passage at hand, Thucydides says nothing of competing perceptions, of different Athenians seeing different things. There are no contending perspectives and so no contending voices. Unified wishing is bound up with unified perception.

And we should note that the perception involved is no simple matter. Were the Spartan army at the gates of Athens or a Spartan fleet (rather improbably) sailing into port at the Piraeus, we could more readily imagine the Athenians looking out and, in some sense, seeing the same thing, perceiving the same threat. But Thucydides at 3.16 tells us that the Athenians perceived a certain attitude on the part of the enemy, seeing behind their preparations a "conviction," a "judgment" about Athenian strengths and weaknesses. At the least, such a perception involves some knowledge—or at least the illusion of knowledge—about the preparations underway in the enemy camp as well as an inference about the motives behind those preparations. But what does it mean for "the Athenians" as a unit to have such a complex perception?[30] Nor is the relationship between unified perception and unified wishing always so straightforward. Consider here the Athenian response to the first news of revolt on Lesbos. The Athenians, Thucydides tells us, "would not listen to the charges, giving greater weight to the wish that they might not be true" (3.3). Here wishing precedes and guides perception. Which, of course, leads us back to a familiar question:

---

30. Aristotle, too, discusses *aisthêsis* as part of his account of deliberation, action, and prudence. Wiggins, "Deliberation and Practical Reason," 236–37; see also Bickford, "Beyond Friendship," 402–3), who translates Aristotle's *aisthêsis* as "situational awareness." I think Thucydides has something similar in mind. What makes Thucydides' account unique and particularly interesting is, again, his presentation of the perception in the context of the simultaneous unity and plurality of *hoi Athenaioi*.

How do (or how can) *hoi Athenaioi* wish as one in this manner? What sort of collective thinking, if any, is at work here?

I do not have full answers to these questions. Indeed, I suspect that it may ultimately prove impossible to draw such answers from Thucydides' work. The ways in which the Athenians, or any other actor(s), most often come to do what they do may, for Thucydides' readers, remain in a sense forever opaque. If Thucydides' frequent decision not to record the "deliberations" of the Athenians is not just a methodological but also a thematic or theoretical matter—and I think this is so—then perhaps we ought to take this opacity as itself an aspect of Thucydides' understanding of human collective action. The silence of *hoi Athenaioi* will, in this way of thinking, signify and embody that opacity.

V. DELIBERATIVE ACTION, SUDDEN ACTION, AND QUESTIONS OF RESPONSIBILITY

We are perhaps the first generation which has become fully aware of the murderous consequences inherent in a line of thought that forces one to admit that all means, provided they are efficient, are permissible and justified to pursue something defined as an end.

—Arendt, The Human Condition

Arendt suggests the danger of the sort of bare instrumentality that, I have argued, marks Athenian action in the earlier stages of the affair of Mitylene. When the end justifies the means, it justifies any means—including indiscriminate if calculated mass murder. When, as Arendt suggests elsewhere, the end does more than justify—when it "produces" and "organizes" the means—then we might say that instrumental rationality becomes all the more dangerous. For if means follow as a matter of course from the end, if end and means are of a single piece with each other, then it must be all the easier to enact the means with little attention to their consequences. Once the end is accepted, action potentially becomes nearly automatic. It can indeed be taken suddenly in the sense developed above. This notion of a nondeliberative exercise of instrumental rationality aptly describes how *hoi Athenaioi* appear in those moments when Thucydides depicts them perceiving, wishing, and acting as one.

Arendt surely does not mean her claim about her generation's full awareness of the danger of this way of thinking and acting to be self-congratulatory; for the rarity of this awareness as Arendt describes it must point to the prevalence of inattention. In ordinary times, no doubt, inattention is the rule and instrumental action, by its very nature, proceeds swiftly and silently, without careful consideration and thus full recognition of its implications and consequences. The moment at which awareness of consequences dawns—most likely a moment of retrospection, of looking backward at what has been wrought—itself suggests a prior period lacking in awareness. Now the Athenians seem to have a moment of dawning awareness not entirely unlike the one Arendt sees in her generation. That moment, of course, comes after the initial harsh sentence has been passed on the Mitylenians: "The next day they experienced immediate remorse and reconsideration about deciding on a savage and extreme resolution to destroy a whole city rather than the guilty ones" (3.36). I want to conclude this chapter by thinking for a moment about the context in which this moment of awareness comes about and what it tells us—or, rather, prompts us to ask—about assigning responsibility for the choices and actions of *hoi Athenaioi*.

Thucydides tells us that the Athenians "debated [*gnomas*]" the fate of the Mitylenians and that they "voted [*edoxen*] in a rage" to put to death all adult males and enslave the women and children. Two things merit notice here. First, Thucydides does not use the language of deliberation. Only after "remorse" arises does he tell us that some Athenians wished it possible for them to "deliberate [*bouleusasthai*] again" (3.36). And importantly, it is only some, not all, Athenians who have this wish. Mitylenian envoys present at Athens, Thucydides says, saw that "the greater part" of the citizens wanted another chance. Along with this greater part must have been a lesser part that would have left matters as they stood. Here, indeed, is the very first mention in the affair of Mitylene of any division in Athens. In this sense, the "debate" held on the first day appears to have been an odd one. Thucydides' account implies that though there was debate, there was no true division. The moment of awareness and repentance seems to separate this rather paradoxically unified debate on the first day from the plurality and deliberation of the second day, when contending voices first truly emerge to speak before the silent demos. This moment, that is, seems precisely to mark the movement from one mode of action to another in Athens.[31]

I argued earlier that plurality and deliberation—as embodied in the Mitylene Debate itself—involve a disagreement not only over means, but also

---

31. Arendt, *The Human Condition*, 229.

over ends. For the first time, the Athenians ask just what is at stake for Athens in Mitylene. Though Thucydides gives us precious little detail about what happens in Athens to bring this about, it seems as if the Athenians, or part of them, come somehow to react with disgust and disbelief at the point to which their mode of acting has brought them. They come late—almost too late—to recognize how "cruel and monstrous" are the consequences of their "decision." This reflection on the true character of the means at which they have arrived brings about a first reflection on more fundamental ends, on what sort of city Athens is and will be, on its goals, its wishes, on its manner of acting in the world. From the standpoint of this moment, Athens's earlier sudden and unified mode of perceiving, wishing, and acting appears unthinking, far from the kind of learning enough prior to acting that Pericles extols in the Funeral Oration. In this context, it only makes sense that Cleon and Diodotus clash not only over what is to be done with the Mitylenians but also over how the Athenians go about making decisions. At stake in the Mitylene Debate is not simply what Athenian action will be, but how Athens as a city comes to act, how it makes decisions.

In Chapter 4, I consider what Cleon and Diodotus, and others, have to say about how Athens makes decisions. Wrapped up in those arguments are questions and claims about responsibility for actions taken, particularly in the context of deliberation. Ought we, for example, to hold accountable the adviser who recommends a course or the demos that chose to follow the advice? In what sense is the idea of "collective responsibility" meaningful? The presence of the sudden mode of action complicates questions of responsibility. If sudden action as the enactment of collective instrumental rationality proceeds, as Arendt suggests, without full awareness, then where does responsibility fit in?

Aristotle's exploration of the difference between involuntary and voluntary action, which provides the context for his discussion of sudden action, suggests a straightforward answer. He holds the distinction between voluntary and involuntary to be one of considerable significance, since, he says, we attach praise or blame to voluntary actions but not to involuntary ones.[32] Involuntary actions include "what is done by force or because of

---

32. Bickford, "Beyond Friendship," builds on Aristotle's notion of *aisthêsis* to suggest that Aristotelian deliberation involves a "paying attention to" or an "awareness" of the particulars of the situation at hand and of one's fellow citizens. The "moment of awareness" I discuss here differs in that it seems to be a necessary prerequisite to or catalyst for deliberation rather than an aspect of deliberation itself. See also note 23 above.

ignorance," while "what is voluntary would seem to be what has its first principle in the person himself when he knows the particular circumstances of the action."[33] Most obviously, actions that are the consequence of a decision or choice by the actor can be called voluntary. Aristotle, though, insists that choice and the voluntary are not coextensive. Because what is voluntary is "a broader notion," there exist actions that are voluntary but not chosen. As he says explicitly in the quotation that heads section II of this chapter, he sees sudden actions as falling into this intermediate category. And so, even if they do not flow from careful deliberation, they cannot be said to flow from ignorance (or force); thus they are as subject to praise and blame as those actions we more fully chose.

Thucydides' account of Athenian action ultimately leads to more complicated ways of thinking about responsibility and about praising and blaming. In addition to the juxtaposition of sudden and deliberative modes of action and the intertwining of these modes with the complex silences of *hoi Athenaioi,* the complications follow in part from the simultaneity of Athenian plurality and Athenian unity as discussed in this chapter and the relation of this simultaneity to the dynamics of Athenian collective identity. I consider those dynamics in the following chapter, taking up the often discussed matter of the Athenian character. My argument there points toward a deeper set of issues regarding responsibility and praise and blame. As we will see, the *History*'s treatment of Athenian character and its relation to speech, silence, and action undermines the sort of firm distinction between ignorance and awareness on which Aristotle relies and leaves us to wonder whether the Athenians, even when they "deliberate," ever come to understand their actions or themselves.

33. Aristotle, *Nicomachean Ethics,* trans. Ross, III.1/1110a.

3

Deliberative Action and Athenian "Character"

I. INTRODUCTION

But not on this occasion alone, but on many others as well, the Lacedaemonians proved the most convenient of all people for the Athenians to be at war with. For as the farthest from them in character (tropos)—the one people being quick, the other slow; the one enterprising, the other timid—they were obliging in general and particularly in the case of a naval power. The Syracusans demonstrated this; for because they were the most similar to the Athenians in character, they also fought the best against them.

(8.96.5)

Thucydides offers this comparison of the Spartans and the Athenians within a few chapters of the point at which the *History* abruptly ends. Amidst the internecine political struggles of the 400 and the 5000 in Athens, a Peloponnesian fleet has engaged and destroyed twenty-two Athenian triremes off Eretria. With Athens itself suddenly left all but undefended by sea, the Spartans have a golden opportunity: they could blockade the Athenian port at the Piraeus and compel an unconditional surrender; or alternatively, they could feign an attack on the Piraeus, thus luring the remaining Athenian fleet away from the shores of Ionia and the remnants of the Athenian empire in Asia Minor (8.96.4). In the event, the Spartans fail to act decisively at all, and Athens survives to begin a slow recovery (8.97).

Thucydides' suggestion that such reluctance is characteristic of the Spartans seemingly confirms the analysis offered by the Corinthians at Sparta in book 1. The Corinthians warn the Spartans to take heed of "what sort of opponents [they] will have in the Athenians" and of "how greatly, let us say totally, they differ" from the Spartans themselves. Where the Spartans are "delayers," the Athenians are "ready to act"; where the Spartans are "the most home-bound of all," the Athenians are "always abroad"; where the Spartans are quick only "to preserve the status quo," the Athenians are "definitely innovators and quick to form their plans and carry out whatever action they resolve" (1.70). Just as Thucydides says in book 8, the Athenians are bold, the Spartans timorous.

The presence of such apparently similar accounts of the Athenians and Spartans near the beginning of the *History* and at its close clearly suggests the importance of some sort of collective "character" for both Thucydides and his speakers. Certainly, students of the *History* have found the idea of collective character to be of more than passing interest. Perhaps the most common approach stresses the consistent contrast between the Athenian and Spartan characters and its importance in explaining the course of the war. Lowell Edmunds, for example, describes this contrast as "programmatic," suggesting that it provides "the terms and concepts" by which both Thucydides and his Greeks "understand events."[1] Others focus more specifically on the Athenian character and the unfolding of its implications over the course of the war. Thus Steven Forde has argued that the "liberation" at the heart of the Athenian character allows for the rise of the Athenian empire but proves "a corrosive incubus," ultimately unleashing an "individualism" that "destroys the city in time."[2]

---

1. Edmunds, *Chance and Intelligence in Thucydides*, 89–90. For similar arguments, see J. H. Finley, *Thucydides*, 121; Pouncey, *The Necessities of War*, 78; and Kagan, *The Archidamian War*, 358. Along these lines, of particular interest is the situation of character as a key variable in a Thucydidean "causal theory of empire" as part of an attempt to make another of the "Great Books" relevant to "today's behavioral science" by Bluhm, "Causal Theory in Thucydides' Peloponnesian War," 32. Such an approach no doubt seemed particularly relevant in the Cold War atmosphere of the early 1960s, when the contrast between Athens and Sparta might be generalized, then mapped onto comparisons of American and Soviet "character." For an insightful account of this apparent "immediate applicability" of Thucydides during the earlier years of the Cold War, see Connor, *Thucydides*, 3–8. Attempts such as Bluhm's to read Thucydides as a scientist of some sort have generally fallen out of favor, as shown by Monoson and Loriaux, "The Illusion of Power and the Disruption of Moral Norms," 285. Cochrane's discussion of the influence of Hippocratic medicine on the *History* remains the most famous sustained account of Thucydides as scientist; Cochrane, *Thucydides and the Science of History*.

2. Forde, "Thucydides on the Causes of Athenian Imperialism," 433 and 442; and *The Ambition to Rule*, 37–38. Euben's discussion of the "corruption" of Athenian collective identity over the course of the war bears a certain similarity to Forde's analysis, though it is significantly different in other aspects; see Euben, *The Tragedy of Political Theory*. The arguments of both Euben and Forde in some sense echo Cornford's account of the tragic fall of Athens, a fall owing in no small part to the flaws at the heart of Athenian character; see Cornford, *Thucydides Mythistoricus*. Connor, *Thucydides*, like Euben and Forde, emphasizes the unfolding of Athenian character over the course of the war, but he focuses on the reader's interaction with the actors' and the historian's perspectives on character. I return later to these issues of perspective.

The common account of Athenian character as a force coursing beneath and driving Athenian politics tends to merge with and reinforce readings that undermine our appreciation of Thucydides as a theorist of democratic politics. First, it fits well with the realist conviction that Thucydides is a theorist of politics between cities who consequently has little to say about politics within the city. If the Athenian character remains constant throughout the *History*, it serves not only as a static point of comparison with the Spartan character but also as a way of accounting for what Athens as a "unit of action" does; there is little reason to pay attention to the superfluities of Athenian "domestic politics," which amount to acting out underlying character traits.[3] Reading the progressive unfolding of the Athenian character as leading to the city's destruction, on the other hand, complements the treatment of Pericles as the model leader. Along these lines, it is possible to explain what happens to Athens in the *History* largely in terms of the tragic disappearance of a great statesman—that is, Pericles, who had been able to harness the potential of that character while containing its dangers.

I here suggest a way of reading Thucydides' treatment of the Athenian character that seeks to situate it more fully within the dynamics of Athenian democratic politics. Once again, I turn to Aristotle and Arendt for help in grappling with the complexities of speech and action in the *History*. My argument proceeds as follows. In the next section, drawing in part from an Arendtian notion of identity, I offer a reconceptualization of Athenian character that focuses on actions rather than qualities or traits. With this conceptual work in place, I turn to consider the role that character plays in two moments of deliberative action in Thucydides' Athens. In section III, focusing again on the Mitylene Debate, I argue that the Athenian character appears as a dynamic aspect of deliberation understood as the interaction through rhetoric of elite speakers and the Athenian demos. Focusing in particular on the collective silence of the demos in moments of deliberative action ultimately reveals a fundamental and irreducible uncertainty attending speakers' claims about the Athenian character. In section IV, with help from Aristotle's *Rhetoric*, I argue that my reading of

---

3. I thus differ from Johnson, *Thucydides, Hobbes, and the Interpretation of Realism*, who argues that Thucydides' reliance on character frustrates realist appropriations because of the unsuitability of character as a scientific concept. The notion of character can in fact be useful to realists when coupled with the idea of the state as the key unit of action. See the use of character—the Russian character, the American character, the English character—by Morgenthau, *Politics Among Nations*, 122–32.

the role of Athenian character applies as well to Pericles' Funeral Oration, which thus appears as a moment of deliberation akin to the Mitylene Debate.[4] In part, my aim here is to challenge the supposed exceptionality of Pericles in Athenian politics. More broadly, I also mean to begin to refocus attention away from issues of leadership or statesmanship by emphasizing Thucydides' consistent appreciation for the powerful presence of the silent demos in Athenian politics, even during Pericles' ascendancy. Then in the conclusion I consider the implications of my approach to the matter of character for how we read the *History* and how we understand the interplay of the perspectives of its author, its actors, and its readers. Here I return to questions of responsibility raised at the conclusion of Chapter 2.

II. RECONCEPTUALIZING ATHENIAN CHARACTER: *TROPOS* AS CHARACTERISTIC ACTION

As we have already seen, we learn of the Athenian character in the pages of Thucydides in two ways: through the words of the author himself, and through the words he chooses to put into the mouths of speakers. Part of understanding the place of character—and speech and action more generally—in Thucydides' work will involve grappling with the juxtaposition of these two perspectives.[5] I address this task directly in the final section of this chapter. For now, though, I will focus on what we might call the perspective of the political actor—of one, that is, who faces the challenge

---

4. I thus consider the Mitylene Debate and the Funeral Oration in an order opposite of that in which they appear in the *History*. Much of the best commentary, by contrast, follows the *History*'s events chronologically; as examples, see Cogan, *The Human Thing*, and Connor, *Thucydides*. Orwin, *Humanity of Thucydides*, 13, on the other hand, defends a nonsequential approach, arguing in part that "the episode that best captures a particular aspect of our problem may occur anywhere in the work." In a similar vein, I find the Mitylene Debate most useful for illuminating the place of Athenian character in Athenian democratic politics. The arguments I offer about it in turn prepare the way for what is likely to be a more controversial reading of the Funeral Oration.

5. Grene, *Greek Political Theory*, 7–8, in a sense had something similar in mind, remarking in his influential study of Thucydides' thought that "as we see the scene and the man as separate, we can ultimately understand the interaction of the two." Thucydides' appreciation for and presentation of the perspective of the political actor caught up in the events of the war has long been recognized by scholars. See, for example, Edmunds, *Chance and Intelligence*, 4; Connor, *Thucydides*, 8; Euben, *Tragedy of Political Theory*, 199; and Ober, *Political Dissent in Democratic Athens*. Farrar, *The Origins of Democratic Thinking*, 188, recognizes the possibility of distinguishing between the role of the "agent" and that of the "critical spectator," but concludes that the *History* suggests that these roles are not as separate as they at first appear.

of speaking and acting in the face of the unknown future. More particularly, I turn in this section to consider how Thucydides' speakers themselves conceptualize the relationship of character to action.

In our everyday discourse, we tend to speak of character as a trait or quality—"he is courageous"—or as a possession—"she has great character." Clearly, some relationship exists between the character mentioned in these locutions and action taken by the individuals involved; no doubt we know of his courage and her character because of deeds we have witnessed or heard tell of. Yet such ways of talking about character fundamentally displace it from these unique deeds. They suppose a quality of the individual that exists independently of what he or she does. In a much-discussed passage of *The Human Condition,* Hannah Arendt diagnoses this manner of speaking about action and individual identity: "the moment we want to say *who* somebody is, our very vocabulary leads us astray into saying *what* he is."[6] For Arendt, "who" suggests one's "unique personal identity" and, it is important to note, can only be found or revealed in one's words and deeds. Saying "what" somebody is, on the other hand, involves indicating their "qualities, gifts, talents, and shortcomings."[7] Because we can and do distinguish these attributes from the unique actions of a person, we can compare across persons. We can, that is, take note of qualities they share with others and, in Arendt's words, "begin to describe a type or a 'character' in the old meaning of the word."[8]

Perhaps the oldest systematic discussion of character—in Aristotle's *Nicomachean Ethics*—seems clearly to follow the same path that our everyday vocabulary takes toward Arendt's "what."[9] Aristotle, of course, grapples

6. Arendt, *The Human Condition,* 181.
7. Ibid., 178.
8. Ibid., 181. Arendt's account of the interplay of speech, action, and identity has, of course, been of considerable interest to, and the subject of intense debate among, contemporary political theorists. See, as a small sample, Fuss, "Hannah Arendt's Conception of Political Community"; Canovan, *Hannah Arendt;* Hansen, *Hannah Arendt,* 47–49; Disch, *Hannah Arendt and the Limits of Philosophy;* Honig, "Toward an Agonistic Feminism"; Villa, *Arendt and Heidegger;* and Pitkin, *The Attack of the Blob,* 157–59. I turn to Arendt mainly for the heuristic value of her concept of action. Euben, *Tragedy of Political Theory,* 37–38, makes a similar use of Arendt's discussion of the "who" in laying the groundwork for his consideration of issues of identity in Greek tragedy. He does not draw directly from Arendt in his insightful analysis of Thucydides.
9. I emphasize that Aristotle offers the first *systematic* discussion of character. As Salkever, *Finding the Mean,* 79n49, points out, Plato occasionally uses *hexis* in a way that is familiar from its central role in the *Ethics.* Note also that Arendt does not directly discuss Aristotle's views on character. Aristotle's work, in fact, figures most prominently at the outset of *The Human Condition,* 12–15, as the inspiration for Arendt's distinctions among labor, work, and action.

with the relationship between action and the *hexeis* that constitute the character of individuals. He makes clear the complexity of this relationship. One's actions exhibit one's *hexeis*, but the actions one takes, particularly as a child, help mold these *hexeis*.[10] Yet whatever the intricacies, character and action remain separate and distinct. Indeed, only as such can we ponder their relationship to each other. Along these lines, translators often render *hexis* as a "state" or "disposition," suggesting that character is some sort of internal matter that shapes and is shaped by action but that remains somehow removed from it.[11] At the end of a very useful discussion of the difficulties of translating *hexis*, Salkever notes that Aristotle defines *hexis* in the *Categories* "as a certain quality [*poion*] 'by virtue of which things are *what* they are.'"[12] We are here clearly removed from the particular actions that make an individual human being a unique *who*.

Students of the *History* have similarly tended to understand Athenian character as a set of qualities independent of the actions the Athenians take. Consider, for example, the Aristotelian cast of Steven Forde's conclusions.[13] As I have noted, Forde, more than most, considers the complex relationship between character and action. Just as Aristotle argues that our *hexeis* depend in part on habits we form in youth (including involuntarily at the insistence of our teachers) Forde locates the origins of Athenian daring in an earlier action forced on the Athenians by the necessity of survival. The Athenians learned to be daring in the pivotal moment before the Battle of Salamis when they abandoned their city in favor of the security of their ships. Such action forged the well-developed character

---

10. Aristotle, *Nicomachean Ethics*, trans. Irwin, 33–35.

11. In their respective translations, Irwin, *Nicomachean Ethics*, and Ross, *The Nicomachean Ethics*, both offer "state." "Disposition" appears in the earlier translations of Rackham, *Nichomachean Ethics*, and Thompson, *The Ethics of Aristotle*.

12. Salkever, *Finding the Mean*, 80; emphasis mine. Salkever himself suggests "personality" as the closest English equivalent to *hexis*, though he immediately notes that this involves "real distortion." Aristotle did not limit the idea of *hexis* to humans: "Thus all organisms insofar as they are substances composed of elements organized or ordered in a certain way, can be said to exhibit a *hexis*," 80.

13. Others have tended toward the causal language of modern social science—one thinks in particular of Bluhm's causal theory of empire (see note 5 above). The roots of this sort of social scientific approach can be found in the work of John Stuart Mill, who in his often neglected *System of Logic* made character central to his vision for a moral science. Mill relied on character as the link in a causal chain tying laws of psychology to the actions of individuals. He called for a science of "ethology" to study this link; *System of Logic*, 562–71. He himself relies on character as the cause of individual action in such political works as *On Liberty* and *The Subjection Women*; see *On Liberty and Other Writings*. In this approach, character as cause and action as effect again remain distinct. For an excellent account of Mill's ethology in theory and practice, see Terence Ball, "The Formation of Character."

that we see in the pages of the *History*. Thucydides and his Greeks subsequently "offer a remarkably consistent portrait of the Athenians, revolving around certain commonly acknowledged core traits." As Arendt suggests, this approach rewards us with the ability to make clear comparisons of character types; thus Forde concludes that "the Athenians are daring in the *History;* the Spartans are the opposite."[14] When, however, we begin to think of character as something consisting of "traits" and of which we can have a "portrait," we to a certain extent disconnect it from action: the Athenians *are* thus and such (something akin to Arendt's "what") rather than the Athenians *do* thus and such (something more like Arendt's "who").

I emphasize this tendency to think of character as a quality or trait or internal state existing independent of action in order to bring into sharper relief the manner in which speakers in Thucydides in fact talk about the Athenian *tropos*. They maintain a rather Arendtian focus on action.[15] They do not make the move to consideration of internal states of mind and the like. Consider a few examples from Pericles' sweeping account of the Athenian *tropos* in the Funeral Oration. The Athenians "associate in private life without undue pressure" (2.37). They "have provided for the spirit the most plentiful respites" (2.38). The Athenians' actions in "foreign policy" also "differ from [their] opponents": they throw open the city to foreigners and depend on "a more relaxed way of life" rather than on harsh discipline to produce soldiers who will defend the city (2.39). As for public affairs, "we Athenians," Pericles says, "ourselves ratify or even propound successful policies" (2.40). Athens stands as "the school of Hellas" because "among us ... any single man would represent an individual self-sufficient for the most varied forms of conduct" (2.41). In short, Pericles offers not a portrait of a set of traits or of a certain internal state but, rather, a vivid description of characteristic actions taken by the Athenians in characteristic ways. The same holds for the Corinthians' descriptions of Athens and

---

14. Forde, "Thucydides on the Causes of Athenian Imperialism," 434.
15. Let me pause here to clarify further my motivation in suggesting the affinity between Arendt's idea of identity and the discussion of Athenian character in the *History*. I do not mean to force the complexity of Thucydides' account into an Arendtian mold. My aim, rather, is to use Arendt's distinction between "who" and "what" and, more generally, her discussion of speech, action, and identity as a heuristic. As will become clear below, although I think Arendt to provide a more useful theoretical backdrop than, say, Aristotle, Thucydides' treatment of character leads us toward its own questions (in part by focusing on the collective level and by emphasizing the instrumentality of character-revealing rhetoric). My hope is that besides setting off these questions, the juxtaposition with Arendt will help suggest the distinctive insights the *History* has to offer and their potential relevance to contemporary discussions of identity and action.

Sparta, which focus on ways of acting, or, in the Spartan case, ways of not acting.

In keeping with this focus on action (or inaction), we can also attend more closely to the term often rendered as "character." *Tropos* in fact appears in a variety of senses throughout the *History*. In 1.6, Thucydides tells us that the Spartans were the first to dress "simply in the present style [*tropon*]." In encouraging the Syracusans to seek alliances elsewhere in Sicily to help in the coming battle with the Athenians, Hermocrates says that the Carthaginians "will want to back us, at least secretly if not openly, or in one fashion [*tropou*] anyway" (6.34.2). And in their famous enunciation of the "Athenian thesis," the anonymous Athenian envoys to Sparta claim that in accepting empire the Athenians have done nothing "contrary to ordinary human behavior [*anthrōpeiou tropou*]" (1.76.2).[16] In each passage,[17] *tropos* suggests a manner, a mode, a means. This accords with the notion that Athenian speakers appeal not so much to an internal character as to a characteristic Athenian manner of acting, a unique Athenian "way."[18]

In Arendt's terms, we might say that Thucydides' speakers, in discussing the Athenian way, refer to "who Athens is." The awkwardness of this locution calls our attention to the initial difficulty of applying this particular notion of identity, developed in regard to the individual, to a city. It is perhaps easier to consider a city as a "what," as possessing certain qualities or having an internal state of a certain type. Plato does something of this sort in the *Republic*, constructing *kallipolis* and comparing it to the four defective constitutions according to the arrangement of the various classes within the city. This approach, of course, allows Plato to compare, by his famous homology, the ordering of the good city with the harmony of the good soul. But Thucydides has different concerns and takes a different

---

16. Where Lattimore offers "ordinary human behavior" to translate *anthrōpeiou troupou*, Crawley has "the common practice of mankind," and Smith has "human nature." Crawley's translation echoes Hobbes, who offers "nothing to be wondered at nor beside the manner of men."

17. And various others. See the uses of *tropos* in 1.97.2, 2.39.4, 5.63.2, 6.35.1, 7.67.2, and 8.27.3.

18. A more elegant translation of *tropos* might be "style." Such a translation might also be more in keeping with the Arendtian cast of much of what I have said thus far. Along these lines, and particularly given the admiration of both Arendt and Nietzsche for Thucydides, see Villa's discussion, *Arendt and Heidegger*, 91, of the similarities between Arendt's discussion of the performance of individual identity and Nietzsche's insistence on the importance of giving "style" to one's character. I have chosen "way" over "style," however, in order to retain the important sense of instrumentality that, as I argue at the end of the next section, is central to Thucydides' understanding of action. As I note there, there emerges on this score an important difference (at least in emphasis) between Arendt and Thucydides.

approach to understanding the city. Unlike Plato, he shows little concern with explicitly elaborating the best regime;[19] he focuses less on the constitution of the city and more on its actions. Here we should keep in mind the insistence of the realists that Thucydides treats the city as a "unit of action." The idea of an Athenian *tropos* refers to the city as a unit acting in a characteristic way.

At the same time, we should not carry this focus on the city as a unit of action so far as to lose contact with the basic plurality of the city. As we saw in Chapter 2, Thucydides and his speakers, in referring to *hoi Athenaioi*, "the Athenians," constantly remind us that Athens is both one city and many individual citizens.[20] In thinking about the Athenian way, then, we must once again attempt to come to grips with the simultaneous unity and plurality of *hoi Athenaioi*. The predominant understanding of Athenian character has allowed commentators to investigate the plurality of the city in part by comparing the Athenian or Spartan qualities of particular individuals. Thus for Edmunds, the "norms" established in the Corinthians' speech allow us "to measure the degree to which an individual manifests the character of a complete Athenian or a complete Spartan."[21] Similarly, Strauss argues: "Cleon is the counterpart of Brasidas because just as Brasidas is an Athenian among the Spartans, Cleon is in a sense the Spartan among the Athenians. As we observed earlier, in another sense Nicias is the Spartan among the Athenians."[22] In keeping with what I have argued here, if we are to draw such comparisons—which can indeed be intriguing—we will do better to think in terms of the actions of individuals and cities. It is Brasidas' actions in Thrace, for example, that put us in mind of the actions which Athens as a city takes. Here, though, I want to consider how the idea of who *hoi Athenaioi* are works in the process by which Athens as a collection of many citizens comes to act as a city—particularly when Athens acts in the deliberative mode sketched in the previous chapter. At its most basic, this involves understanding Athenian speakers' appeals to the Athenian *tropos* as political rhetoric.

---

19. On this point, see Orwin, *Humanity of Thucydides*, 173; and my own discussion in Chapter 6.

20. Farrar, *Origins of Democratic Thinking*, 158, similarly speaks of "the two aspects of the political community, entity and collectivity" in the context of describing what she takes to be "Pericles' role" in Athens, though her understanding of that role differs from the one I develop in the following section.

21. Edmunds, *Chance and Intelligence*, 90.

22. Strauss, *The City and Man*, 12. For similar points, see Orwin, *Humanity of Thucydides*, 122f.; and Connor, *Thucydides*, 41.

III. DEMOCRATIC POLITICS AND THE RHETORIC OF CHARACTER I: THE MITYLENE DEBATE

Aristotle defines rhetoric as "the faculty of observing in any given case the available means of persuasion."[23] I have something similar in mind in using the term, though I will also use rhetoric to refer (as we often do in everyday discourse) to speeches as the products of speaker's judgments about what will persuade and what will not. To say that arguments about the Athenian *tropos* work as rhetoric is, first of all, simply to say that speakers choose such arguments as means of persuasion in given cases. Thus during their speech at Sparta in book 1, for example, the Corinthians choose to make arguments about the Athenian and Spartan ways of acting, presumably because they think that such arguments will in some way help carry their proposal for action against Athens.

By comparison, earlier in book 1, the Corcyreans come to Athens seeking help in their fight against Corinth but do not make arguments about the Athenian way. At first glance, this is somewhat surprising. The Corcyreans present the Athenians with what they claim to be an attractive and relatively risk-free opportunity. Aiding them in their war against Corinth means helping a city that has been wronged without breaking the thirty-year treaty with the Peloponnesians (1.35). It also means gaining the use of the Corcyrean navy in the inevitable war with the Spartans (1.33). We might well expect the Corcyreans to appeal to the Athenians' supposed penchant for daring action, arguing that seizing such an opportunity would be fully in "character." On closer inspection, though, the Corcyreans perhaps have sound rhetorical reasons for eschewing such means of persuasion. They emphasize their relative isolation in Greece (1.37), recognizing that they have had few contacts with other cities and thus have no allies on whom to call. Unlike the Corinthians, who can confront the Spartans as friendly critics (1.69), the Corcyreans do not have the kind of relationship with Athens that would allow them to offer the sorts of characterological descriptions offered by the Corinthians. We might well conclude that making such arguments requires a familiarity with the audience that the Corcyreans simply lack.[24] Appeals to the Athenian *tropos* seem, in this sense, unavailable in the given case.

---

23. Aristotle, *The Rhetoric and Poetics*, 24.
24. By contrast, the Corinthian speakers at Sparta suggest that precisely their familiarity with the Spartans allows them to draw the unfavorable contrast with Athens: "And let no one think that this is said out of hostility rather than as criticism; for criticism is directed toward

We can apply this way of thinking about rhetorical strategy to the Athenian assembly speeches that Thucydides records. Not surprisingly, among the Athenians—who are surely familiar with one another—arguments about the Athenian way abound. Consider, again, the Mitylene Debate. Cleon and Diodotus, as we have seen, clash over two broad issues, both of which involve the use of claims about the Athenian *tropos* as means of (attempted) persuasion. First, they make arguments regarding the place of justice and expediency in Athenian action. Such arguments, of course, are a central and recurring theme in the *History*. Second, Cleon argues that the Athenians talk too much, whereas Diodotus defends the practice of careful deliberation as essential to the making of sound decisions. In making these latter arguments, Cleon and Diodotus join an ongoing Athenian discussion about the workings of Athenian decision making. I consider this thread of discussion in great detail in Chapter 4. Here, two examples will suffice to make the point. In the Funeral Oration, Pericles, of course, treats deliberation as a central aspect of the Athenian *tropos*. Later, Nicias and Alcibiades, in debating whether the Athenians should sail to Sicily, disagree again about the worth of deliberation and the relevance of the motives of advisers (6.9; 6.16). Simply put, all of these Athenian speakers weave into their rhetorical strategies appeals to what we might call the Athenian way of political life. They have, again, apparently settled on such appeals as "available means of persuasion."

This basic idea—that appeals to the Athenian way work as rhetoric in particular moments of decision—leaves us with important questions about the place of the Athenian *tropos* in Athenian democratic politics. How do arguments about the Athenian way work to persuade the Athenians gathered before Cleon and Diodotus in the Athenian assembly? What can we learn from such arguments about deliberative action in the *History*? And what can we learn about the Athenian *tropos* itself by considering the claims that speakers make about it and the reaction of the Athenian demos to those claims, especially since the demos remains silent throughout? As a starting point, we might recall Josiah Ober's argument that the rhetoric of ancient elites provides evidence for the political inclinations and political power of the ancient demos.[25] Ober restricts the application of this

---

friends who are in error, accusations toward enemies who are at fault" (1.69). Friends critique, enemies accuse. Coming to Athens, the Corcyreans, having been neither friends nor enemies, can neither critique nor accuse.

25. See my discussion of Ober's arguments in the Introduction; Ober, *Mass and Elite*, 44.

approach to the fourth-century orators.[26] But Marc Cogan had earlier suggested a very similar way of reading the speeches in Thucydides. Cogan argues that the principle of "rhetorical deliberation" serves as the "bridge" by which individual actions translate into social actions in the *History*.[27] Thucydides' conception of deliberation as "rhetorical" allows his account to reflect certain "extrarational peculiarities" of audience and speaker, including emotions, prejudices, and "intellectual habits" or "the character of the audience."[28] The speeches represent speakers' attempts to influence the "subjective reality" of the situation in part by drawing from their understanding of this character. The reader can work in the opposite direction: "The specific content of a [rhetorical] problem and its solution on a given occasion are the result, then, of those particular facts that are proper to that occasion and no other; it is our knowledge of the general structure of rhetoric that enables us to discover (or recover) these particularities."[29] Like Ober, Cogan thus argues that, knowing which rhetorical strategy speakers have taken and which strategies have succeeded, careful students of Thucydides can infer information about the audience. In a sense, Cogan sees the rhetorical choices of Athenian speakers as offering a way to resolve the silence of the Athenian demos. We can, for example, recover the traits of the audience's character, though these traits remain "unarticulated" precisely because, as "constants which operate without explicit statement," they influence what the successful speaker must say.[30]

Of course, as speakers' frequent references to various aspects of the Athenian *tropos* clearly show, "character" is at times articulated; speakers explicitly discuss it. Cogan's own discussion of "the character of the Athenians when sitting in assembly" suggests as much. Drawing on the speeches of Pericles, Cleon, Diodotus, Nicias, and Alcibiades, he argues that "we have considerable and remarkably consistent testimony [about this character] in the speeches."[31] But if we find the testimony *in the speeches,* then it must be part of speakers' attempts to shape how the audience understands the situation or, to borrow Cogan's term, the "subjective reality" of the situation. The rhetorical implication of character thus goes deeper than Cogan allows. Speakers in the *History* do not merely draw

26. Ober has, though, considered the rhetoric of Thucydides' speakers and Thucydides' own critique of "democratic knowledge" in *Political Dissent in Democratic Athens.*
27. Cogan, *The Human Thing,* 197.
28. Ibid., 201 and 205.
29. Ibid., 203.
30. Ibid., 201.
31. Ibid., 206.

on their knowledge of the character of audiences to shape their speeches; they use their speeches to try to shape the audience's understanding of that character. Surely this is what the Corinthians are up to when they tell the Spartans how different their actions are from those of the Athenians; the Corinthians hope to influence how the Spartans see their past actions and, it follows, how they will act now.

So, too, in the Mitylene Debate. In this and similar moments of deliberative action, *hoi Athenaioi* appear simultaneously as a plurality of citizens and as a unit of action. Though divided, the Athenians come together to search for what can unite them, if only in the sense of deciding what, in fact, they will do with the captive Mitylenians. Such moments are indeed the "bridge" by which the Athenians find unity from plurality, and discussions of the Athenian *tropos* stand as central in this process of "bridging." This *tropos*, though, does not exist as a background constant that defines the Athenians as a unit; or as a fixed point of reference for Cleon and Diodotus as they choose what to say; or, finally, as an unchanging standard to which true "leaders" may recall an unruly or misguided demos.[32] Rather, the rhetorical strategy of discussing the Athenian way involves an attempt to offer authoritative interpretations of how Athens has acted in the past, of the things the Athenians have sought to do and the way in which they have sought to do them. By describing what they take Athenian ends and means to have been, Cleon and Diodotus seek to gain rhetorical footing for saying what Athenian ends and means should be now.

Here it may help to return to Arendt's distinction between the "who" and the "what." We can now highlight the similarities and differences between her treatment of individual action and identity and the place of the Athenian *tropos* in Athenian politics in the *History*.[33] We might say that Cogan's way of reading the speeches in Thucydides—and, analogously, Ober's way of reading fourth-century oratory—treat that which unites the Athenians as a "what." Speakers make use of their knowledge of what the Athenians are—their consistent traits or qualities or beliefs or tendencies—to shape their appeals. The approach I have been suggesting, on the other hand, would have us see the speakers in Thucydides as

---

32. As I argued in Chapter 1, the idea that the Athenians should act as a unit can be seen as part of the assumed backdrop to moments of deliberation such as the Mitylene Debate. So, too, might the idea that the Athenians have a characteristic way of acting. My point here is that the *content* of the Athenian way cannot be seen as a background constant, since speakers make distinct arguments about that content.

33. Again, I do so with the careful proviso that my intention is to use Arendt as a starting point, not as a conceptual framework for corralling the complexity of the *History*.

offering accounts of "who" *hoi Athenaioi* are in terms of the characteristic Athenian way of acting. The Athenian *tropos* thus emerges in the speeches of particular Athenians as interpretations of past actions taken by the city. Consequently, it is always open to change through the offering of alternative accounts (as we see in the Mitylene Debate) or as the Athenians act anew. Arendt seems to have something similar in mind when she speaks of "the impossibility . . . to solidify in words the living essence of the person as it shows itself in the flux of action and speech."[34]

Making a related point, Arendt asserts that the "disclosure" of "who" a person is "can almost never be achieved as a willful purpose."[35] In a limited sense, this holds true for Thucydides' Athens as well; *hoi Athenaioi* as a "unit of action" do not set out with the purpose of disclosing—or, in more contemporary jargon, "performing"—the Athenian *tropos*. But unlike Arendt, who suggests that purposefulness belongs not to action but to work and labor, Thucydides does present action, in its deliberative as well as its sudden mode, as inherently instrumental.[36] In moments of deliberative action, this instrumentality emerges on two levels. First, as a "unit of action," *hoi Athenaioi* gather in order to settle on means to achieve their ends in the world. In the case of the Mitylene Debate, the immediate question is not who the Athenians are, but what shall be done with their captives.[37] The arguments of the Mitylene Debate are, to put the matter rather crudely, tools by which the Athenians might decide whether to kill or spare the Mitylenians.[38]

   34. Arendt, *The Human Condition*, 181.
   35. Ibid., 179.
   36. Arendt has often enough been criticized for reducing politics and action to speechifying. Though Arendt makes plenty of disparaging remarks about instrumental activity, she does concede that identity-disclosing action can be and often is intertwined with means–end activity; see *The Human Condition*, 182. While recognizing these Arendtian "acknowledgments," Dietz suggests that "Arendt's theory cannot conceptually vindicate either the emancipatory value of purposeful performance or the practical purposefulness of politics"; see "'The Slow Boring of Hard Boards,'" 880. As I argue in the text, Thucydides clearly retains the instrumentality of politics that Dietz and others fault Arendt for eschewing.
   37. Saxonhouse, *Athenian Democracy*, 59.
   38. Here, again, my argument bears some resemblance to realist readings of the *History*. Keohane, "Realism and the Study of World Politics," 165, suggests that Thucydides as a realist saw states as "carefully calculating costs of alternative courses of action and seeking to maximize their expected utility." Such claims suggest a lively sense of politics as a means for the pursuit of the city's ends—a sense that I think Thucydides shares. Such claims also, however, continue to overlook disputes within cities over means and ends and, in particular, the possibility that the city's calculations may go beyond "utility" to include considerations of, say, justice. Thucydides' actors, of course, often take up the issue of justice as a possible end (as Cleon and Diodotus do in the Mitylene Debate), though we may well despair over how seldom they choose to pursue it.

Cleon and Diodotus raise the question of the Athenian way as part of their attempt to influence the answer to that question. Here we find the second aspect of instrumentality in Athenian deliberative action. There are particular Athenians who purposively seek to disclose the Athenian *tropos* to their fellow citizens. In pursuit of their own ends as politicians, Cleon and Diodotus speak as if it *were* possible "to solidify in words" the Athenian way.[39] For Arendt, an agent's identity most likely "remains hidden from the person himself" and appears most "clearly and unmistakably to others" encountered in human plurality.[40] In Thucydides' presentation of democratic politics, the plurality emerges, as it were, within the agent, within the "unit of action" that is the city. To the silently gathered demos, Cleon and Diodotus appear as "others" who claim to see the Athenian way clearly and who use this claim as an instrument for securing influence among their fellow citizens.

Let me pause briefly here to summarize the course of my argument about the place of the Athenian *tropos* in democratic politics in the *History*. Thucydides portrays deliberation as the interaction of contending speakers and silent demos in search of what Athens as a city is to do. In the course of this search, speakers make rhetorical appeals to the Athenian *tropos*, seeking to persuade the Athenians that what they as a city have done in the past reveals a way of acting that should guide them in the immediate future. But the interpretations that speakers thus offer are imminently contestable and, in the example of the Mitylene Debate, immediately contested. Though they may produce a decision about what is to be done, moments of deliberative action thus leave undecided the content of the Athenian way. In part, this follows from the basic ambiguity of *hoi Athenaioi* as a unit of action. Through deliberation, the city as many seeks unity in acting; but its inherent plurality, marked by the division between speakers and demos, persists in the openness of its actions to alternative interpretations. In part, too, it follows from the fact that the political speech that constitutes deliberation simultaneously incorporates both revelatory and instrumental aspects. The words with which speakers claim to reveal Athenian character are at the same time instruments by which those speakers attempt to shape Athenian character.[41]

---

39. And, so far as the reader can tell, they may actually believe they have described the "living essence" of the Athenian way, though most would undoubtedly be more likely to accept Diodotus' sincerity rather than Cleon's.

40. Arendt, *The Human Condition*, 179.

41. This way of thinking about democratic politics in the *History* complicates the evaluation of Cleon and Diodotus offered by Saxonhouse. Drawing on the arguments he makes about

As moments of deliberation reach their denouement, Thucydides reinforces the simultaneous decisiveness and indecisiveness created by the presence of contending elite voices by leaving intact the powerful silence of the assembled demos. Let us focus once more on the arguments that Cleon and Diodotus make about the place of speech in the Athenian way of political life. Viewed in the light of the two speakers' purposes, both these arguments make rhetorical sense. Cleon wants the Athenians to recognize themselves in his attack on deliberation and in this instance to act differently, to refuse to rethink the sentence passed on the Mitylenians. Diodotus, on the other hand, intends the Athenians to understand this as an instance when the standard Athenian practice of discussion and an Athenian willingness to reconsider previous decisions will yield the proper policy. What, then, can we glean from the Athenians' decision about their self-understandings and more generally about this aspect of the Athenian *tropos*?

Given that the Athenians choose to follow his advice on what to do with the Mitylenians, our immediate inclination might be to say that their action embodies and confirms Diodotus' understanding of deliberation as a crucial aspect of the Athenian way of political life. But how do we know this? Thucydides tells us nothing about the impact of the specific arguments made by Cleon and Diodotus: "And after these proposals were made opposing one another with very even strength, the Athenians clashed in their opinions after all, and in the show of hands the resolutions were nearly equal, but that of Diodotus prevailed" (3.49). Mainly, we learn here that the vote was very close, so perhaps we can say that some Athenians have accepted Diodotus' argument while others have not. But even this is conjecture. Perhaps those who voted for Diodotus' proposal indeed accepted his arguments and acted accordingly. Alternatively, perhaps they have accepted what Diodotus has to say about expediency (and, again, acted accordingly), while rejecting what he has to say about deliberation. As for those who voted with Cleon, perhaps they accepted his arguments about deliberation but not his insistence on the importance of expediency. The possible permutations go on and on. Thucydides does not offer us

---

the value of deliberation, she calls Diodotus "the true democratic theorist from antiquity"; Saxonhouse, *Athenian Democracy*, 75. Diodotus, on this argument, stands on the democratic side, that is, the side of debate, division, and plurality; and Cleon on the undemocratic side, that is, the side of unity in the city. While this is, in a sense, true of the particular arguments each makes, in another sense it fails to account for the fact that both Cleon and Diodotus set out with the purpose of uniting the city. Perhaps we can say that Diodotus has a more lively Thucydidean sense of the fact that the Athenians are—and must be—both many and one.

any conclusive analysis of Athenian opinions or, for that matter, his own interpretation of the meaning of the decision taken. His account thus emphasizes the manner in which both the persistent silence of the Athenian demos and, consequently, decisions made by the demos resist any authoritative interpretation. The Athenians' action, both at the moment of acting and in the future, remains open to the same sort of interpretations offered by the speakers in the Mitylene Debate itself. Some, probably those who support Cleon, will continue to claim that the decision taken by the Athenians appears as a perfect example of the mutability of Athenian democracy; others, most likely those who side with Diodotus, may continue to see it as confirming the value of democratic deliberation in Athens. Deliberation has here fulfilled its fundamental purpose of producing action, but just what that action means and thus what has been learned or revealed about the Athenian *tropos* remains an open question. I now turn to Pericles' Funeral Oration as another instance in which the Athenians themselves take up the question of who they are in the context of deciding what they should do.

IV. DEMOCRATIC POLITICS AND THE RHETORIC OF CHARACTER II: THE FUNERAL ORATION

Pericles, breaking with tradition, only briefly discusses the Athenian ancestors at the outset of the Funeral Oration,[42] and moves quickly to "set forth by what sort of training we have come to our present position, and with what political institutions [*politaea*] and as the result of what manner of life [*tropos*] our empire became great" (2.36).[43] He thus embarks on what Forde has rightly called "the most famous discussion of Athenian character."[44] As part of the reconceptualization of the Athenian *tropos* offered above, I drew from some of the claims Pericles makes about *hoi Athenaioi*. My aim in this section is not to examine those claims in more detail, but rather to build on the account of deliberation offered in the previous section in order to suggest a reorientation of our approach to the Funeral

---

42. On Pericles' break with the traditional funeral oration or *epitaphios logos*, see Orwin, *Humanity of Thucydides*, 16; and Loraux, *The Invention of Athens*, who argues that the atypicality of Pericles' oration as recorded by Thucydides makes it suspect as a source for generalization about the genre.
43. I draw here from Smith's translation. Lattimore, rather oddly, seems to omit any translation of the reference to the Athenian *tropos* in this passage.
44. Forde, "Causes of Athenian Imperialism," 434; *The Ambition to Rule*, 18.

Oration. My broader purpose in turning to the Funeral Oration is to suggest how we might move beyond a reading of Athenian politics that focuses on the presence or absence of Periclean leadership. To that end, I argue that the Funeral Oration stands as a moment of deliberative action and democratic politics, not unlike the Mitylene Debate, in which the Athenian *tropos* becomes a subject of political rhetoric aimed at persuading the Athenians to act in a particular manner.

Any such argument must confront some obvious facts that make the Funeral Oration stand out: in the Mitylene Debate two speakers contend for influence in a situation that demands immediate action, whereas in the Funeral Oration a single speaker rises on what appears to be a strictly ceremonial occasion. That the single speaker is Pericles only deepens the difficulty. As I noted in the Introduction, given the silence of contending voices when he speaks, Pericles seems to stand apart from other Athenian speakers. This fact, again, no doubt facilitates the conclusion that Pericles somehow speaks for a united Athens and that the Funeral Oration stands as some sort of "explicit act of self-identification."[45]

Especially given the reading of character outlined above, we must question the idea of an underlying Athenian "self" that is fixed and unified enough to be "identified" in this manner. In fact, the Funeral Oration itself is a moment of plurality—or, better, another instance of the simultaneous unity and plurality familiar from the Mitylene Debate. Thucydides presents not simply one Athens, but one Athenian speaker and many Athenians who do not speak. From this perspective, only the absence of a second speaker differentiates Pericles' appearances in the *History* from a moment like the Mitylene Debate. And we need not presume that a single speaker means a united and acquiescent audience. In its silent presence, the Athenian demos here, too, retains the powers of decision and division. Pericles, no less than any other speaker, faces the basic challenge of choosing persuasive rhetoric.

But just what is Pericles trying to persuade his fellow citizens to do? Here Aristotle's division of rhetoric into three types—judicial, deliberative or political, and epideictic or ceremonial—proves useful. Commentators at times discuss the Funeral Oration as a prime example of the third category.[46] Reading rather narrowly, this classification seems correct enough.

---

45. Jansson, "Identity-defining Practices in Thucydides' *History of the Peloponnesian War*," 159.

46. On Pericles' Funeral Oration as epideictic rhetoric, see, for example, Kennedy, *The Art of Persuasion in Ancient Greece*, 155; and Connor, *Thucydides*, 67.

In the *Rhetoric*, Aristotle writes that "the ceremonial oratory of display either praises or censures somebody."[47] Pericles surely means in part to display the Athenian *tropos* and, by extension, to praise it. If we prefer more contemporary constructivist jargon, then we can say that Pericles indeed seems to aim at identifying Athens or perhaps at a performance that reveals the Athenian way. At the same time, classifying the Funeral Oration in this manner as epideictic understates certain deliberative aspects of both the context and the speech.

The audience for epideictic oratory, Aristotle says, consists of "observers," who "merely decide on the orator's skill" to determine a winner.[48] In introducing the Funeral Oration, though, Thucydides tells us that Athenian tradition dictated that "a man chosen by the state [*poles*], known for wise judgment and of high reputation" deliver "an appropriate speech of praise" (2.34.6). Based on his stature and importance in the city—on his political standing—Athens has recognized him in advance as a skillful and thus worthy speaker for this occasion. Pericles is not so much a contestant seeking a prize as a politician with a wonderful opportunity to speak to the demos without the potentially disruptive appearance of counterarguments. The Funeral Oration allows Pericles to speak before an audience of Athenians who have, in this sense, already passed on his qualifications to speak to them and who might thus heed what he has to say. But we should emphasize the "might." He can hope to sway his audience, but again, he must hit upon the correct means of persuasion if he is to achieve his purpose.[49]

Judging by the Funeral Oration itself and thinking again of Aristotle's tripartite division, that purpose seems to be as much deliberative as ceremonial. Aristotle further distinguishes between the three kinds of rhetoric according to the moment in time on which they focus. Judicial rhetoric centers on the past: "one man accuses the other, and the other defends himself, with reference to things already done." Deliberative or "political" rhetoric concerns the future, "things to be done hereafter." Epideictic rhetoric "is, properly speaking, concerned with the present, since all men praise or blame in view of the state of things existing at the time." Aristotle adds,

47. Aristotle, *Rhetoric and Poetics*, 32.
48. Ibid.
49. Loraux, *Invention of Athens*, chap. 1, similarly discusses the selection of the orator as part of her broader argument that the funeral oration, with its aristocratic overtones, was nonetheless adapted to suit the democratic polis.

almost in passing, that the ceremonial orator may "find it useful also to recall the past and to make guesses about the future."[50]

Now Pericles' oration no doubt recalls the past, if in an immediate sense more so than in thinking of the ancestors. It also praises the fallen in light of the present and addresses the future.[51] Regarding the latter, he does not so much "guess" about the future as call on the Athenians to imagine a particular future and, more immediately, to do what they must to make that future real. This chiefly means persevering in the war by acting in the proper Athenian way: "emulate [those who have fallen], judge that happiness is freedom and freedom courage and do not stand aside from the dangers of the war" (2.35). Pericles' oration does not neatly or completely fall in Aristotle's category of deliberative rhetoric; unlike the Mitylene Debate or the Corinthian speech at Sparta, the Funeral Oration does not concern a particular proposal or policy. Still, the context and the speech do have political or deliberative aspects. Pericles sets out to use his influence to bring about a certain sort of Athenian action in the immediate future. We can say that Pericles' oration not only partakes of the epideictic kind of rhetoric, but also contains a full measure of the deliberative or political kind.

The Funeral Oration thus stands as a moment of deliberative action in a way familiar from our consideration of the Mitylene Debate. The juxtaposition of Athenian plurality and unity looks different here: there is only one speaker. The interplay of speech as an instrument for collective decision making and speech as revealing collective character looks different, too: here, the revelatory role seems more central.[52] But we should approach these differences as existing within a broadly similar presentation of deliberation as the interaction of elite speaker and silent demos through rhetoric. As with the Mitylene Debate, Thucydides leaves us to wonder whether

50. Aristotle, *Rhetoric and Poetics*, 32.
51. On this point, see Connor, *Thucydides*, 68.
52. Drawing again on Dietz's critique of Arendt's noninstrumental view of action (see note 59 above), we might say that Pericles intends the Funeral Oration as a "purposeful performance" with "emancipatory value." By displaying the Athenian *tropos*, he means to "emancipate" the Athenians from grief and fear and lead them toward a brighter future. One of the benefits of reading the Funeral Oration—and speech more generally—as purposive or instrumental is that we can gain some critical purchase on such rhetorical ploys. We might, for instance, see Pericles' "purposeful performance" as manipulative rather than emancipatory. Along these lines, see Nietzsche's curious description of "Pericles' panegyric" as a "grandly optimistic, deceptive image"; Nietzsche, *Human, All Too Human*, trans. Helen Zimmern (New York: Russell and Russell, 1964), 257. Perhaps the plague that immediately follows in part reveals the deception or unravels the manipulation. Certainly it leaves Pericles fighting for his political life.

the Athenians have accepted the speaker's particular arguments. After Pericles offers his glowing description of the Athenian way of life and issues his call for the Athenians to act accordingly, to become lovers of the city and to redouble their efforts in the war, Thucydides once more preserves the basic silence of the demos, offering only, "such was the funeral that occurred in this winter" (2.42). He tells us nothing of whether the Athenians accepted Pericles' description of the Athenian *tropos*; he merely records that description and moves on to the next summer's actions.

Whatever the stature of Pericles, we should thus read his Funeral Oration as another attempt to define the "identity" of *hoi Athenaioi*, not as a simple expression of that identity. In this sense, Pericles faces the same task as any other Athenian who seeks to lead the demos, and his role in Athenian politics is fundamentally like that of any other would-be elite. He must draw from his political judgment and rhetorical skill to try to persuade the assembled Athenians to accept his account of who they are as a unit of action and thus to follow his advice for the immediate future. Once he has spoken, the impact of his words remains unclear. The subsequent actions taken by the Athenians remain open to interpretation by future actors. So, too, do Pericles' words themselves. The plague that shortly ensues seems to lead the Athenians to question the authority of Pericles and his understanding of the Athenian way. He soon finds himself in the assembly attempting to reinterpret and thus reestablish his relationship with the demos (2.60). Later, as we will see in Chapter 4, we seem to hear echoes of the Funeral Oration, as speakers try again authoritatively to (re)define the Athenian way. It certainly makes sense to think of Pericles' speeches providing handy, albeit not foolproof, rhetorical resources to later speakers as they attempt to gain the support of the demos. This is the stuff of democratic politics in the *History*. Understanding what Thucydides' has to tell us about democracy in part means grappling with how demos and speakers—even the mighty Pericles—navigate the fundamental uncertainty of acting in a world of "characters" who are in a sense fundamentally unknowable.

V. CONCLUSION: PERSPECTIVES ON CHARACTER

We should not forget, though, the other perspective on character that emerges near the end of the *History*. In the passage quoted at the outset of this chapter, Thucydides himself seems to look beyond the changeability that dominates what I above referred to as the perspective of the political actor. In 8.96 he clearly privileges one understanding of the Athenian *tropos:* in the context of Spartan "slowness," he calls the Athenian way "quick." He seems, too, to offer what amounts to a nascent theory of Athens' defeat based on this understanding. In short, Thucydides here speaks from his perspective as historian in an authoritative manner about the Athenian way. What are we to make of such an authorial comment and of its placement near the very end of the *History*?

To begin to suggest an answer, let me turn briefly to an argument offered by W. R. Connor. Connor holds that by putting the initial comparison of Athenian and Spartan character in the mouths of the Corinthians, rather than in his own words, Thucydides "can retain his distance and remain taciturn."[53] For the reader, the Corinthians' arguments present a challenge that emerges from the juxtaposition of the two perspectives presented in the *History*. From the hindsight of history, readers know that Athens will lose the war. From the more immediate perspective of one listening to the speech of the Corinthians, it would appear, on the contrary, that the vigorous Athenians should rather easily defeat the plodding Spartans. Connor suggests that Thucydides' restraint thus makes the Athenian character something of a puzzle for the reader: How could it fail to produce victory? In a sense, 8.96 provides Thucydides' answer, but only after the reader struggles to find his or her own.[54]

The understanding of the place of the Athenian *tropos* in politics that I have developed here suggests that we take Connor's argument a step further. If for the reader the Athenian *tropos* presents a puzzle in the way Connor suggests, it must appear all the more puzzling to the actors themselves—both elites who speak and ordinary citizens who do not. Like Thucydides, the reader can ponder the Athenians and their actions with hindsight. The Corinthians, the Spartans,[55] and most important for my

---

53. Connor, *Thucydides*, 41.

54. Thucydides does suggest earlier (relatively earlier, at any rate), at 7.55.2, that the Syracusans and Athenians are "similar in character [*homiotropoi*]." As Connor notes, though, only at 8.96 does he develop the comparison at any length and offer his account of its implications and effects. It is also true that Thucydides throughout the *History* provides the context in which readers might puzzle over the Athenian character. His account of past Athenian actions in the "archeology" and "pentekontaetia" of book 1, for example, provides the basis for Forde's analysis of Athenian "daring." As Forde points out, Thucydides himself tells us that the other Greek cities feared the daring that had "come into being" in Athens during the Persian wars (1.90.1). Ultimately, though, this fear rested on a particular interpretation of Athenian action and Athenian character drawn by other Greeks. Again, by leaving his own authoritative comments until book 8, Thucydides allows the reader to witness—and to participate in—the ongoing interpretation and reinterpretation of the meaning of Athenian action, past and present.

55. And other, less notable Greek cities, as I make clear in Chapters 4 and 5.

purposes the Athenians themselves "explore" the Athenian way in the process of dealing with a future that is unknown and a past that is always open to interpretation and reinterpretation. From this standpoint, what Connor describes as Thucydides' "restraint" will have been more a matter of necessity imposed on him by the subject matter. If his reader is to understand how collective "character" works as a dynamic subject of deliberation, the *History* must show how it works from the perspective of the political actor. In particular, if we are to understand how the rival interpretations of contending speakers combined with the persistent silence of the Athenian demos work to render the Athenian way unknowable from the perspective of politics, Thucydides must himself remain silent, must withhold until near the end his summary judgment about who the Athenians are.

Arendt seems to have something similar in mind in comments she makes about the imitation of action and actors in Greek drama. While the "universal meaning" of a play is revealed by the chorus, "the intangible identities of the agents in the story, since they escape all generalization and therefore all reification, can be conveyed only through an imitation of their acting."[56] The reification of the agent occurs only after the action, in the backwards glance of the storyteller.[57] We must be careful here. Thucydides insists that he has not engaged in "patriotic storytelling" but has rather sought an "accuracy" (*akribeia*) that truly allows his work to be a possession for all time (1.22). Yet the "accuracy" that makes Thucydides' account more than just a good story, and thus the power of his own summary analysis in 8.96, does not derive from any Archimedean objectivity on his part.[58] Rather, it comes in large part from the juxtaposition of his perspective with that of the political actor, allowing each to temper the other.

I have dwelt here mainly on the perspective of the political actor, immersed in the present, struggling to understand an uncertain past, seeking

---

56. Arendt, *The Human Condition*, 187–88.

57. Ibid., 184. Disch, *Hannah Arendt and the Limits of Philosophy*, 127–28, discusses Arendt's notions of storytelling and the storyteller in depth and considers Arendt's own use of the *History* "as a model of the kind of historical writing she is trying to achieve." In this context, she provides a helpful discussion of Arendt's understanding of Thucydidean versus Archimedean objectivity.

58. Just what Thucydides means by "accuracy" has been the subject of much scholarly debate. For a brief account of the difficulties of interpreting 1.22, see Orwin, *Humanity of Thucydides*, 207–12. See also the discussions of Thucydidean objectivity in Connor, *Thucydides*, 8; and Euben, *Tragedy of Political Theory*, 194–98. Arendt herself suggests that Thucydidean objectivity consists in his making "articulate the standpoints and interests of the warring parties"; see Arendt, *Between Past and Future*, 51–52.

a way into the unknown future. I have done so first and foremost because I take prevailing readings of collective character and democratic politics in the *History* to be in need of a certain tempering. As I suggested at the outset, those readings contribute to Thucydides' relative obscurity as a theorist of democracy. They also tend to simplify the question of what happens to Athens over the course of the war, placing responsibility for the city's fall with the Athenian character itself or with leaders incapable of managing that character. If we wish, with the advantage of hindsight, to construct a narrative that centers on the Athenian character, we must complicate it with an accompanying appreciation for the challenges of political judgment that character poses to political actors—including both vocal elites and silent demos. In the next chapter I turn to more fully pursue that task.

4

The Silence of the Demos and the Challenges of Political Judgment: On the "Decline" of Athenian Politics

I. INTRODUCTION

But it is right to expect us the speakers ... to take a somewhat longer view than you whose attention is brief, especially since we are accountable when we give advice while you are not accountable when you listen.

—Diodotus (3.43) (trans. Smith)

Other than what we learn from his brief appearance in the *History*, we know little of this Diodotus. His name means something like "the gift of god," and some have thought him a figment of Thucydides' historical imagination, fashioned to provide a foil for Cleon. We have seen in passing Diodotus' response to Cleon's attack on speech: there can be no other means, he says, "to throw light on that which still belongs to the dim and distant future" (3.42). In the passage above, Diodotus turns his attention from the flaws of Cleon's argument to the foibles of the Athenian demos. Athenians, though they properly bear responsibility for the actions they choose, tend to blame the one who offers advice. The prudent adviser, then, will struggle to see as far ahead as possible, however dim the future may seem. By the time of the Mitylene Debate, the Athenian assembly has become, on Diodotus' telling, a dangerous place for one who would lead.

Along these lines, we might read Thucydides as telling (with the help of the possibly fictitious Diodotus and others) a story of Athenian political decline. If the Athenian character, insofar as it is a changeable subject of deliberation, cannot account for what happens to Athens, then changes in the process of deliberation itself may. Some recent readings of the *History* emphasizing the way in which political speech serves to constitute "communities" lead us in this direction. Put in the terms I have been using, these readings see speech deteriorating over the course of the war, coming to serve increasingly poorly as a way for the Athenians (or any "community") to learn what makes them one, for plurality to yield unity. In the end, all that remains is a quasi-Hobbesian struggle among the many or of each for himself, in which speech is a tool for personal gain.[1] Taken too far, any such argument about the declining ability of speech runs afoul of the consistent complexity of speech in the *History*.[2] We will, that is, have difficulty saying that political speech degenerates over the course of the *History* from its proper role as constitutive of community into mere rhetorical maneuvering. The instrumental and constitutive roles of speech intertwine throughout, as rival speakers vie for the support of the silent demos precisely by offering accounts of what Athens means and of what constitutes the Athenian way. The relation and relative importance of those roles may change, but political speech on Thucydides' telling inherently involves both.

Diodotus' lament itself offers a further complication to any story of Athenian political decline. As I noted in Chapter 3, Diodotus here not only responds to Cleon's attack on deliberation, but also enters into an ongoing discussion of Athenian political life. Athenian speakers, that is, routinely make the workings of democratic politics a subject of their rhetoric. In trying to cement their standing in Athens, they offer their own accounts of the proper relationship between advisers and demos, treating that relationship as an aspect of the rhetorically contestable Athenian way. Thus understanding deliberative action in Thucydides' Athens requires us to grapple with the arguments that speakers make about deliberative action

---

1. Euben, for example, sees Thucydides as making the point that "only in a community collectively constituted and maintained can human motives of whatever kind and however self-referential be a rational or coherent basis for thought and action." According to Euben, Thucydides traces the change in speech from peacetime, "when men have neither the pretext nor desire to act or speak in ways that corrupt their common life," to war, which ultimately leads to the destruction of communities constituted through speech and hence to the end of coherent collective action; thus revolution at Corcyra and, ultimately, the oligarchic coup at Athens. White, *When Words Lose Their Meaning*, offers something of a similar argument, finding Thucydides tracing the decline of a "culture of argument" that exists in a healthy form in Athens and indeed throughout Greece at the beginning of the war, allowing for moral argument and moral agreement. As this culture declines, White argues, it becomes less and less possible for speakers to introduce justice into considerations of what is to be done, and collective political judgment suffers and falters. I return (briefly) to address White's reading in Chapter 5, Section II; I consider the Corcyrean Revolution and the coup at Athens in more detail in Chapter 1.

2. Euben himself recognizes that this sort of tale is a bit "too neat," for "even within a healthy polis men are rivals, as well as friends, involved in complex strategies of persuasion in which the inherent ambiguity of moral terms is integrated in disparate ways." Euben, *Tragedy*, 189.

and the import of those arguments in the context of the silent power of the Athenian demos.

I take on this task in the present chapter, exploring claims made by Athenian advisers about the way the Athenians make decisions and thinking about how those claims might fit together into a narrative of change or decline in Athenian politics. In part, my conclusions will be familiar ones: we will have difficulty constructing such a narrative precisely because the nature of Athenian politics remains contestable. No matter how convincing the words of any given speaker may seem, the persistent silence of the Athenian demos destabilizes any putatively authoritative interpretation. But I also want to add a new wrinkle, inspired by Diodotus' complaint about the difficulty and danger of advising the Athenians in the face of the unknown future. I here work towards a Thucydidean understanding of the challenges of political judgment posed to the political actor by the uncertainties of collective identity, deliberative action, and political speech developed in the last two chapters. I orient my discussion around the interaction of the Athenian demos with two advisers often thought to be widely divergent in political judgment: the mighty Pericles and the hapless Nicias.

II. THE PERICLEAN VISION OF DEMOCRATIC POLITICS

As I have already suggested, the most prevalent reading of what happens to Athenian politics during the war centers on the figure of Pericles as exceptional leader. This reading finds indirect support from the silence of contending voices and the silence of the Athenian demos when Pericles speaks, but its most explicit textual support comes in the eulogy of Pericles. Thucydides writes, in C. F. Smith's translation, that Pericles "led [the Athenians] rather than being led by them" and that his influence amounted to "a government ruled by its foremost citizen" or, in Hobbes's translation, a "monarchy" (2.65). Here we might first apply what I said in Chapter 3 about Thucydides' retrospective comments on Athenian character in 8.96. Eulogies, after all, always look backward; by definition, those who eulogize speak from hindsight. Thucydides' comments should not stop us from thinking about Pericles' influence from the more immediate perspective of politics, where it may appear significantly less "monarchical."

What is more, Thucydides within the eulogy itself offers indications that Pericles' "rule" was not so simple a matter as the application of great skill in shaping and controlling the rather inert matter of the demos. Pericles "owed his position," Thucydides tells us, "to his recognized standing and ability." The "strength of his high reputation" allowed him boldly to oppose the Athenians. Such passages suggest that Pericles' influence depended indeed on a sort of skill, but on a skill in interacting with, rather than managing, the demos. His standing had to be recognized by someone, his reputation taken into account by those he would oppose. In short, the eulogy recognizes the demos as an active party in Athenian politics. What Thucydides writes in 2.65 from the perspective of history seems to urge us to consider as well the perspective of the political actor; thus we can turn to what Pericles himself has to say about his political place in Athens.

Perhaps the most central passage for understanding Pericles' perspective on Athenian politics and his place in it comes in the final Periclean speech that Thucydides records. Admonishing the Athenians for turning on him anger roused by the trials of war and plague, Pericles declares: "And yet I, the object of your anger, consider myself a man inferior to no one in judging what is necessary and explaining it; furthermore, a lover of my country and above money" (2.60). The words are striking. They seem to provide clear evidence of that ability to upbraid the Athenian demos with which Thucydides credits Pericles. What other politician could dare to engage in such "unabashed self-praise"?[3] A basic tenant of Greek rhetoric held that orators in law courts should disclaim special skill in speaking; witness Socrates' downplaying his rhetorical ability in Plato's *Apology*.[4] Surely the same advice holds for speakers in democratic assemblies. Claiming an elite position surely risks offending and alienating an audience of supposed political equals. Claiming a special skill in speaking might well set such an audience on its guard against rhetorical maneuvers. What might Pericles be up to here?

On a common reading, this passage provides a model of the statesman

---

3. Connor, *Thucydides*. 65. Others, too, have been struck by the tone of this passage and by Pericles' third speech more generally. Grene, *Greek Political Theory*, 87, notes Pericles' "calm arrogance." Saxonhouse, *Athenian Democracy*, 67, says Pericles "even becomes a bit petulant" with his fellow citizens. Westlake, *Individuals in Thucydides*, similarly notes Pericles' "unconciliatory attitude" and concludes that "this is the speech of a brave man" (37).

4. At the outset of the *Apology*, Socrates dismisses the idea, advanced by his accusers, that he will deceive the jury. The implication of this idea, he says, is "that I am a skillful speaker." His accusers will soon be "confuted, when it becomes obvious that I have not the slightest skill as a speaker." Plato, *The Last Days of Socrates*, 45. Kennedy, *The Art of Persuasion in Ancient Greece*, discusses this passage in a similar context.

by which future leaders might be measured.⁵ This sort of reading, again, downplays the "historicity" of Thucydides' presentation of Athenian politics and of Pericles' speeches in particular. Pericles no more serves as the direct mouthpiece of Thucydides than do the Corinthians of the first book. Thucydides portrays him as a speaker in a particular rhetorical context—that is, as a participant in a particular moment of deliberative action in Athens. As such, we need to read Pericles' self-description more broadly as his proffered understanding of the Athenian practice of deliberation and of the role of the adviser in that practice. Let me, then, return to a closer examination of Pericles' attempt to save his position with the desperate and angry demos.

Pericles clinches the argument that begins with his "unabashed self-praise" as follows: "And so, if in thinking that I rather than others was endowed with these qualities, however modestly, you were persuaded to go to war, I could not reasonably be charged with misconduct" (2.60.7). Now clearly Pericles intends the Athenians to accept as true the conditional with which he begins: when they followed his advice and went to war, they indeed believed that he was beyond others in knowledge, expositional skill, and a sort of honest patriotism. Furthermore, Pericles implies that the Athenians allowed themselves to be persuaded precisely because they saw in him these three qualities. But what should this post hoc description of how the decision to go to war was taken have to do with assessing blame in the present? Thucydides provides us with no direct confirmation that the Athenian demos understands the decision to go to war as a matter of following a leader with the particular qualities that Pericles claims. Moreover, even if the Athenians did once think Pericles to have qualities that added to the basic persuasiveness of his advice, it is possible that they now simply see that they were mistaken. Of course, Thucydides has Pericles deny precisely this. Thus his "unabashed self-praise": he did and still does possess these qualities. And so, as the argument goes, the Athenians are not to blame for following Pericles' advice in the first place, nor, he says, should they blame him if his advice now seems faulty.

Who if anyone does Pericles mean for the demos to hold accountable for Athens's misfortunes? We can see what the answer must be from a

---

5. Pouncey, *The Necessities of War*, 78, for example, finds in Pericles' self-praise "a set of standards needed to move nations by political leadership, with which he can measure the performance of prominent politicians in the work." See also J. H. Finley, *Thucydides*, 151; and Kagan, *The Peace of Nicias and the Sicilian Expedition*, 358.

passage in Pericles' first speech, in which he counsels war against the Peloponnesians: "I charge those who stand persuaded [by me] that you support our common resolutions, even if there are setbacks or else not to claim their intelligence as a contribution to our successes. For the outcome of situations can follow a course as absurd as the plans of man, which is just why we are accustomed to blame chance for whatever turns out contrary to calculation" (1.140). Pericles envisions, and demands that the Athenians recognize, a collective responsibility that follows from the decision to take a speaker's advice. Everyone who comes to favor a course of action has a hand in the judgment that course represents and must participate in any praise or blame that results. We shall attend in a moment to echoes of this notion of collective judgment and responsibility in the postplague speech, but we can see even now how it is implied in Pericles' argument there. According to that argument, the Athenians' judgment in going to war was based on the belief that Pericles possessed certain qualities that made his advice particularly persuasive. That belief still holds; if the Athenians' judgment has not worked out as they wished, the fault lies neither with Pericles—who still has what it takes to be a good adviser—nor with the demos, which was right in choosing an adviser based on knowledge, expositional skill, and honest patriotism. Rather, all must face the fact that the best decisions, taken in the most suitable manner, may still lead to difficulty. To put the point a bit differently, Pericles means the Athenians to see that the fault lies not in the way they have deliberated and decided in the past, not in their seeking out advisers with certain qualities, nor in their choosing as an adviser Pericles in particular, but in the imponderable way in which the best-laid plans often fail.

Pericles' first and third speeches share an emphasis on collective responsibility, but there remains an obvious difference. In his first speech, Pericles engages in none of the "unabashed self-praise" we hear in his third speech. He does claim a certain personal constancy. "Athenians, I am of the same opinion as ever" (1.140), he says by way of prelude to his demand for a similar constancy on the part of the demos, a willingness to accept that collective responsibility just discussed. He makes no claims, however, about the personal qualities that distinguish him from others, no mention of his knowledge, his speaking skill, his patriotism, his honesty. We need to ask why Pericles does make such claims in the third speech, and here the context is crucial. After the plague, Pericles' position in Athens comes under fire. The demos has turned on him, and he is seeking a way to assuage its anger. In part, he turns to the same expedient that other speakers throughout the *History* hit upon, offering an account of the Athenian way of political life and his position in it. If we somehow accept the truth of this account, then Pericles indeed appears as a masterful, even exceptional, leader, revealing to a demos turned unruly and antagonistic in the face of its suffering not only the true heights of his own stature but also something about themselves—namely, why they have followed him in the past. In the immediate political moment, though, the truth of Pericles' account of Athenian politics is precisely what is at issue, and the silent Athenian demos stands as the immediate arbiter. Pericles constructs an interpretation of the past, of the way deliberation in Athens has worked, and he hopes the demos will accept it. If they do, then they may feel a sense of collective responsibility that diverts their wrath from Pericles. If they do not, Pericles will bear that wrath alone.

But Pericles' (re)construction of the past Athenian way of political life serves another purpose beyond the immediate assuaging of the anger of the demos; he also intends it as a guide for future Athenian action. Lowell Edmunds argues persuasively that Pericles bases his war policy on an understanding of the constancy of human intelligence (*gnome*) as the only effective bulwark against the vicissitudes of chance. Indications of this understanding run throughout his first and third speeches and merge with Pericles' claims regarding how Athenian politics do and should work. Thus in a passage from the first speech already cited, it is because "the course of events" can move as "perversely" as "the plans of men" that it is so important for the Athenians to stand behind common decisions. Plans may often go awry, and what we see as "fortune" may make matters worse, but plan we must. What is more, we must stick with our plans in the face of setbacks. This is surely, too, the central point of the postplague speech. Pericles thus attributes the current state of mind of the Athenians to what they perceive as the dashing of their war plans: "for the spirit is cowed by that which is sudden and happens contrary to all calculation." But the Athenians must persevere: "since you inhabit a great city and were brought up with a way of life [*ethesin*] to match it, you must be willing to hold out even in the greatest misfortunes and not wipe out your fame" (2.61). And, of course, their endurance must take the form of continuing Pericles' moderate war policy and thus continuing to respect Pericles as the foremost adviser. In this third speech, Pericles' advice about the proper actions to take and his claims about the Athenian way of political life thus both demand a certain stability, a continuing of things as they have been. We must continue along with the plans we have made even in the face of chance, and that means continuing to exercise our collective intelligence, continuing to deliberate, in the way we did in making those plans. If I was accepted as adviser before and my plans were followed, nothing in the vicissitudes of war and plague should cause you to be angry with me now or to change course in the future. Pericles' attempt to evade blame for his advice in the past is simultaneously a claim to the position of adviser in the present and for the future.

Rather than showing the exceptional leader standing somehow above the fray, Pericles' third speech thus clearly suggests the tenuous basis of political influence in Athens. Would-be leaders must find words that simultaneously respect the political equality of all citizens while persuading those same citizens to accept one of their own as in a sense unequal in importance and influence. Thucydides accordingly does not present Pericles as arrogantly defying the demos with "unabashed self-praise." Rather, he shows us a politically chastened Pericles who is trying to get the Athenians to understand their mode of politics in a way that will at once absolve him of personal responsibility for the past and secure his influence in the immediate future. Whatever the impact of his claims about himself on future Athenian thinking about the relationship of adviser and demos—and we will want to attend to the possibility of such impact presently—Pericles needs the Athenians to apply the standards he offers here and now, to him. The situation demands that Pericles exercise what political judgment and skill he has in finding a new way to persuade the demos that he did and still does have what it takes to be a good adviser.

The third speech is often read as showing Pericles' exceptional skill in managing the demos. In fact, it provides the clearest example of how Pericles' skill and position are political, not managerial. Like any other leader, he must find a way to persuade the Athenians assembled before him to accept his influence. He no doubt has greater ability in this regard than do other Athenian elites. Thucydides certainly suggests as much, both directly in the eulogy and indirectly through the silence of contending voices during the time of Pericles' preeminence. In the end, though, Pericles, too, must contend with the basic challenges of Athenian politics. Though he may well for a time succeed in rendering Athenian democracy merely nominal, even then he must consistently appeal to the demos, which in its silent presence provides the persistently political context for his "rule by the first man."

THE SILENCE OF THE DEMOS   103

III. PERICLES AND THEMISTOCLES

Taken from a broader perspective, Pericles' self-praise reflects the *History*'s thematization of deliberation as the interaction of elite speakers and silent demos. Future Athenian speakers, as they attempt to find words that will persuade the demos, make similar claims about the workings of democratic politics in Athens, and I turn later to consider the extent to which they operate within the framework that Pericles lays out. Before proceeding, though, I want to consider in more detail just what Pericles claims about himself and about Athens' way of making decisions. To do so, I turn to the contrast Thucydides develops between Pericles and Themistocles, the Athenian hero of the Persian Wars.

Themistocles exits the *History* just as Pericles takes center stage. Thucydides' eulogy of Themistocles immediately precedes his recording of Pericles' first speech. We have, though, briefly met Pericles before. In the interval between the final decision to go to war and the first invasion of Attica, the Peloponnesians, looking to establish "as good a reason as possible for going to war," demand that the Athenians drive out "the curse of the goddess" (1.126). The source of that curse implicates Pericles' family, and Thucydides tells us that the Peloponnesians hope, in vain, to diminish his standing in Athens (1.127). The Athenians respond with demands that the Lacedaemonians drive out the curse of Taenarus and the curse of Pausanias. Thucydides segues from the career of Pausanias, which explains the latter curse, to a discussion of the end of Themistocles' career.

Surely a link exists between Pausanias, a Spartan hero during the Persian Wars, and Themistocles, but the transition here seems forced or at least purposeful. For the reader, the chapters spent on Pausanias (1.128–35) are necessary to explain the curses; those devoted to Themistocles' adventures in Persia (1.136–38) are not.[6] Beyond reflecting Thucydides' clear interest in the great individuals of Greek history, it seems reasonable to think, as many have suggested, that Thucydides offers Themistocles as a comparison point for other Greek—and in particular other Athenian—leaders. I will later consider the striking comparison with Alcibiades. But Thucydides also perhaps digresses on Themistocles in order to prepare us for his presentation of Pericles. We might most obviously compare the eulogies Thucydides offers of the two—eulogies that are in fact comparable

---

6. On this point, see Palmer, *Love of Glory and the Common Good*, 89–91; Gomme, Dover, and Andrewes, *A Historical Commentary on Thucydides*, 1:26–27; Bury, *The Ancient Greek Historians*, 127–28; and Forde, *The Ambition to Rule*, 69.

in tone and length. I want here, though, to pursue a different course, comparing what Thucydides says of Themistocles to what Pericles says about himself in the postplague speech. Now clearly, I must be careful in this, for the two descriptions issue from different perspectives: one from the author of the *History*, one from words put into the mouth of a political actor. But the difference in perspectives will in fact turn out to reinforce the basic contrast suggested by the descriptions themselves.

First, Pericles claims for himself and Thucydides attributes to Themistocles a sort of knowledge directly relevant to action, captured in both descriptions by *ta deonta* (what is necessary, what is called for). Thus Pericles tells the Athenians that he thinks himself "inferior to no man in judging [*gnomai*] what is necessary [*ta deonta*]" (2.60). Themistocles, according to Thucydides, "was certainly supreme in his immediate grasp [*autoschediazein*] of what was necessary [*ta deonta*]" (1.138). Both Themistocles and Pericles on these accounts know what is to be done, but the varying verbs seem to suggest some difference between the two. J. H. Finley, for one, locates the difference in changes in the intellectual climate of fifth-century Greece. Thucydides found it "almost incredible" that Themistocles could see *ta deonta* so clearly. The same ability appeared less incredible in Pericles, who as "the friend of sophists and philosophers" could apply what he had learned in such intellectual circles.[7] According to Finley, then, Themistocles' ability struck Thucydides as unusual precisely because Themistocles lived before the learning that made Periclean knowledge possible. And this may well be an accurate account of Thucydides' understanding of the difference between Themistocles and Pericles.

Still, Thucydides has Pericles himself make no such claims about the intellectual basis of his knowledge. This seems a wise enough rhetorical strategy; to speak approvingly of sophists and philosophers might alienate a good portion of his audience. Indeed, Pericles' claim to knowledge seems particularly well suited for a speech to an assembly of citizens. His use of *gnomai*, with its connotations of judging or determining, suggests the process of deliberation—precisely the activity in which an assembly should engage. Here we can recall Edmunds' work on Pericles' conception of *gnome* as a faculty of planning, of rationally applying human intelligence to the uncertainties of the future. The key contrast with the claims that Thucydides makes for Themistocles in fact centers not so much on learning and study as on planning and deliberation and, more particularly,

---

7. J. H. Finley, *Thucydides*, 96–97.

on the time that such activities require. Themistocles' knowledge is instantaneous and comes "without study"; he needs only "the briefest deliberation." His is a "natural ability" or capacity (*ischyn, dynamei*) that expresses itself immediately (1.138). I should not want to say that Thucydides thinks Pericles lacks a similar ability. In the context of speaking to the Athenians, though, Pericles does not claim a natural power that separates him from his fellow citizens. He is merely, he says, "not inferior" to anyone in Athens; at most, he claims to play a valuable part in a group of fellow citizens engaged in the collective task of deliberating on what to do.

This difference becomes clearer when we consider another apparent similarity between the eulogy of Themistocles and Pericles "self-praise." Pericles claims not only the ability to determine the proper measures but skill in "explaining [*hermeneusai*]" them. He goes on to say that "one who has ideas and does not instruct clearly [*saphos didaxas*] is on the same level as if he had not thought of them" (2.60.6). We should note carefully the Greek that Thucydides has Pericles use here. *Hermeneusai* suggests our hermeneutics, and it has the connotation of interpreting or putting in words; *didaxas*, from *didasko* (the root of our didactic) suggests teaching or instruction.[8] In both these formulations, speaking ability appears as a tool for communicating knowledge. Speech takes a subordinate position; speaking ability proves useful insofar as it exists separately from and serves knowledge of *ta deonta*. Surely these formulations imply some sort of inequality, but only that which exists between one who knows and one who does not.

To this we can compare Thucydides' claim about Themistocles' expositional skill, that "whatever he was engaged in he was capable of explaining" (*hexegesasthai;* from *hexegeomai*)" (1.138.3). *Hexegeomai* carries the notion of making clear or showing, but also of ordering or leading. Thucydides and his speakers, in fact, use various forms of it throughout the *History* to refer to situations of leadership or command, most often to describe Athenian "supremacy" over the "allies."[9] This notion of a sort of speech that does more than teach—that orders as well—fits with the account Thucydides gives of Themistocles' role in the rebuilding of the Athenian walls after the Persian Wars. When the Spartans objected, Themistocles "proposed]*hekleuen*]" that the Athenians send him to Sparta (1.90). The

---

8. Blanco thus translates 2.60.6 as "the man who has ideas but can't teach them might as well not have any at all." Yunis, *Taming Democracy,* discusses at some length the idea of Pericles' advising the demos as a sort of instruction.

9. See, for example, 1.71.7, 1.76.1, and 3.55.4.

verb used here connotes something more than proposing. It can, like *hexegeomai*, mean to order or command. Crawley renders it as "told," and Thucydides uses various forms of it to describe military commanders giving orders to their troops and again in 1.91 when Themistocles secretly sends word to the Athenians to detain the envoys that Sparta has sent to investigate the building of the walls. The upshot of this, I think, is that Themistocles uses his ability "to expound" *ta deonta* from a position of power, as a tool of command. Though Pericles holds the position of *strategos*, in speaking to the deliberating demos he claims the ability not of a commander who orders, but of a fellow citizen who has relevant knowledge to pass along and who has the skill necessary to do so.

Pericles also claims what we might call a certain honest patriotism. This, he suggests, is a necessary supplement to knowledge of *ta deonta* and the ability to communicate that knowledge to others: "the man able to do both [i.e., see what is necessary and explain it] but ill-disposed toward his city cannot make any declaration with the comparable loyalty; and if he has that as well but he is conquered by money, for this alone he can be bought in entirety" (2.60.6). Only if a speaker is honest and patriotic in this sense can the demos know that his offering of the proper measures is genuine, not directed toward some selfish ends but rather toward the good of the city.

Thucydides makes no claim of honest patriotism for Themistocles; in fact, he does not comment directly at all on the matter. But the part of Themistocles' career on which Thucydides bases his praise deserves special attention on this score. In the eulogy, we see Themistocles as the exile, banished from Athens, sought by both Athenians and Spartans to answer the accusation that he was involved in Pausanias' plot to betray all of Greece to the Persians. Turning to Persia, he employs his "native intelligence" in the service of Artaxerxes. Indeed, Thucydides offers his praise of Themistocles in the context of Artaxerxes' own appreciation of Themistocles' insight. Even the Periclean honest patriot might have reason to flee unjust prosecution. Themistocles appears to go the extra step, proving disloyal by selling his skills to Persia. Certainly he is not the model of "unselfish devotion" to the polis that Pericles claims to be.

The point I want to make, though, is not so much that Themistocles appears unpatriotic as that the question of honest patriotism as framed by Pericles simply does not arise in Thucydides' consideration of Themistocles' career. Consider the end of the eulogy of Themistocles: "Such were the ends of Pausanias the Lacedaemonian and Themistocles the Athenian, the most famous Hellenes of their time" (1.138.6). In the next paragraph we meet Pericles as "the first man in Athens at that time" (1.139.4). Both Pericles' self-praise and Thucydides' introduction of him place central importance on his status as an Athenian. That Themistocles was an Athenian, on the other hand, remains somehow secondary or incidental; what matters are the skills he possessed; these skills, whether applied in Athens or in Persia, distinguished him as an individual Greek.

That Thucydides employs two different perspectives in the passages at hand, as I suggested earlier, only reinforces the contrasts between Themistocles and Pericles. Thucydides speaks of Themistocles in the authoritative voice of the historian. He describes a great man of action who quickly sees what must be done and who can, when necessary, direct others to do it. For whose benefit he exercises these abilities—his own, that of Athens, of Greece, even of Persia—is largely irrelevant. Themistocles as an individual stands independent of any particular political setting. On this score, we should note again that Thucydides' account of Themistocles does seem a digression; Themistocles is not enmeshed in the action of the *History* proper.

Pericles, on the other hand, speaks from the perspective of the political actor describing himself to other political actors. He has, so he says, the right qualities for an adviser. He has knowledge that can aid the city in its determination of what is to be done. He has the ability clearly to lay before his fellow citizens this knowledge as well as the honesty and patriotism that mark a commitment to the common good. These claims, of course, cannot be taken in the same way as those which Thucydides makes about Themistocles. Even if he sees Themistocles' abilities as "almost incredible' (to borrow again from J. H. Finley), Thucydides means to present Themistocles to the reader as he in fact was. Pericles' claims about himself have a different status in the *History*. The truth of those claims stands or falls not with our evaluation of the accuracy or veracity of the historian, but with the judgment of the deliberating demos. Because the demos remains silent, we cannot know whether Pericles' claims have been accepted in detail or not. As they appear in the *History*, Pericles and Themistocles are measured by different means, from different perspectives. Thucydides' inclusion of the eulogy of Themistocles has the effect of reinforcing the fact that Pericles, however skilled he might be, must make the best arguments he can, hoping his words will have the immediate effect of persuading his fellow citizens to follow his advice. But words spoken can have lives of their own. I turn now to think about the impact of Pericles' "self-praise" on the future of Athenian politics.

IV. PERICLES' HEIRS: CLEON AND DIODOTUS

As we have already noticed in Chapter 2, after Pericles' final speech, Thucydides does not return us to the Athenian assembly, does not record another moment of Athenian deliberative action, until the Mitylene Debate. I have already considered some of the arguments made by Cleon and Diodotus about the workings of democratic politics in Athens: Cleon's attack on deliberation; Diodotus' concern with the lack of collective responsibility among the Athenians. Here I return to these matters to think about how they relate to Pericles' vision of Athenian politics.

With his defense of democratic decision making and his brave defiance of the demagogue Cleon, Diodotus has drawn nearly universal admiration from Thucydides' readers. Arlene Saxonhouse, for example, has called Diodotus "the true democratic theorist from antiquity."[10] Among Thucydides' speakers, she contends, only Diodotus appreciates two key principles of democracy: first, division in the polis makes for healthy deliberation, and second, occasionally the tendency of democratic politics to produce a little instability may be for the best. After all, Diodotus' arguments seemingly spare a good many innocent lives by convincing the Athenians to think again. Against this democratic reasonableness, Cleon's demand for Athens to stand firmly united behind the initial sentence appears both "antidemocratic" and dangerous. There is, of course, nothing particularly shocking in finding Diodotus a better democrat than Cleon. Saxonhouse, though, makes another, bolder claim. There is, she argues, a "way in which we must see Cleon as the consequence of Pericles."[11] Cleon's speech in the Mitylene Debate echoes Pericles' rhetorical aim in both the Funeral Oration and, particularly, the third speech. Both Cleon and Pericles, Saxonhouse argues, seek to fashion Athens into "an unchanging uniformity that remains itself," thereby removing the very plurality and political space within which democracy might work.[12]

I have suggested, too, that Pericles attempts, particularly in the third speech, to unite the Athenians in part by (re)constructing a stable understanding of the Athenian way of political life. And Cleon does face a basic rhetorical task not unlike the one confronting Pericles in the postplague speech: both seek to convince the Athenians to reaffirm a policy on which they have already decided. Cleon's discussion of Athenian politics in a

---

10. Saxonhouse, *Athenian Democracy*, 75.
11. Ibid., 73.
12. Ibid., 70.

sense follows from his rhetorical challenge. The Athenians' decision to reconsider the sentence passed on the Mitylenians the day before reflects just the sort of changeability that Cleon says mars Athenian democratic politics. He intends his account of the Athenian way of political life to deter the Athenians from changing their minds in the case at hand. Of course, in the same way, Diodotus' claims about how politics should proceed in a democracy reinforce his arguments from expediency for sparing the Mitylenians. The overturning of ill-considered decisions is (or should be) part of the normal course of political life in a democracy; no harm will come from the Athenians changing their minds in this case. From this point of view, both Cleon and Diodotus are heirs of Pericles' rhetorical strategy of offering claims about the Athenian way of making collective decisions. And, as we will see presently, in their speeches both seem to echo aspects of Pericles' account of Athenian politics as the interaction of the demos with a certain sort of adviser. In short, which man—Cleon or Diodotus—stands nearer Pericles in the substance of his political thinking will ultimately prove a very complex question. Beyond exploring this question, we will need to ask, too, about the extent to which we can draw conclusions about the influence Pericles exerts after his death based on what we take to be partial echoes of his words in the speeches of others.[13]

Cleon aims his attack on deliberation partly at rival speakers like Diodotus, but also at the Athenians more generally. Just before he turns to argue more directly about the justice of punishing the Mitylenians, Cleon admonishes the Athenians that they act more like "men seated for entertainment by sophists [*sophiston*] rather than to deliberate [*bouleuomenois*] for the city" (3.38.7). With this claim Cleon does not dismiss deliberation altogether. In fact, in this brief passage he seems to make a positively Periclean point. Pericles holds that speech or deliberation serves simply as the means through which those who know what is to be done communicate it to others. Speech is necessary to politics but always subordinate to knowledge; its necessity flows from the fact that those who know must have a way to teach those who do not. We might read Cleon's wish for *bouleomenois* in place of *sophiston* as saying that the Athenians have allowed speech to escape its proper position and have thus subordinated knowledge

13. In short, I mean to take seriously the possibility suggested by Saxonhouse's claim that we ought to see "Cleon as the *consequence* of Pericles." Saxonhouse's argument works mostly at the level of comparison. She finds and describes key similarities between what Cleon and Pericles say and important differences between the words of Diodotus and Pericles. But in the passage quoted above, she suggests a firmer link between Cleon and Pericles and with this the possibility of holding Pericles in some sense responsible for Cleon and his words.

to sophistic rhetorical games. On this reading, the solution should be simple: speech must be put back in its proper place in order to right the Athenian way of political life; the Athenians must recognize speech as a tool of knowledge once again. One could even imagine Cleon claiming a direct link with Pericles, saying something like, "Athenians, the great Pericles knew that words must serve to guide us toward what must be done, not to divert or amuse us."

Cleon, though, says nothing of the sort. In part this is because he in fact means to offer a more fundamental critique of deliberation by pointing to a deep incompatibility between knowledge of *ta deonta* and speech. The Athenians, he says, are guilty of "considering future activities on the basis of fine speeches about their feasibility and events that have already happened on the basis of splendid criticism, instead of using your powers of sight to give greater credibility to what has been done than what has been heard" (3.38.4). Now Pericles might well have spoken of speakers representing future activities as feasible—based, of course, on their knowledge of *ta deonta*—and meant it as an account of how politics should work in Athens. Cleon, on the other hand, wants to oppose reliance on what is heard, on able speakers' representations, with "what has been done." Cleon's point is that because all Athenians can see facts and deeds, there is no need in democratic politics for able speakers, who in fact only cloud the vision of those who listen to them. He thus suggests that those who deliberate should attend to what they see or what they know to be true from their own experience instead of paying heed to "fine speeches."

This is, in a sense, a very egalitarian argument. It is also quite crude, and Cleon has long been recognized as a rank demagogue. Everyone can see facts and deeds; there is no need for the special skills of the eloquent: these are powerful appeals in a democracy, especially one in which the vast majority of citizens never speak. Cleon makes this point more explicitly near the beginning of his speech. The "alarming" tendency of the Athenians constantly to change measures, he says, reflects their failure to realize that "ignorance [*amathia*] combined with self-control is more beneficial than cleverness [*dexiotes*] combined with intemperance; and that compared with more intelligent men the less gifted usually run their states better" (3.37.3). We should understand the opposition of *amathia* and *dexiotes* in the context of the arguments considered in the last paragraph. Those who are *amathia* are unlearned, but they do see facts and deeds. Within a clear recognition of their limits, and without needing to make or even to hear long-winded speeches, they can yet make judgments about what is to be done. *Amathia* and *dexiotes*, in effect, represent two sorts of knowledge: that of the unspeaking common citizen who takes counsel, and that of the shrewd sophist who uses the power of speech to play tricks on the demos. There can be no combination of the knowledge truly relevant to deciding what should be done and the knowledge of the able speaker. One or the other will dictate the Athenian way of politics, and Cleon demands that the Athenians choose the former. In so doing, and without ever mentioning Pericles by name, he clearly steps away from the Periclean idea that knowledge of *ta deonta* can and indeed must coexist with speaking ability. In Cleon's Athens such a combination seems impossible.[14]

As I noted in Chapter 2, Cleon by speaking either falls victim to his own argument and becomes a sophist, or operates implicitly from the idea that he has a relevant knowledge that others lack and can communicate it to them; in other words, either he is the sort of speaker he attacks, or he is in fact relying on the notion of politics that Pericles advances and that he seems to reject. Arguments that attack speech and that counsel silent action undermine the position of speakers. In his own account of the Athenian way of political life, Diodotus very briefly points to this incoherence. If Cleon's attack on deliberation through speech is anything other than self-serving slander, if it is meant as a serious account of how politics works in Athens, then it reveals its speaker to be "dull of wit." There is no "other way the future and its uncertainty can be considered" (3.42.2). Words are necessary to deciding what to do. Though Diodotus makes no mention of him, this point echoes Pericles: knowledge by itself is not enough; speech is necessary to turn individual knowledge into collective judgment and action. To use Cleon's terms, there is no seeing the "facts" without hearing accounts of them.

Diodotus devotes much more space to the concerns he has about the decline of collective responsibility in Athens and the accompanying tendency of the demos to turn on its advisers. Here he is responding to a brief remark that Cleon makes about a sort of speaker who "is motivated by profit when he fashions his attractive speech and attempts to mislead. In such contests as these, the state awards others the prizes yet bears the risks itself" (3.38.2–3). If we can, from a certain perspective, see Cleon's attack on speech as a move away from Pericles' account of Athenian politics, his argument here clings to an aspect of that account. He offers honesty—in

---

14. We might say that Cleon thus in general favors the sudden mode of Athenian action over the deliberative mode of action, thinking that the latter is, in a sense, a contradiction in terms.

the sense of being beyond money—and patriotism—in the sense of having the city's best interests in mind—as criteria for judging speakers in precisely the way Pericles claims them as personal qualities that deem him worthy of the demos' support.

Similarly, if Diodotus' brief account of the role of speech echoes Pericles, then his response to Cleon on this matter differs from the Periclean account of Athenian politics. Speakers who attack other speakers' motives "are the hardest to cope with," Diodotus contends (3.42). Indeed, such attacks have already produced a climate of suspicion. The Athenian way of politics already involves raising charges against speakers on the least suspicion of corruption, no matter what the quality of their advice. In this climate, "the result is that straightforward good advice is no less suspect than bad" (3.43.2). Diodotus seeks here, of course, to discredit Cleon's earlier personal attack. In making this immediate point, though, he moves away from an important aspect of Pericles' description of Athenian politics. Attending to the motives of speakers proves to do more harm than good. Rather than an aid in choosing whose advice to follow, considerations of honesty and patriotism tend to obscure the basic question of whose advice is best. Diodotus envisions a politics where such considerations have no place, where "the good citizen" proves himself "the better speaker" and where the quality of advice given matters above all (3.42).

And so the matter of the descent of Pericles' argument about Athenian political life appears more complex than Saxonhouse's praise of Diodotus allows. Cleon disparages the unproblematic relationship between knowledge and speech that Pericles championed, but he champions the importance of honest patriotism in Athenian politics. Diodotus responds by reasserting the importance of speech as a way of reaching political judgments, but seeks to jettison any concern over the motives of speakers. Neither Cleon nor Diodotus accepts without qualification the list of qualities that Pericles attributes to himself as a good adviser. And neither holds to the simple notion of a collective responsibility shared by advisers and demos. Cleon means precisely to set the demos against its advisers (at least all of its advisers save one), and Diodotus seems not to share Pericles' hope that collective responsibility can be reestablished: "If those who make proposals and those who accept them suffered equally, you would judge more carefully. But as it is, in accordance with whatever temper you fly into, there are times when you make mistakes and penalize the judgment of your advisor alone and not your own, however many may have shared responsibility for the error" (3.43). So long as speakers like Cleon exist,¹⁵ so long as speakers' motives are an issue, the would-be adviser can only try to look further ahead and hope that his advice is in fact sound.

Attending to the apparent echoes of Pericles' final speech, we might say that the Mitylene Debate witnesses a shattering of the Athenian way of political life as Pericles understood it. Cleon and Diodotus engage in what appears from the vantage point of history as a competition over Pericles' legacy, each seizing on only part of his description of the relationship between adviser and demos. It certainly makes sense that they should do so. The smart politician will imitate what appears to have worked in the past, borrowing arguments and ideas as appropriate, and aligning when possible with respected predecessors.¹⁶ While Pericles has been gone from the Athenian political scene for several years, we have no reason to think that his words, his ways of thinking, or, more generally, his specter, have simply vanished. From our point of view, Cleon and Diodotus would be foolish not to treat his ideas and arguments as possible—indeed likely—means of winning favor with the Athenians.

This makes it all the more odd that neither Cleon nor Diodotus ever mentions Pericles by name. While we think we hear echoes of Pericles, nothing in the Mitylene Debate explicitly indicates that Cleon and Diodotus, in choosing their arguments, had his ideas in mind. Just as Thucydides tells us little or nothing about the accuracy or impact of any speaker's account of the Athenian *tropos,* so he gives us no indication that the silent mass of ordinary citizens accepted Pericles' account of the Athenian way of political life. And so we do not know whether the Athenians have the ideas of their great leader in mind when they hear Cleon and Diodotus speak. Pericles and his words are, in this sense, at once hanging in the air as the Mitylene Debate unfolds and, at the same time, nowhere to be found. His posthumous responsibility for Cleon, or for Diodotus, or for what they together have to say about Athenian politics, must then remain a matter of considerable uncertainty. From our perspective as readers, once that perspective is tempered with a sense of the perspective of the political actor, the question of Pericles' responsibility—of the consequences of his words—remains open, a matter for careful thought but not for certain resolution.

---

15. See Orwin's discussion of Diodotus' "proposed reforms" in Athenian political practice, including ridding the city of demagogues like Cleon, as "utopian"; *Humanity of Thucydides,* 159–60.

16. As something of an exception that proves the rule, consider Al Gore's failure to capitalize on the continuing popularity of Bill Clinton during the 2000 presidential election.

Thucydides' account and the manner in which he at once suggests and denies the influence of Pericles' words points to an analogous uncertainty for the political actor regarding the future of one's words and deeds. Consider, again, Pericles' perspective. Faced with personal political disaster, he offers in his final speech a bold account of Athenian politics centering on the role of the adviser, with himself as the ideal individual to fulfill that role. Given its immediate impact, this tack seems sound. But how will his words be used? Will other speakers in other contexts mangle and manipulate what he says? If Pericles uses certain arguments to persuade the demos, will that demos be vulnerable to appeals that draw selectively on those arguments? Can he know the future of his rhetoric? How? Ought he to feel responsible for what happens two years later? Will he be held responsible? Diodotus is right to say that those who would advise must "look somewhat further ahead." But he is also right in saying that the future remains "dim and uncertain," not only because of the basic unpredictability of human affairs but also because of the way in which the silent presence of the demos destabilizes the would-be authoritative claims of any speaker. Pericles cannot know what either the demos or future speakers will make of his words; he surely cannot simply foresee the Mitylene Debate. But insofar as he is concerned about his future as an adviser and about Athens's future as a city—and about the sort of historical judgments I have been considering—he must try.

V. NICIAS, ALCIBIADES, AND THE RHETORIC OF COMMAND

The impact of words spoken cannot be controlled by those who speak. Though politics demands that the effort be made, no speaker can define once and for all the Athenian way of political life or dictate, or even know with any certainty, the impact of a proffered definition. The speaker, Thucydides' work implies, must hope to see the future clearly, knowing, if wise in a Thucydidean way, that this is impossible. But this does not exhaust the challenges facing the Athenian political actor. If the ultimate uncontrollability of political speech makes the future uncertain, it similarly renders the past, in a sense, opaque. The speaker—and as we will see, those who listen and decide—must look backwards as well as forwards, and nothing in either direction is clear. Political judgment must be retrospective as well as prospective. To think about these challenges more fully, I turn to poor Nicias and his struggle with Alcibiades.

Perhaps more than any other moment in the *History*, the debate over the expedition to Sicily centers the question of the adequacy of the political way of democratic Athens. From the vantage point of history, a sense of doom seems to hang over the assembly in which Nicias and Alcibiades clash. Thucydides will not let us draw the conclusion that the expedition was simply ill fated from the beginning.[17] Discussing Athens's course under Pericles' successors, who "even resorted to handing over affairs to the people's pleasure," Thucydides writes that "the expedition to Sicily [was] a mistake not so much in judgment about those they were attacking as because the senders did not subsequently make decisions advantageous for the participants" (2.65). The decision to send the expedition was not in itself wrong. Still, we can surely say that had the Athenians agreed with Nicias to call off the expedition, the disaster would not have occurred. Why do they not? Why does Nicias fail in his attempt to dissuade the demos?

By the time Nicias rises to speak about Sicily, we have reason to doubt his political acumen.[18] We have already encountered him once, attempting to outwit Cleon. With the latter clamoring for action on Pylos and brashly claiming that if he were in command he would end the matter forthwith, Nicias offers to give him just that opportunity by resigning his command. Thinking that failure is inevitable, Nicias thereby seeks to snare Cleon in a trap of his own making. When Cleon succeeds at Pylos beyond anyone's expectations, Nicias appears partly the unfortunate victim of chance, partly a political bungler (4.27–41).

This hardly gives us confidence that he can successfully handle the

---

17. On Thucydides' judgment regarding the decision to sail to Sicily and the tension some see between 2.65 and the opening of book 6, see, among others, Orwin, *Humanity*, 118–19; Connor, *Thucydides*, 158n2; Hornblower, *Thucydides*, 148ff.; and Palmer, *Love of Glory*, 94. All argue, as I have, that Thucydides does not simply condemn the expedition to Sicily as so much foolishness. For a contrasting view, see Cornford, *Thucydides Mythistoricus*, 51, who argues that "to Thucydides, from first to last, the Sicilian enterprise was an irrelevant diversion" that would lead the Athenians to tragic disaster.

18. Then, too, even the most casual reading of the commentary predisposes the contemporary reader toward a less than positive evaluation of Nicias; he enjoys an almost unanimous reputation for political bungling. "It is not the practice of Thucydides," Westlake, *Individuals*, says, "to be indulgent towards incompetent leadership, and . . . he shows no indulgence toward the shortcomings of Nicias" (210–11). Palmer, *Love of Glory*, also tells us of Nicias' "incompetence," which "looms large," and of how he "fails spectacularly" (101–6). Kagan, *Peace of Nicias*, goes further, arguing that Nicias, "for whom subtle and tricky argument was hardly a strong suit," should have kept quiet about Sicily; his efforts to dissuade the demos only made matters worse (186, 190–91). Connor, *Thucydides*, concludes, more generously, that Thucydides' account of the Sicily debate leaves us with "doubts about the wisdom of (Nicias') leadership" (164). I mean the arguments that follow to temper these sorts of judgments with a fuller appreciation of the challenges Nicias faces.

difficult rhetorical task he faces in his clash with Alcibiades. The decision to go to Sicily has been made; Thucydides reports an assembly called for the purpose of making preparations. Nicias must, then, first convince the Athenians to reconsider their decision and then convince them to change it. His directly substantive argument is that Athens needs to take care of what it has rather than risk all by seeking more. But in the first of his two speeches in the assembly on Sicily, Nicias also makes arguments about his place as an adviser. In the context of the words of Pericles and of Cleon and Diodotus, we can think of these arguments as offering his understanding of how politics works in Athens.

Proponents of the expedition could easily raise an argument against Nicias analogous to Cleon's claim about the inability of a democracy to be steadfast. "We Athenians talk too much," they might say, "and that leads us to change our minds too often. We have decided to go to Sicily, let us get on with it." The role of speech and continued debate, though, plays little part in the speeches of either Nicias or Alcibiades. Nicias says merely that the Athenians "ought again to consider" the question of whether to sail to Sicily and that they should not "with little deliberation" undertake "a war that does not concern us" (6.9.1). Alcibiades does not directly dispute this point.

Rather, to the extent that Nicias and Alcibiades consider the Athenian way of deliberation and decision making, both of them focus on the motives of would-be advisers. Nicias' arguments on this score concern both his own motives and those of Alcibiades. Regarding the former, Nicias' account is complex or, one might say less generously, confused: "And yet I myself derive honor from such actions and am less fearful than most about my own person, although I think that he who takes his person and property into account is just as good a citizen; it is exactly such a man who would wish for his own sake that the affairs of his city prosper as well. Nevertheless, neither in the past have I said what was contrary to my judgment nor do I now, but I will speak in whatever way I judge best" (6.9.2). Nicias seems mostly to want to say that he has set aside personal gain in favor of honestly advising the Athenians on the interests of the city. This makes good rhetorical sense: the general who will command the expedition might be expected to favor it; that he does not adds weight to the possibility that it might be a bad idea altogether. More broadly, the appeal to honesty and patriotism as indications of the value of a speaker's advice echoes the arguments of both Pericles and Cleon. We might speculate that the Athenians were familiar with such arguments and might thus be more prone to accept them. All of this makes the middle part of Nicias' argument difficult to comprehend. By saying that he does not fault those who take concern for their private interests, he appears to weaken his claims about himself. What force can remain behind his claim that he follows the best interest of the city contrary to his own interest when he says that one can easily enough see that personal and civic interests are, in a sense, intertwined?

We might consider two possible explanations for this turn in Nicias' argument. On the one hand, from his earlier encounter with Cleon, Nicias does appear as something of a bumbler; perhaps he simply does not have the political savvy to recognize how seriously confused this argument sounds. On the other hand, we might recall that along with Pericles' and Cleon's appeals to honesty and patriotism, we—and more important, the Athenians—have heard Diodotus as well. Nicias' claim that he is an honest adviser for the city's good sounds like Cleon and especially Pericles, but his claim that he does not fault anyone for taking account of his private interest suggests Diodotus' rejection of speakers' motives as a basis for political decisions. Thucydides' report of the Mitylene Debate and its aftermath gives us no indication of the impact of the accounts Cleon and Diodotus offer of Athenian politics. Like Pericles' description of the ideal adviser in the postplague speech, what both Cleon and Diodotus have to say about the motives of speakers seems to hang in the air. As readers, we do not know whether the Athenians have accepted what one or the other—or neither—has said; Thucydides has given us no precise indication of what the silent demos has made of these arguments. Perhaps Nicias, similarly not knowing which vision of Athenian politics has prevailed, attempts to cover all bases. Though on its face rather strained, his argument points to a problem facing all speakers in Thucydides. They must attend to the immediate and future impact of their words, must look into the unknown future. But they must also peer into an opaque past. Nicias' seeming indecision about whether to follow Cleon or Diodotus points, I think, to the challenge of political judgment for all speakers. This challenge follows from the way in which the interaction of elite speakers and silent demos destabilizes both the future and the past of Athenian politics.

Nicias himself immediately turns from his attempt to have it both ways by following (speaking from our perspective as readers) both Cleon and Diodotus on the matter of speakers' motives. His only slightly veiled attack on Alcibiades makes it clear that Nicias does indeed mean for the Athenians to take honesty and patriotism into account. He thus turns near the end of his first speech to warn the Athenians against "anyone here" who is "pleased at being chosen to command" but who is, in fact, "too young for a command" (6.12). Both these criticisms of Alcibiades are fairly straightforward. Without mentioning him by name, Nicias charges Alcibiades with "thinking only of himself," with looking to the expedition and his command of it as an opportunity to profit and thus as a way to sustain his expensive avocation of raising horses. He clearly means for the Athenians to use the motives of speakers as a way to judge the quality of their advice. Here there is no hint of the idea that one can seek private interest and the good of the state simultaneously: the Athenians must not "allow this person to show off as an individual by endangering the city" (6.12). As for Nicias' other argument, the reminder of Alcibiades' youthfulness works on two levels. First, as we have seen, Nicias suggests forthrightly that Alcibiades is too young to command; age should be a factor in who leads Athens. Then, too, Nicias "call[s] on their elders" to stand up to the young and not to be "shamed" into voting for the expedition against their better judgment (6.13). He thus suggests a division in Athens of which we have not previously had any indication.

Alcibiades responds to Nicias' attack on his youth and to the suggestion that the old should restrain and guide the young with what amounts to a single argument. The Athenians must reject Nicias' "division of the young against old (6.18.6). His own case is an example of the rule that "youth and age can do nothing without each other" (6.18.6). The Athenian way of doing things—"our well-tried order," Alcibiades says—demands that young and old work together. As for the expedition to Sicily, then, the Athenians should "make full use of the services of both men"; Alcibiades, who is young, and Nicias, who "appears fortunate," make a potent combination of commanders (6.17). Alcibiades thus seizes on Nicias' claims to make a powerful counterargument: Nicias seeks to divide you, but I say we can work together.

His response to Nicias' claims about his motives is more interesting. Most basically, Alcibiades says that motives do not in fact matter. Thus, whatever the charges made about his private life and ambitions, the Athenians should "consider whether my public management can be matched by anyone" (6.16). In a sense, this echoes Diodotus' rejection of arguments about speakers' motives: what matters, according to Diodotus, is the quality of advice. Likewise, for Alcibiades, what matters is the impact on the city of his actions. But Alcibiades wants to go further. Nicias had left open the possibility that a leader's self-interest might be the same as the city's good. The individual who looks to prosper will want the city to prosper, too. Alcibiades turns this point around. His private actions, however egoistic they appear, redound to the glory of Athens. His seven chariots caused the other Greeks to believe Athens "to be even greater than its real power"; his providing of choruses "points to strength" in the eyes of foreigners (6.16). Such great deeds performed by a private individual serve, too, as powerful public policy. If the city wants to prosper, it should allow, indeed welcome and even aid, the ambitions of an Alcibiades.

All of this points to more fundamental changes that Alcibiades wants to work in the Athenian way of political life. Pericles had demanded that the Athenians bear together the burden imposed by misfortunes and setbacks, that they not blame their advisers alone. Diodotus lamented the fact that the Athenians did not have such a sense of collective responsibility and the consequences for speakers. Alcibiades seems to enter into this train of arguments, though in the context of his claim that his own self-interested actions are in fact in the best interest of the city. He wants no part in a responsibility shared equally by all. After all, "failures do not share their adversity evenly with others" (6.16.4). Why, then, should the individual who fares well and thus benefits the city, as Alcibiades does, share the credit? Should not the Athenians "submit to the arrogance of the successful" (6.16.4)? The outlandish things Alcibiades does as a private individual rightly place him above other Athenians, though they are unlikely to realize this so long as he lives. Only after the death of great men does their city pride "itself on men who were no aliens or failures but belonged to it and excelled" (6.16.5). In the meantime, the Athenians must, as we said above, accept Alcibiades' ambitions and judge him by his actions. Given what he has said, these actions no doubt include not only his work as *strategos* but also such apparently private actions as the exhibition of horses and chariots. All of these mark Alcibiades as a cut above the rest and, in particular, as well suited to command an expedition to Sicily.

And we should note carefully that all of Alcibiades' arguments about his public and private acts, about his ambitions, in fact revolve around the issue of whether or not he should command. Thus his conclusion: the Athenians should "make the most of the services" of both he and Nicias. Clearly, Alcibiades means the Athenians to think his services more valuable than those of Nicias. What Nicias has to contribute is his "reputation of good luck"—hardly the most glowing praise. Most significant, though, is the change in the relationship of demos to prominent individual entailed by Alcibiades' focus on the issue of command. This focus appears in Alcibiades' first words: "Athenians, I more than others am entitled to command, which must be my first point because of Nicias' attack on me, and I consider myself deserving as well" (6.16.1). Nicias, then, by reluctantly but decisively attacking Alcibiades, appears to open the door for the move Alcibiades makes. In discussing the role of motives, Nicias turns from the claim that he would never advise the city against his own best judgment to the claim that Alcibiades' youthful selfishness makes him unfit to command.

The change is subtle but, given Alcibiades' response, significant. Consider the contrast between the account of Athenian politics in Pericles' postplague speech and Alcibiades' argument here. Pericles as the knowledgeable speaker with good motives demands a special place as adviser. Cleon and Diodotus seem to work within this basic way of thinking about Athenian politics. Alcibiades, too, seeks to advise the Athenians. Thus the latter half of his speech consists of an analysis of the Athenian empire and a denigration of the Sicilians. But he wants the Athenians to understand him not only as one who speaks in the interest of the city but also as a doer of great deeds. He has done things that awe Athens' enemies, both as a general and as a private individual. On this basis he demands his proper place, demands that the city allow him the opportunity to do more glorious deeds for himself and, by extension, for Athens. In a sense, his advice about the Sicily expedition simply extends his argument about the need for Athens to give him such opportunities.

After Alcibiades speaks, Nicias makes a last-ditch attempt to change the Athenians' minds by offering an exaggerated account of the necessary armament and supplies. This second speech apparently fails completely. Consequently, Nicias seems even more inept as adviser; but let us, again, consider the context of his failure. Thucydides tells us that Nicias decided "that he could no longer dissuade them with the same arguments" (6.19). With his first words—the Athenians, he says, are "intent on making the expedition at all events"—Nicias cedes complete victory to his opponent (6.20). And the surrender goes beyond the question of what should be done. In this second speech, Nicias chooses the rhetorical strategy of a general requisitioning troops and supplies. Perhaps Nicias simply lacks the rhetorical skill to make any other argument. Or perhaps he has, again, made a fateful calculation about the thinking of the Athenians sitting silently in front of him. He seems to assume that Alcibiades has succeeded in changing the issue from one of advice to one of command. From this perspective Nicias' realization that the same arguments will no longer work—if they ever would—makes a certain sort of sense. His only hope is to appear as a commander realistically assessing what the expedition requires, showing his judgment about the enemy and what might be required to defeat them. In short, Nicias wagers that in the wake of Alcibiades' arguments the Athenians see him solely as a commander, and he speaks accordingly. In doing so, he responds to the basic dilemma facing all speakers: to find a way to sway the demos without knowing with any certainty the impact of words already spoken and arguments already made. Perhaps we can try to imagine other arguments that Nicias might have made; surely, though, we must be sympathetic to the task he faces.

VI. CONCLUSION

If the Mitylene Debate seemed from our perspective as readers to mark the disintegration—at least in the words uttered by Cleon and Diodotus—of Pericles' vision of deliberative action in Athenian politics, then, from that same perspective, the Sicily Debate seems to usher in an altogether un-Periclean relation of adviser to demos. Indeed, Alcibiades forwards an understanding of the leading citizen as commander rather than adviser. This new relationship between prominent individual and demos is not entirely unknown to Thucydides' Athens; more than one commentator has noted parallels between Alcibiades and Themistocles.[19] Here we can say that the former describes himself in a way that recalls Thucydides' eulogy of the latter. Alcibiades would have the Athenians see him in the same way Thucydides sees Themistocles: as a brilliant individual, able to see what must be done and, when necessary, to command others to do it. For whom Themistocles did great deeds—Athens, Persia, himself— seemed to matter less in Thucydides' eulogy than the deeds themselves. Alcibiades' attempt to overturn the importance of motives suggests that he aims at something similar. Above all, he demands that the Athenians grant him the opportunity to exercise his skills through command. That his pursuit of glory merges with the common good of Athens is little more

---

19. I thus noted above that Palmer, *Love of Glory*, 89–91, explores the link between Themistocles and Alcibiades. For similar comments, see Westlake, *Individuals*, 212–15. Forde, *Ambition to Rule*, claims that Alcibiades is "actually more extreme" than Themistocles in his ambition and in his willingness to let that ambition work for or against his home city (70). Connor, *Thucydides*, on the other hand, points to the Syracusan Hermocrates as a "new Themistocles" (198), as does Orwin, *Humanity*, 167.

than a happy coincidence. Ultimately, Alcibiades wants most to have the Athenians recognize him as a great man, just as Thucydides recognizes the greatness of Themistocles.

It seems at first glance as if Alcibiades succeeds. Nicias comes to the point of presenting himself as a commander ready to carry out the presumed ends of the city rather than as an adviser questioning ends as well as means. And the Athenian demos enthusiastically reaffirms its decision to sail for Sicily. Thucydides' account of the Sicily Debate thus tempts us to say that the pressures of war bring about a fundamental change in the Athenian way of politics. The rhetoric of advising deteriorates into confusion. That confusion makes way for the return of the rhetoric of command. But when we attend to the particularities and immediacy of politics, we must be careful in moving from the rhetoric of speakers to conclusions about political reality in Athens. That Nicias comes eventually to speak in Alcibiades' terms points toward a judgment that Nicias has made about what arguments have worked and so what arguments will now work best. As I have argued, we can discuss the quality of that judgment; we ultimately cannot, though, say with any certainty whether it was right or wrong.

We must also remain wary when interpreting the decision of the Athenian demos to sail for Sicily. The demos retains power over the course of Athenian affairs and over individual politicians. This power is at once blunt and subtle, for the decisions of the demos, while final, are also, as we have seen, irreducibly open to interpretation. The demos votes to sail to Sicily, but this tells us nothing about the particular impact of Alcibiades' assumption of the mantle of command. From Thucydides' account, we simply do not know whether the Athenians have indeed accepted a return to Themistoclean politics.[20] So much is familiar from Chapter 3. We have seen more clearly in the current chapter how the persistently silent presence of the Athenian demos yields deep uncertainty for those who would advise the Athenians. Cleon and Diodotus know that Pericles tried to define Athenian politics in a particular fashion. They do not know which of his words the demos has taken to heart; they must thus choose their own words carefully. So, too, Nicias seems to grapple with the uncertainty of Athenian political discourse. In this way, the very bluntness of the demos' power,

20. Thucydides does, it is true, emphasize the momentary unity of the Athenians following the Sicily debate, saying that "all alike fell in love with the expedition" (6.24). Indeed, one might say that at this moment the Athenians appear all too unified. Again, though, this momentary unity of passion tells us little about whether the Athenians are unified behind a particular understanding of the expedition to Sicily or of Alcibiades' role in Athenian affairs.

by destabilizing any supposedly clear understanding of Athenian political life, shapes in a more subtle, implicit way the challenge of political judgment that any assembly speaker confronts. Surely Alcibiades faces the same challenge. When he rises to speak in response to Nicias, he cannot be certain what argument to make; he cannot know precisely what his fellow Athenians are thinking. The seemingly undemocratic silence of the Athenian demos in a sense here produces a paradoxically democratic outcome. However much he might wish, Alcibiades cannot simply issue Themistoclean demands.

The aftermath of the Sicily debate confirms that Alcibiades cannot simply evade the power and judgment of the demos; no more than Pericles or Nicias can he with his words control the meaning of Athenian politics or his own place in it. The desecration of the stone Hermae occurs on a night not long before the expedition is to set sail. Informants connect Alcibiades with the act, and accuse him as well of "scurrilous celebration of the Mysteries." Seizing the opportunity, Alcibiades' political enemies suggest that he means to end democracy, pointing toward "the undemocratic licentiousness of his conduct in general" (6.28). There is a certain irony in Alcibiades' response. Whether from confidence in his innocence or simply in his persuasive power, he calls for the Athenians to put him on trial immediately, before the fleet sails. Thucydides tells us that Alcibiades pointed out that it was "more sensible not to send him out on so great an expedition, facing such an accusation." But did not Alcibiades himself argue in the Sicily Debate that such accusations ought to be set aside? Has he not himself claimed that the issue was one of command, not of personal behavior? The Athenians, urged on by Alcibiades' enemies, in fact do exactly what Alcibiades earlier suggested they should. Despite their questions about his devotion to Athenian democracy, they send him out in command of the fleet, expecting, no doubt, that he will do great deeds.

Soon enough, of course, the Athenians recall Alcibiades for trial. When, like Themistocles before him, he flees to Sparta, the Athenians try him in absentia and sentence him to death. There surely follow some familiar lessons for would-be advisers of the Athenian demos. One can try to shape the adviser–demos relationship, but the demos will have the final say, and the adviser must always remain on guard. Alcibiades seeks in the Sicily Debate to establish his independence from the demos, to place himself as commander above the fray. He cannot. In the end, he only eludes the power of the demos by removing himself—much as Thucydides removes Themistocles—from the scene of Athenian politics.

Thucydides' account of the early stages of the Sicily campaign thus affirms the silent power of the Athenian demos over the politicians who struggle to advise it. In doing so, it also reminds us that the demos faces challenges of its own. Most basically, the demos must in moments of deliberation make judgments about the claims made by speakers. Speakers explain their perceptions of the situation at hand; they offer different accounts of the ends at stake for the Athenians and of the means to achieve those ends. And as we have seen in this and the last chapter, they offer accounts of what "Athens" means, of how "Athenians" act and interact. Consider the sorts of questions that the speeches discussed in this chapter might raise for the Athenians. Some call for determinations about past actions: Has Pericles accurately described why we have followed his advice? Is Cleon right, have we shown a tendency to change our minds too often? Others demand that the demos peer into the future, trying to foresee the consequences of following a line of advice supported by certain arguments: If we accept Diodotus' advice, does that mean rejecting, with him, any concern with the motives of speakers? Does following Alcibiades to Sicily mean accepting him as "commander," perhaps never again to have mere "advisers?"

It is tempting to say that Athens meets disaster because the demos, having momentarily accepted Alcibiades' claims, cannot stay the course. The Athenians, in the end, cannot abide a mode of politics that allows such a character so much unambiguous power.[21] Put differently, Athenian politics deteriorates when the adviser–advised mode of deliberative action loses its coherence, when Periclean politics give way to Themistoclean politics. The *History* invites us to such speculations. But it always undermines them, always calls us back to the uncertainty and complexity and immediacy of politics seen through the eyes of the political actor and to the fundamental ambiguities of democratic politics. From this perspective, Sicily stands not as the end point of a long decline of democratic deliberation in Athenian politics, but as another moment in the ongoing struggle by both elite speakers and silent demos to control the ultimately uncontrollable course of Athenian politics.

21. Orwin, *Humanity,* seems to have something of this sort in mind: "In their distrust [of Alcibiades], the Athenians leave their Sicilian expedition in the hands of the one man whose unquestioned justice and piety repel distrust and who, acting on Melian hopes, incurs for himself and the whole armada a Melian fate" (126). On the notion of Nicias as more "Melian" than "Athenian," see my comments in Chapter 2.

5

Justice and Empire:
Athenian Silence and the Representation of Athens Abroad

I. INTRODUCTION

To this point I have for the most part focused my reading of Athenian democratic politics in the *History* on the interactions of Athenians in the assembly. The last two chapters in particular have centered on what I in Chapter 2 called the "deliberative mode" of Athenian action. Consideration of that mode of action centers our attention on the struggle of elites to win political influence and the manner in which the Athenian demos, by the silent power of its presence, problematizes all elite attempts to control the meaning of politics, action, and identity in the city. A full understanding of Athenian democratic politics, though, also requires attention to those moments in which silence prevails in the Athenian assembly. I turn in Chapter 6 to address more directly what I have called the "sudden mode" of Athenian action. In the present chapter I turn my attention to moments of Athenian action that appear at first glance to exist somewhere between sudden action and fully deliberative action, focusing in particular on the conference at Sparta in book 1 and the Melian Dialogue in book 5. In such moments, though Thucydides reports no speeches given at Athens itself, Athenians do speak elsewhere. At a theoretical level, beyond grappling with this juxtaposition of the silence of *hoi Athenaioi* at home with the appearance of Athenian "envoys" abroad, understanding these moments requires thinking about the complex manifestations of Athenian plurality and Athenian unity as the Athenians come to act in the Greek world. More immediately, these moments bring to the fore the question of justice in the context of Athenian empire.

II. ATHENIAN JUSTICE AT HOME AND ABROAD

The language of justice appears in the pages of Thucydides chiefly in the realm of "international relations." This is not, of course, to make the more eccentric claim that justice reigns in the Greece that Thucydides portrays. Rather, I mean to point to the seemingly simple fact that speakers in the *History* refer to justice almost exclusively in the context of arguments about how one city does or should act toward other cities. This observation holds both when cities interact with one another through speech—as at Sparta in book 1, at Plataea in book 3, and at Melos in book 5—and when the citizens of a single polis gather to determine what to do. More particularly, for the Athenians, be they at home or abroad, questions of justice merge with the central issues of war and empire. Have the Athenians practiced justice in dealing with their "allies?" (How) ought justice to be considered in dealing with vanquished foes? More broadly, what role should considerations of right play in a war among cities of equal and unequal degrees of might?

To this focus on justice as an aspect of "foreign policy," we can compare the apparent absence of analogous questions about Athenian "internal politics."[1] As we have seen in Chapter 4, the discussion of democracy by Athenian speakers revolves around problems of collective political judgment. In reflecting on their way of political life, the Athenians repeatedly struggle with the broad question of how their politics does and should work and, more particularly, with questions about the proper relationship between advisers and demos as the city comes to make decisions. We can no doubt imagine justice in internal politics becoming a concern for the Athenians as well. The Athenians, that is, might well exercise their collective judgment in consideration of the "right" or "just" distribution of political power and political roles. They might, for example, ask whether it is just that some citizens seem to have more influence over the city's decisions than others. But for the most part they do not.[2] Justice, again,

---

1. Thucydides himself does not suggest any sort of clear distinction between "foreign policy" and "internal politics." Though I use the contemporary distinction for the sake of clarity here, much of the present chapter (and Chapter 6 as well) will be concerned with questions that Thucydides' account poses regarding the intertwining of the interactions of the Athenians in Athens and actions taken by Athenians and others in the course of Greek affairs.

2. Outside Athens, the Syracusan Athenagoras hints at an argument for democracy based on justice; in democracy, he says, the people "individually and collectively, have a fair share," while oligarchy "offers the many a portion of the dangers and is not simply greedy over the benefits but takes all away and keeps them." But he also has recourse to arguments based on the demos' collective political capacity: "the rich are the best guardians of property while the wise give the best advice, but for hearing and then judging the people are supreme" (6.39).

figures chiefly as one among many competing aims (including security, glory, and power) that Athens might pursue in its dealings with other cities. In this sense, democratic politics and democratic political judgment in Thucydides' Athens apparently exist prior to considerations of justice. The Athenians, that is, seem to pursue justice (and, again, other goals) by way of a democratic politics the justice of which they do not seriously question.

In the context of even the most cursory examination of later Greek political thought, this seems a strangely incomplete way of thinking. In the *Republic*, of course, Plato will find justice to be a certain harmony inherent in the ordering of *kallipolis*. Each individual has a proper place, a proper position in the just city, which must not be abandoned or exceeded. "This doing one's own work," says Socrates, "is justice."³ As the critique in book 8 goes, the equality and license that animate democracy, allowing everyone to do what they please, make for precisely the sort of disharmony and disorder that the just city overcomes. Neither Thucydides nor his speakers concern themselves with the justice of democracy in this manner. No doubt the ordering of the polis, the assignation of political roles to various sorts of citizens, becomes an issue in Athens, but, again, it does so chiefly because of its implications for the exercise of collective judgment, not as a standard for critiquing the fundamental (in)justice of the city.

Then, too, neither Thucydides nor his speakers explore the theoretical arguments from justice that might in fact be made for democracy—the sorts of arguments that Aristotle, for example, reviews in book III of the *Politics*. Democrats and oligarchs, Aristotle says, agree that justice consists of equality for equals and inequality for those who are not equal. They disagree, though, about the meaning of equality: for democrats, equality issues from "free birth"; for oligarchs, from equal wealth. There follow "oligarchic and democratic justice" as contrasting principles for the formation of governments. And for Aristotle, there follows the conclusion "that none of the principles on which men claim to rule ... are right"; all are in a sense incomplete.⁴ As Arlene Saxonhouse has noted, "issues of equality"—and hence, following Aristotle, of justice—"seldom surface" in discussions of democratic politics in the *History*. Rather, Thucydides "presents us with ancient democracy as a challenge of decision-making as a group of citizens deliberating about public policy."⁵

That approach to understanding democracy and its problems means

3. Plato, *Republic*, book IV, line 433b.
4. Aristotle, *Politics* III.9–13.
5. Saxonhouse, *Athenian Democracy*, 85.

that, from a certain point of view, Thucydides largely remains silent on basic foundational issues of and arguments about justice. He does not take up in an appropriately Platonic or Aristotelian way "the question of the best regime."[6] I suspect, too, that his apparent lack of sustained concern with democracy as the embodiment of a certain understanding of equality and justice helps account for Thucydides' relative contemporary obscurity as a theorist of democracy. Insofar as recent democratic theory often directs its focus precisely toward issues of equality and justice, particularly in the context of diversity and difference in the citizen body, Thucydides apparently asks different questions. Justice figures in the *History* as an aspect of "public policy" rather than a principle of democracy itself.

But the fact that the practice of democratic politics thus precedes consideration of justice hardly renders the relationship between democracy and justice unproblematic. A host of important questions surround justice toward others understood as a potential end for the democratic city. How does justice bear on "the challenge of decision making?" Does it make the exercise of political judgment in Athens more complex or difficult? What bearing does the fact that the Athenians practice a *democratic* politics have on their pursuit of justice? Nor should we rule out the possibility that the choices the Athenians make about justice return to have some impact on their practice of democracy. Might not a certain way of acting toward other Greeks influence by some subtle means the way the Athenians interact with one another? If, as has often been said, the Athenians follow a rather harsh foreign policy, might not such harshness help account for the eventual downfall of democracy itself? Let me begin to sort out these complex and important issues by considering two—seemingly quite different—accounts of that last possibility.

Clifford Orwin detects throughout Athenian speeches an "Athenian thesis" on justice and empire, a thesis first offered by the anonymous Athenian envoys who speak at Sparta in book 1. Those envoys famously defend the Athenians' acceptance of their hegemonic role as by no means "remarkable, nor contrary to ordinary human behavior"; and they defend their continued refusal to "let it go" as motivated by the "great forces of prestige, fear, and self-interest" (1.76.2). The variations on this thesis range

---

6. Along these lines, Orwin, *Humanity of Thucydides*, 172, considers Thucydides' "failure to *articulate* the best regime" (emphasis mine). He goes on to argue that Thucydides undermines the very possibility of such articulation by downplaying the role of choice in "domestic politics" and by calling "our attention to characters who deprecate the importance of this question" by subordinating it to the problem of stability.

from the one offered by Diodotus, which comes closest to Thucydides' own "humanity"; to the claim made by the Athenian speakers at Melos that among both gods and men the strong rule when they can and the weak suffer what they must, with justice a concern only where power is equal. These basic Athenian convictions, Orwin argues, eventually return home to infect Athenian "domestic politics." In particular, in the arguments by which Alcibiades claims the role of commander in Athenian politics, Orwin detects a strident version of the Athenian thesis.[7] Thucydides' entire narrative confirms that external affairs always will work according to the Athenian thesis. But to introduce such ideas about justice—or, rather, about the irrelevance of justice—into domestic politics proves disastrous. If it is to remain whole, the city must practice a sort of hypocrisy, acting toward other cities in a manner in which its citizens must never act toward one another.[8] In back of Athenian foreign-policy decisions thus lurk principles that must not be allowed to enter into discussions of the practice of democracy.

That feedback of this sort occurs, that the Athenians overcome their prudent hypocrisy in favor of a thorough-going abandonment of justice that destroys them, we might take as indicative of Thucydides' appreciation of justice on a grander scale. Perhaps the internal dissolution of Athens follows as a fitting and proper punishment for the Athenians' earlier flouting of justice throughout Greece. Nearly a century ago, F. M. Cornford gave expression to precisely this sense of just retribution. Beneath Thucydides' detached prose, Cornford detected the outlines of an Aeschylean tragedy. Buoyed by success at Pylos—success that Thucydides seems to present as due essentially to good fortune—the Athenians fall victim to an admixture of hope and erotic fervor. At Melos, Cornford argues, the Athenians exhibit a "pathological state of mind" that leads them to want more and more and thus passionately to desire Sicily.[9] In their hubris, of course, they reach too far and learn through their sufferings in Sicily and civil strife at home the lesson that Herodotus in his *Histories* and Aeschylus in

---

7. See Sections IV and V of Chapter 4, where I offer my own reading of Alcibiades' arguments as developing in the context of earlier speakers' discussions of the Athenian way of political life.

8. "In practice," Orwin writes, "the introduction of the Athenian thesis into domestic politics proves disastrous." Theoretically, though, "on Thucydides' showing it is not so clearly true that the Athenian thesis is inapplicable to domestic life as that no city dare admit its applicability. The good of the city demands a healthy dose of that hypocrisy so scorned by the noblest Athenians and by Alcibiades in particular" *Humanity*, 195.

9. Cornford, *Thucydides Mythistoricus*, 183–84.

his *Persae* drew from Xerxes' failed invasion of Greece. To ignore the restraints of justice and moderation, as the Athenians by their own admission do, is, in the cautionary tale Cornford finds in Thucydides, to risk the most horrible disaster both abroad and, ultimately, at home.

Much separates the arguments of Orwin and Cornford. Most significantly, Orwin's account of the link between foreign policy and the demise of Athenian democratic politics leaves behind the "mythical" elements and tragic passions of Cornford's reading. Still, the two share a conviction that what Athens says about inter-Greek affairs and how Athens acts toward other cities can have deleterious consequences on the Athenians' interactions with one another. Note well that this conviction rests on the shared assumption that we can identify what Athens says and what Athens does with regard to justice. Orwin thus finds an "Athenian" thesis regarding the relations among cities; Cornford detects an "Athenian" state of mind at Melos. Now what I have had to say in previous chapters should put us on guard against such arguments. They posit an Athenian unity that remains elusive and problematic, given the way in which the silent presence of the demos destabilizes any attempt to say authoritatively what "Athens" means. As we will see again momentarily, the way in which elite speakers and silent demos interact in moments of deliberative action again complicates any attempt to find an Athenian understanding of foreign affairs issuing forth from the Athenians assembled on the Pnyx. Surely we must temper accordingly any rendering of the consequences that such an understanding might later have for Athenian democratic politics.

But that familiar move will not prove conclusive in this instance. Precisely because justice appears as an aspect of "foreign policy," of how Athens acts toward other cities, it draws us outside the confines of the imperial city itself. Most obviously, we find at key moments Athenian envoys in other Greek cities making arguments about Athens, its actions, its principles. Both Cornford and Orwin, in fact, emphasize the importance of these envoys' speeches as reflections of Athenian unity. Where Cornford finds the envoys straightforwardly venting a raging passion that unifies Athens at the moment and that ultimately brings about disaster,[10] Orwin hears in the words of the envoys a latent unity of Athenian thinking, the full implications of which will only be known when Alcibiades makes the Athenian thesis present in Athens itself.[11] Differences aside, Cornford and

---

10. Ibid.
11. Orwin, *Humanity of Thucydides*, 91, 123.

Orwin thus both suggest that outside the Athenian assembly, we can indeed find and identify an Athenian position on justice that in turn allows us to search for its effects in Athenian domestic politics. In the persons of the envoys, they argue, Thucydides reveals to us an Athenian unity on foreign policy external to any debates or disagreements or disunity in Athens itself.

Such arguments rest on a basic conviction about the relationship between Athenian envoys and Athens itself, a conviction straightforwardly set forth by one of Thucydides' earliest if not always most perceptive critics. The blunt language of the Athenian envoys at Melos strikes Dionysius of Halicarnassus as more appropriate for an "oriental monarch" threatening the more civilized Greeks than for Greeks addressing their own kind. Dionysius, though, puts the blame not on the speakers but on Thucydides for suggesting that anyone speaking for Athens could possibly say such things: "For the views and statements which the leaders of the cities and the men entrusted with such great power [seem] to hold and express before [other] cities on behalf of their own city, these all men look upon as shared by the city which dispatches them."[12] The words of the envoys cast Athens—a city that in fact respected the gods and exerted a "humanizing influence" on Greek life—in a most unrealistic light. Dionysius finds the Melian Dialogue unconvincing precisely because it fails accurately to reflect what he takes to be truly Athenian views. Most important for my purposes here, he explicitly argues that everyone takes envoys in general and these envoys in particular as representatives of Athens. However divided the Athenians may appear when assembled on the Pnyx, there exists at the moment of Melos a unified Athenian position to be announced to the Melians. Envoys speak "on behalf" of their city, surely expressing what their fellow citizens have determined at home.

Let me be clear here. I do not mean to accuse either Orwin or Cornford of unthinkingly following the arguments of Dionysius.[13] Indeed, they stand out among contemporary commentators for their reflections, however brief, on the relation of anonymous envoys to home city. A position akin to that taken by Dionysius in fact informs most commentary, though it seldom comes in for explicit discussion. I want in the remainder of this chapter to introduce a series of complications to this standard notion by, again, trying to think about the relation of envoys to Athens from something like the perspective of Thucydides' Greeks themselves. I will eventually claim

---

12. Dionysius, *On Thucydides*, 397.
13. Cornford, *Thucydides Mythistoricus*, 178 and 185, cites and quotes Dionysius when discussing the Melian Dialogue. Orwin does not.

that we need to think of the envoys not so much as representatives of Athenian unity but, rather, as political actors in their own right, enmeshed in particular political and rhetorical situations. More positively, I want to use the issue of the envoys' status to think about the relationship between deliberation in Athens and *hoi Athenaioi* as a unit of action in the world of Greek affairs. This approach allows me to edge closer to the difficult matter—left unconsidered since Chapter 1—of how we ought to understand Athenian action in its sudden mode, when the silence of contending voices and the silence of the demos come together to render *hoi Athenaioi* as a whole utterly silent.

III. TALK OF JUSTICE IN THE ATHENIAN ASSEMBLY

Earlier I pointed toward one potential complication for the argument that anonymous envoys represent Athens. If the consideration of justice and empire in the Athenian assembly proves analogous to the Athenians' consideration of democratic politics, we will find it difficult to identify a single Athenian way of thinking or acting. Though the point will, again, not prove conclusive, such an analogy does in fact hold. As a consequence, we will not find emerging from the give and take of speakers and demos something that the envoys might in turn represent to other cities. Rather, arguments made in Athens about justice and empire amount to (potentially endless) attempts authoritatively to interpret for the silent Athenians an aspect of the Athenian way of life, of the Athenian *tropos*.[14] To trace fully all the twists and turns of such arguments would go beyond my present purposes. Here I want briefly to make two points that should be relatively familiar from previous chapters. First, in the context of a broad framing of the issue, the arguments we hear in the Athenian assembly about justice and its role in prosecuting the war and managing the empire change over the course of the war. Second, none of those arguments amount to an authoritative statement of Athenian thinking on these central issues of foreign policy. I briefly compare the speeches of Pericles and Alcibiades for the former point; for the latter, I turn to the Mitylene Debate.

In his first and third speeches, Pericles grapples—as will subsequent Athenian speakers—with the relevance of justice as a standard for judging

---

14. Let me quickly note that neither Thucydides nor his speakers refer to foreign policy as an aspect of the Athenian tropos. I am drawing the analogy here—and will try to substantiate it. In Sections V and VI, having such language at hand will prove helpful.

past Athenian actions and as a guide for the immediate future. More to the point, he refuses to apply standards of justice to what Athens has done. This basic irrelevance follows, Pericles' first speech suggests, from the aggression and intransigence of Athens's enemies. The Spartans have refused "arbitration" and "discussion," eschewing treaty provisions that provide for the legal resolution of disputes among equals (1.140). Their turning to war rests on their own preemptory condemnation of the Athenians, leaving the latter with a simple choice between freedom and a "subservience" imposed not through the justice of arbitration but by "command" (1.141.1). The place of justice in Pericles' thinking thus merges with his portrayal of the war as essentially defensive. Whatever they have done in the past, the Athenians must defend themselves now. If the Spartans will not allow for the consideration of Athens' past actions in the proper forum, if they opt for a war of aggression rather than peaceful negotiation based on the merits of their grievances, then they themselves have taken the justice of what the Athenians have done off the agenda. The Athenians have neither the need nor the time for a searching consideration of the rights and wrongs—whatever they may be—of the imperial past, so Pericles offers nothing of the sort. The realities of the present demand attention.

In the postplague speech, Pericles makes the same point about the basic irrelevance of past (in)justices for a city fighting a defensive war. At the same time, his arguments reflect the broader rhetorical tack of the speech as revelatory. As we saw in Chapter 4, Pericles—war and plague having brought him to the brink of political disaster—responds by "revealing" to the Athenians for the first time the "real" reasons they have followed him. Along similar strategic lines, he now tells them "somewhat plainly"—certainly more plainly than before—that the empire amounts to "a tyranny." Then, too, the Athenians may not realize—for Pericles has "not mentioned it"—that this tyranny extends so widely, particularly given Athenian naval power, that "there is *no one* . . . to prevent you from sailing with the naval forces you have at your disposal" (2.62; emphasis added). The stakes are thus higher than the Athenians think; they go beyond "one issue alone, slavery instead of freedom," to include "loss of empire" and "danger from those whose hatred you incurred during your rule" (2.63).

With these revelations (in addition to his revelations about the real basis of his influence in Athens), Pericles means to (re)secure his own position by heightening the Athenians' appreciation of the need for a firm defense and by convincing them to persevere despite hardship. Such arguments also help clarify—for the demos and for we readers—Pericles' argument about justice. While it may seem to have been "unjust [*adikon*] to acquire" such a position in Greece, he says, it is certainly "dangerous to let go" (2.63.3). In keeping with his strategy of revelation, Pericles comes much closer here than in his first speech to admitting that Athens has acted unjustly. But he also holds more firmly than ever to the argument that the aggression Athens faces makes all that irrelevant. The Athenians must leave behind any concern over what they have or have not done. In a sense they can do this precisely because the Spartans have attacked them. So far as justice goes, the past matters little in the face of the (heightened) dangers of the present.

In urging on the Athenians' passion for Sicily, Alcibiades, like Pericles, treats justice as essentially irrelevant to the prosecution of war and empire. Indeed, he will never directly refer to *dike*, though his concluding words suggest its role in the understanding of the war to which he calls the demos: "I have no doubt whatsoever in my mind that a city never inactive would be soonest ruined by change to inaction, and that men who conduct their affairs with the least violence to their normal character and customs, even if these are less than ideal [*cheiro*], are the ones who live in the greatest security" (6.18.7). Certainly we hear in these words an echo of Pericles' claim that nothing matters but the avoiding of destruction. But clearly, too, Alcibiades means for the demos to reject Pericles' defensive war for an offensive one, for a war strategy that focuses on activity rather than inactivity. In the course of such arguments, Alcibiades suggests a different stance toward Athens' past. As the passage cited above indicates, he says that Athens must continue to act as it has acted before, adding to the empire by the same means used to acquire it. Earlier he has thus argued that Athens cannot "regulate the amount of empire"; the Athenians must sail to Sicily to strengthen their power (6.18.3–4). This new strategy surely forfeits the possibility of breaking cleanly with possible past injustices. Alcibiades admits as much; the Athenians must continue to act as they have, even if that means acting in something less than an ideal way. Standards such as justice remain irrelevant in this understanding of the war; that irrelevance, however, follows not so much from Spartan aggression as from a conscious Athenian decision. We might say that though he proclaimed such questions irrelevant, Pericles nonetheless offered (or argued that the Spartans were offering) a glimpse of exoneration through a turning away from the possibly unjust past toward a just self-defense in the present. In urging an offensive war, on the other hand, Alcibiades means for the Athenians to confront directly their questionable past and to affirm it in the present.

Notwithstanding their broadly similar framings of justice as irrelevant, Pericles and Alcibiades depict the nature of that irrelevance and its implications for Athenian actions in significantly different ways. Even this rather schematic comparison reminds us that we will find no fully consistent Athenian position on such matters that the Athenian envoys might in turn (re)present when they appear in other cities. We should remember, too, the difficulty of ascertaining whether the arguments of Pericles and Alcibiades reflect "Athenian" thinking at the particular moments when they speak. Pericles, after all, only speaks because he senses the anger of the Athenians, anger directed at him and his moderate, defensive war policies; he responds to a moment of division and discord, a moment of Athenian plurality. Alcibiades, of course, faces opposition as well; he speaks in response to Nicias' arguments about the dangers of going on the offensive. But the fact that the Athenians may disagree among themselves at any given time regarding the role of justice is perhaps most evident in the Mitylene Debate, during which Cleon, Diodotus, and those Athenians gathered silently before them reconsider the sentence initially passed on the captured Mitylenians.

The familiarity of the arguments about justice that Cleon and Diodotus advance does little to diminish their power to shock. We should expect Diodotus, the advocate of leniency, to be the champion of justice; yet it is Cleon, of course, who calls on justice in demanding that the Athenians confirm their initial decision. At its most basic, Cleon's "justice" amounts to a lust for revenge of the sort initially felt in Athens toward the Mitylenians. "Return to your feelings during the ordeal," Cleon demands, and "punish them now as they deserve" (3.40). He goes on to offer what he insists are compelling reasons for such wrath. The Athenians have treated the Mitylenians better than the other allies, but they have revolted nonetheless. They have worked deliberate injury on Athens, injury that demands just retribution. But beyond this bare vengeance, Cleon also points to fundamental questions about the empire—questions that he says are raised by the rebellion of allies like the Mitylenians: "if they were right to revolt, you would be ruling when you should not" (3.40.4). The Athenians cannot, as Pericles argued, simply defend their empire without regard to its ethical implications. In this instance, the actions the Athenians take will reflect on the basic justice of the empire. By not giving the Mitylenians their due punishment, the Athenians will be so much as admitting that their rule has no just foundation. Cleon thus argues that the current situation demands from the Athenians an answer to the question that Pericles suggested they could avoid even asking.

Or does he in fact so argue? In the very next breath, Cleon seems to step back from the issue of justice and return to a position that seems to echo Pericles' third speech: "if you then see fit to [rule an empire] even when it is wrong, why, it stands to reason that you must also punish [the Mitylenians] in your own interests" (3.40). Here Cleon poses the question not as a matter of justice, of right and wrong, but more basically as a question of safety and hence expediency. Indeed, in addition to his vulgar appeal to vengeance, he has throughout worked on this accompanying argument from expediency. Thus in the midst of his harangue about the dangers of democratic deliberation we find the lament that the Athenians "do not bear in mind that [they] hold [their] empire as a tyranny," and hence do not face up to the deadly serious challenge posed by rebellious subject cities (3.37.1). That challenge demands harsh treatment of the Mitylenians, not only from the standpoint of justice, but also to stave off future rebellions: "If you take account of the allies . . . do you think there is any who will not revolt on the slightest pretext when either success brings freedom or failure brings no fatal consequences?" (3.39). Cleon thus seeks to unite appeals to justice and to expediency behind a single course of action, as he clearly indicates when he "sums up": "by following me, you will act both justly and expediently toward the Mitylenians" (3.40). Again, the backdrop of Pericles' declaration of the simple irrelevance of justice reveals the complexity (or confusion) of Cleon's claims. On the one hand, Cleon seems to argue, as Pericles did, that the past justice or injustice of the empire matters not a whit; indeed, he goes beyond Pericles' "somewhat plain" suggestion and positively affirms that the empire exists as a tyranny. From such a point of view, the Athenians face a simple question of expediency: How can they best defend themselves? On the other hand, Cleon wants to take advantage of the Athenians' lust for vengeance and to appeal to their desire to see the empire as just in itself.

This attempt to cling to what sounds like a more strident version of Pericles' insistence on protecting the empire, all the while playing to some (perceived) self-righteous Athenian sense of justice, would seem to suggest two possible responses for the advocate of leniency: a critique, on the one hand, of Cleon's account of justice, or, on the other hand, a critique of his reading of the expedient in this particular case. It is disconcerting that Diodotus chooses the latter strategy, declaring that "the debate, if we are sensible, is not about [the Mitylenians'] guilt but about the right planning for ourselves" (3.44), and arguing on the basis of the failure of capital punishment as a deterrent. Could he not just as easily challenge Cleon's account of justice? Surely on the previous day, the Athenians acted as if justice meant vengeance, pure and simple; but in the meantime they have had serious regrets, doubting a decree that seemed "cruel and monstrous." Cannot Diodotus say something like "Cleon's reckless rhetoric reflects yesterday's anger; let us consider, indeed, the justice of punishing the Mitylenians, but let us do so in the spirit of sober reflection which has brought us together today"? The conviction that Diodotus indeed has some such rhetorical option underlies, to take one recent example, the criticism of James Boyd White, who contends that Diodotus here contributes to the breakdown of that culture of moral argument that moderated the horrors of war in the early years. In the struggle to define the place of justice in Athens's political language, Diodotus cedes victory to Cleon. By thus affirming the irrelevance of injustice, he leaves Athens with a rhetoric "without limits or standards or permanent values."[15] The arguments of the envoys at Melos mark "the next natural stage in the development" of this rhetoric.[16] Surely we must hold Diodotus in some way responsible.

Not that he is without defenders. On the one hand, Strauss some time ago contended that Diodotus subtly weaves an argument from justice into his more obvious appeal to expediency. Developing this thought, Orwin argues that Diodotus applies the "Athenian thesis" to the Mitylenians; in other words, their actions issued from a compulsion that mitigated their guilt.[17] That Diodotus must hide this argument follows from his own conclusion that, in Athenian politics, even the good speaker must have recourse to subterfuge (3.43). On the other hand, Ball suggests a simpler defense more attuned to the immediate exigencies of the situation. Cleon having "cut the ground from beneath [his] feet" on the issue of justice, and time being dangerously short, Diodotus must make do with the rhetorical resources ready to hand. To save the lives of the Mitylenians, he turns to an argument that, while not entirely to our taste, gets the job done.[18]

15. White, *When Words Lose Their Meaning*, 76.
16. Ibid. White's argument here assumes precisely the reading of the envoys as "representative" of "Athens," which I want here to call into question.
17. Orwin, *Humanity of Thucydides*, 142–57.
18. Terence Ball, "When Words Lose Their Meaning." As the next few sentences suggest, I find Ball's defense of Diodotus largely convincing, though the case does not admit of any sort of final closure. Thus where Ball says that Diodotus "has no way out except to beat Cleon at his own game" (628), I should want to say that Diodotus' options remain uncertain, given that—as I say in the text—we cannot know for sure how fully the Athenians have accepted Cleon's claims.

Along these lines, we should recall the tentative conclusions drawn in Chapter 4 about the challenges of political judgment that would-be Athenian advisers face. Surely in the heat of political action, especially given the persistent silence of the demos, Diodotus cannot know how successful Cleon's argument has been, cannot know whether an attempt to redefine justice will work. He cannot take the time to make what appears to be the more difficult argument, particularly in the context of Pericles' earlier dismissal of considerations of justice. And perhaps, too, we should not blame Diodotus for any future arguments, in Athens or elsewhere, that seem to echo his. After all, he does not appear alone in the Mitylene Debate; Cleon's speech as well resounds with more than a little harshness, contains its own rank appeals to expediency. In the end, how can we or he know with any certainty which arguments will, as it were, stick in the Athenian mind?

In this way, the Mitylene Debate and the commentary on it again point out the irreducible plurality of understandings lurking within any apparent unity issuing from the Athenian assembly. The by now familiar conclusion must be that at any moment in which we see the Athenians engaged in deliberation in the assembly—or having deliberated, making a decision—we should be wary of saying that they hold the empire to mean this rather than that, or that they understand the import of justice for their actions in a single manner. In addition to the changing way in which Athenian speakers depict such matters over the course of the war, we should remember that, in the context of the interaction of speakers and silent demos, no single political speech, nor any single interpretation of one political speech, can express what "Athens" thinks. That Thucydides allows no such clarity about democratic politics in Athens should provide a reason for pause in thinking about what happens when Athenians appear in other cities. Considerations of justice and empire in Athens, that is, should cause us to doubt the notion that something called "Athens" can be unambiguously "represented" abroad. To repeat, though, such doubts hardly prove conclusive. It may be, after all, that Thucydides turns to the envoy's speeches precisely as a device for expressing a unified Athenian position on specific matters of "foreign policy."

IV. THE STATUS OF ATHENIAN ENVOYS

My approach to uncovering the plurality that renders problematic any simple notion of Athenian identity has involved thinking about how speakers and speeches in the Athenian assembly appear from the perspective of the political actor. Here I want to ask after the status of the anonymous envoys—and, in the following section, their speeches—from a similar perspective. First, though, let me point toward two possible understandings of the envoys as individuals in which they might appear as representatives of Athenian unity. On the one hand, that the envoys remain anonymous suggests the possibility that Thucydides means them to appear simply as typical Athenians. That is, insofar as they have no independent identity in the pages of the *History*, perhaps the envoys embody and give voice to a sort of generic "Athenianism." We might even think this particularly likely in the case of democratic Athens, where citizens consider themselves equals; where one citizen can easily stand in for another, perhaps any citizen can and—in some sense, inevitably does—stand in for the city. On the other hand, barring this slippage of democratic equality into a sort of democratic identity, we might understand the Athenians to have charged the envoys precisely with the task of representing Athens. Though Thucydides records no exercise of democratic decision making in these instances, perhaps we can detect in Thucydides' presentation of them some indication of a more formal or procedural link to their home city. We need, then, to attend both to the status of the envoys as Athenians and to Thucydides' account of their missions.

In identifying their speeches as "major expositions" of the Athenian thesis, Orwin emphasizes the common anonymity of the Athenians who speak at Delos in book 4, at Sparta in book 1 and at Melos in book 6. Yet Thucydides, by the very terms he uses to describe them, suggests some sort of distinction between the first speaker and the latter two. He refers to the Athenian who goes to Delos as "a herald [*kerykos*]" (4.97, 4.98). The Athenians who speak at Sparta and Melos he calls "envoys [*presbeis*]" (1.72; 6.84). That latter term—*presbeis*—belongs to a family of words that, besides denoting an envoy or ambassador, can connote rank, honor, or privilege. It surely makes sense that Athens would entrust important missions to prominent individuals or that membership on such a mission would raise one to a certain rank in the city. Thucydides, of course, says nothing of the sort. He offers no kind of direct personal description of either herald or envoys. His choice of separate terms, though, does indicate that we cannot simply lump Delos, Sparta, and Melos together according to the anonymity of Athenian speakers. And the choice of *presbeis* contains, I think, just the hint of a nascent particularity, a more specific identity that might distinguish the "envoys" from the more fully anonymous "herald."

The manner in which Thucydides records the three speeches also suggests that we should think of the envoys, and not the herald, as in some sense particular rather than generic Athenians. Thucydides reports the message carried by the herald to the Delians at some length, but entirely in indirect discourse. Moreover, the "speaker" throughout remains "the Athenians," Thucydides using the third person plural, just as he does when reporting Athenian actions in the course of the narrative. Thus the "speech" begins: "the Athenians sent their own herald ... and stated that they had done no injury"; and later continues "the law of the Hellenes was, they said," with "they" again referring to "the Athenians" (4.98). As befits a message bearer, the herald thus serves as a mouthpiece for the Athenians; as a particular Athenian, he himself remains silent. By the instrument of the herald, the Athenians make themselves present to speak at Delos. By contrast, Thucydides records the Athenian speeches at Sparta and Melos in direct discourse. He gives us, that is, the actual words of the envoys. The latter have their own voice; they make themselves heard; they engage in debate and dialogue. This contrast further suggests a particularity attached to the envoys that must call into question the notion that they are simply generic Athenians who represent by making present their home city. Despite their anonymity, they have an undeniable presence of their own—and thus a certain distance from Athens or "the Athenians"—that the simple herald lacks.

If we cannot take the envoys as by their very identity reflecting Athenian thinking, what of the possibility that they have been charged with the task of representation by the Athenians? Here let us think about the routes by which our anonymous Athenians come to speak. We have seen, for example, that the Athenians do send (*pempousin*) the herald to Delos for the express purpose of delivering a specific message.[19] Now Thucydides tells us that the Athenians who rise at Sparta to defend their city against the charges made by the Corinthians had come "on other business" (1.72). In keeping with their anonymity, he says nothing of what this other business might have been. Clearly, insofar as they are envoys they have not come on what we should think of as a private errand. They arrive in Sparta on some sort of mission for Athens, but that mission does not involve showing "how great the power of their city was" (1.72), as Thucydides describes their purpose in speaking. "Our mission," the envoys themselves say, "was not intended for debating your allies but for the business for which our

---

19. I consider more directly the role of another such herald in the next chapter when I return more directly to consider *hoi Athenaioi* as a unit of action.

city sent [*epempsen*] us" (1.73.1). By thus contrasting the envoys' official mission with their purpose in speaking, Thucydides prompts the reader to wonder, as the Peloponnesians might well wonder, whether we have heard what *the* Athenians think or what *these* Athenians think. He thus makes "Athens" both present and strangely distant, strangely absent, in the words of the first set of envoys.

Thucydides leaves much less room for doubt about the mission and purpose of the Athenian participants in the Melian Dialogue. Before attacking, the commanders of the expedition "sent [*epempsan*] envoys [*presbeis*] to make proposals to the Melians" (5.84). They have a relatively clear mission—"to make proposals to the Melians" or, more specifically, to propose unconditional surrender (5.84).[20] Here, though, we should note carefully who has assigned them this task. Unlike their counterparts at Sparta, the envoys at Melos take their orders not from the city itself, but from *strategoi* chosen by the city. Thucydides even gives us the commanders' names: Cleomedes and Teisias. By thus interposing another link in the chain of command, Thucydides injects another and different sort of particularity into the appearance of the envoys. We can ask—and perhaps more important, imagine the Melians asking—some very simple but important questions. Who are these Athenians who speak? Do they speak for the mass of Athenians who remain silent at home? For Cleomedes and Teisias? Only for themselves? Are these, in fact, generic Athenians voicing what everyone in their city thinks? Or are they simply particular Athenians sent by particular *strategoi* to deal with this particular situation?[21] When we arrive at such questions, at such possibilities of particularity, we find another bit of trouble for any attempt to take these envoys as unambiguous representatives.

V. THE ATHENIAN ENVOYS ON THE POSSIBILITY OF JUSTICE

Thus far I have considered two difficulties for the notion that the anonymous envoys in some sense espouse an "Athenian" position on justice.

20. The translation is Smith's. Lattimore translates *presbeis* as "representatives." As the argument of this chapter suggests, I find the idea of the envoys as representatives problematic.
21. Similar questions might be raised regarding the status of the Melians with whom the Athenian envoys argue. Thucydides reports that "the Melians did not bring [the Athenian envoys] before the common people but told them to speak to the officials and a small group about their reasons for coming" (5.84). And so the Melian people no more directly consider their fate than do the Athenians in the assembly. This adds another layer of complexity to the Melian Dialogue, discussion of which I have omitted here, given my focus on Athenian democratic politics.

It is difficult to say that one understanding of the empire and its implications reigns among Athenians at any given time; besides this, we must question the equation of the Athenian envoys with *hoi Athenaioi*. Though the envoys remain nameless, the manner in which they appear as individuals in the *History* marks them as something other than simply generic citizens of their home city. And the way in which they come to speak rules out any simple account of their formal relationship to Athens, any notion that the envoys merely dutifully carry out a straightforward mission, mouthing the words that the otherwise silent Athenians have told them to speak. Now that latter sort of particularity points toward one further complication in the relation between the envoys and "Athens." To take the common reading of the envoys seriously, we must assume that they present to other cities an Athenian point of view, that they reveal to others what the Athenians think. But this oversimplifies the actual rhetorical situations in which the envoys operate. The comparison with the herald at Delos again proves suggestive. The Athenians who speak at Sparta and at Melos do not simply mouth an Athenian statement, as the herald at Delos does. Rather, as I said in passing above, they engage in argument, in debate, in what we have come to call in the case of Melos a "dialogue" with other speakers. Given what happens when would-be advisers speak in Athens, we would expect the particularities of these rhetorical engagements to shape what the envoys say. In this sense, the envoys may find themselves forced to innovate, to make arguments that would not have appeared in Athens itself or in any message carried by a herald. I turn now to consider such possibilities, beginning with the envoys at Sparta.

In responding to the Corinthians' attempt to stir the reluctant Spartans to action, the envoys develop two related but distinct themes.[22] They claim, first, that in taking and holding the empire, Athens has done nothing "remarkable" or "contrary to ordinary human behavior [*anthropeious tropou*]" (1.76.2). By this line of argument, the envoys mean to counter the portrait of Athens offered by the Corinthians—that is, their description of the Athenians' pursuit of empire as grasping, bold, daring, and restless. To the claim that these "characteristics" mark Athenian action as distinctive and distinctly dangerous, the Athenians respond simply that they have done nothing out of the ordinary. They have acted as any city would, following a "law" or "rule" or "thing" long established by the actions of others:

---

22. I have discussed the arguments of the Corinthians and the rhetorical strategy they employ in Chapter 2.

"the weaker is kept down by the stronger" (1.76.2). The rhetorical force of all this rests on establishing two things. First, the envoys must establish this "practice" as truly "common." Hence the general argument that it has "ever been established" and the more specific claim that the Spartans, too, act according to it in dealing with their Peloponnesian allies (1.76.1).[23] Second, the Athenians need to show that their city has indeed acted in the commonly accepted manner. Hence they dwell at some length on the rise of the Athenian empire in the wake of the Persian Wars (1.74–75).

The rhetorical strategy the envoys thus follow mirrors that of those Athenian speakers who attempt to buttress their own position by offering accounts of the Athenian *tropos*. By (re)interpreting past actions, they seek to establish an authoritative way of doing things, which they can then use to evaluate and guide present actions. The Athenian envoys at Sparta enter into an analogous discussion of the prevailing manner in which a Greek city—or any city—deals with its counterparts. They do so, we should note, in direct response to the Corinthians' account of past Athenian actions; the Corinthian speech not only prompts the Athenians to speak on a subject outside their official purview but also shapes the line of argument they pursue. Furthermore, this sort of argument, this appeal to an accepted *tropos*, also allows for claims of innovation, as in the analogous situation in Athenian "domestic politics." In response to the "argument of justice" raised by the Corinthians, the envoys retort that such an argument "never yet, when there was any opportunity to gain something by might, deterred anyone who propounded it from taking advantage" (1.76.3). Adherence to this standard way of acting would exonerate the Athenians, but they make a bolder claim. Should any city, they say, go beyond common practice and prove "more observant than they might have, considering their power, then they are to be commended." Precisely this sort of going beyond what Greeks would ordinarily do, this stepping away from the ordinary practice of imperial cities, marks Athens. Or so, at any rate, the envoys seek to prove by describing, for example, how the Athenians have allowed their subjects access to the Athenian courts (1.77). Instead of using their strength to rule in their own interests, the Athenians have been "more observant of justice" than anyone should have expected.

In forwarding this first theme, then, the envoys situate themselves—or

23. See also the Athenian claim that should the Spartans "overthrow us and obtain supremacy," they would find themselves hated just like the Athenians (I.77.6) Again, the suggestion here is that a common way of doing things exists among the Greeks and that Athens has acted—and suffered—according to it.

find themselves situated—in a discussion among Greeks about how Greek cities do or should act toward one another. But a second theme appears as well, intertwined with the notion of an established practice from which innovation is possible and, at first glance at least, in some tension with it. The envoys at several points speak of Athens and all other imperial cities as in some sense compelled to rule over others. Thus the Athenians "were compelled" to advance the empire "especially out of fear, then prestige as well, and later out of self-interest" (1.75.3). The action that was neither "remarkable" nor "contrary to the common practice" involved "yielding" to these same "strongest motives" (1.75.2). Thus far, the two themes can coexist and even reinforce each other. The envoys seek to buttress their claims about common practices by locating the roots of such practices in basic human compulsions.

The potential problem arises when the Athenians claim to have worked some innovation. Here again is the core of that claim, this time including the appeal to compulsion in which the envoys situate it: "And they are to be commended who, yielding to the instinct of human nature [*anthropeia physei*] to rule over others, have been more observant of justice than they might have been, considering their power" (1.76.3). And here is Clifford Orwin on the apparent tension, even incoherence, of this sort of argument: "Again and again the representatives of Athenianism contradict themselves, rejecting on the one hand the possibility of acting against 'necessity' conceived as advantage, and claiming on the other to do so."[24] How are we to reconcile the idea that human nature—through fear, honor, and interest—compels cities to rule without regard to justice with the claim that Athens manages to act as no other city does or can? If common practices have their roots in human nature, how is it that they can be altered by the Athenians or anyone else? The Athenians, Orwin contends, "recurrently grapple" with this "dilemma of their thesis."

Now this dilemma, this tension, surely calls to mind the debates on the relative places of *nomos* and *physis* that swirled through fifth-century Greek intellectual life. The sophists in particular explored the contrast between "laws" or "conventions" or "traditions" (*nomos*) on the one hand and "nature" (*physis*) on the other.[25] The realm of *nomos*, a creation of humans, allows for change through human action and interaction. By contrast, *physis* stands before human action, guiding it. Now clearly, if we take *nomos* and

---

24. Orwin, *Humanity*, 196.
25. See Lebow, "Thucydides the Constructivist," 553–54, for a discussion of attempts to locate Thucydides in the context of the *nomos*–*physis* debate in fifth-century Athens.

physis to their respective extremes—as some sophists apparently did—then contrast yields to sharp antithesis. If we take man-made *nomoi* as constantly in flux, not just as changeable but as *easily* changeable, and *physis* as necessary and absolute, we can hardly combine the two. But the envoys at Sparta try to do just this, to appeal to both tradition and nature, to changeable practices and unchangeable instincts.[26] As we will see, the envoys at Melos similarly have reference to both *nomoi* and *physis*. (How) do they manage to do so without falling into a blatant self-contradiction that might destroy the rhetorical power of their speech?

The envoys at Sparta resolve (or avoid, if you prefer) the dilemma by refusing to take "law" and "nature" to such extremes. They do not suggest that the "common practice" of imperial cities is infinitely malleable. Certainly they say that Athens has innovated by going beyond or, we might say, by altering, that common practice. But the power of their argument comes from the claim that such innovation in fact occurs very rarely and thus deserves special note and praise. Most of the time, the "established" rules hold. Likewise, in speaking of "human nature," they refer to "motives" and "instincts," never, notably, to "necessity." And they seem to allow room for successful struggle against *physis*. If humans, as they say, "yield" to the drive to rule, then might not they also possibly "overcome" such a drive? Indeed, the notions of *tropos* and *physis* that the envoys advance work together to form an essentially coherent argument, whether or not we find it persuasive. Human nature pushes cities in a given direction, and common practice tends to follow. But that direction is not—in this speech—strictly necessary: human nature can be overcome, the determined city can deviate from what most do, can practice justice more than it would have to.[27] There is only a contradiction here if we go to extremes, if we refuse to see human nature and human practice blending into a shade of gray. The envoys construct a rhetorical balance—precarious though it may be—between convention and nature. They thus situate Athenian imperial action at once in the context of general human drives and, as it were, at once both inside and outside the context of common Greek practice.

To put the point simply, the Athenian envoys at Melos eschew this balancing act by subsuming the realm of common practice under a much

---

26. This, in part, involves the idea that *tropos* refers to the realm of *nomos*. Here, of course, see Chapter 2 and my argument that, from the perspective of the political actor, the Athenian *tropos* emerges from political interaction. See, too, Connor, *Thucydides*, 173n41.

27. In this way the Athenian envoys in book 1 are perhaps best understood as, in Donnelly's terminology, "strong realists." Donnelly, *Realism and International Relations*, 12.

more extreme understanding of nature or *physis*. The climactic moment of the dialogue comes when the Melians suggest that the gods favor the just over the unjust, and, too, that the Lacedaemonians will come to their aid out of a sense of "kinship" and "honor" (5.104). The Athenian response contains, at least nominally, the same two themes we found in the speech at Sparta: "According to our understanding, divinity, it would seem, and mankind, as has always been obvious, are under an innate compulsion [*physeos anagkaias*] to rule wherever empowered. Without being either the ones who made this law [*nomon*] or the first to apply it after it was laid down, we applied it as one in existence when we took it up and anyone else who attained power would act accordingly" (5.105.2). Neither gods nor men, and of these latter, certainly not Spartans (5.105.3), respect justice; neither will do anything to help the Melians. The strong imperial city will do what it will do, and justice be damned—or, better, justice is simply irrelevant. Clearly, this passage has a different cast, a different tone than the speech of the envoys at Sparta. What appeared there as a common practice (*tropos*), from which the Athenians deviated by pursuing justice, is now more firmly a law (*nomos*). And having "found" that law already "in existence," the Athenians have no intention of changing or going beyond it. Indeed, here, no one "established" this "law"; it follows from nature. And here, too, nature, which the envoys at Sparta envisioned as an instinct or a set of motives, now yields a "necessity." Surely the Athenians mean to portray changing such a law not simply as difficult but as impossible.[28]

With the speech at Sparta in mind, we might ask what accounts for this more complete subjection of human practice to human nature. One possibility is that the envoys' words reflect a general coarsening of discourse among Greeks. In describing the breakdown of common meanings in Corcyra, Thucydides says that "war is a violent teacher" (3.82). Perhaps the Athenian envoys at Melos, whether or not they represent general Athenian opinion, have begun to learn its lessons. On the other hand, we should also consider some of the particularities of the Melian Dialogue. For example, we might reasonably enough argue that the format of the exchange adds to the Athenians' bluntness. The anonymous envoys favor a dialogue precisely because it allows for plain speaking without "noble

---

28. Compare my reading to that of Werner Jaeger, *Paideia*, 401–2, who says that the Athenians here simply take *nomos* and *physis* to be distinct. Again, insofar as *nomon* refers back to *physeos anagkaias*, I take the envoys at Melos to be saying that *nomos* is necessity.

phrases" and "lengthy and unconvincing speeches" (5.89).[29] With the power of the Athenian forces near to hand, they simply wish a setting in which to make clear the brute facts. Indeed, in the event, the dialogue form seems to lead to an increasing bluntness, the Athenians growing more and more impatient with the recalcitrant and stubbornly hopeful Melians.

These reflections on the dialogue format point, too, to the obviously different status of the audiences that the two sets of envoys address. The Spartans in book 1 certainly stand in a more powerful position than the lowly Melians. Sparta appears as something like Athens's equal; surely the envoys cannot be so blunt with them. Indeed, rather early on in the Melian Dialogue the Athenian speakers assert that the Melians know "as well as we do that in human considerations justice is what is decided when equal forces are opposed" (5.89). Athenians might discuss some possibility of justice with Spartans. They will not countenance such pleas from Melians. As with the format chosen, the audience with which the envoys interact shapes or intertwines with the arguments they make. Given the context in which they speak, in short, we should not be surprised that the envoys at Melos seem to speak more harshly, more bluntly than those at Sparta.

In fact, by the end of the dialogue, we ought perhaps to be asking not why the Athenian participants turn so entirely to arguments from strict necessity, but why they retain the language of *nomos* at all. Why not drop altogether such language, which, after all, continues to suggest the realm of human practice, a realm where the pursuit of justice and the introduction of some counterargument by the Melians might be possible? Here the answer lies, I think, in the chief similarity between the situations in which the two sets of envoys speak. The envoys at Melos, like the envoys at Sparta, find themselves in the rhetorical context of Greek intercity relations. Their apparent aim, we should remember, is to *persuade* the Melians, and they must do so within that context. By clinging to the notion of a *nomos* established among cities, they can simultaneously try to alter its relationship to *physis*. They can try to persuade the Melians that necessity rules the actions of all imperial cities and thus that Melos can have no

---

29. The Melians themselves are responsible for the exchange taking place in private; they "did not bring [the envoys] before the common people but told them to speak to the officials and a small group" (5.84). The Athenians suggest that the Melians, being fearful of a public setting, ought to protect themselves from the persuasive lure of "a continuous persuasion" and thus ought to agree to respond "immediately to whatever is said that sounds unfavorable" (5.85). The Melians submit to such a format with a certain wariness but little objection.

hope. As at Sparta, the fact that Athenian envoys confront other speakers from other Greek cities shapes what they can and do say.

And here we find, again, a final complication telling against the notion that either set of Athenian envoys simply gives expression to or represents or reflects an opinion or view or feeling that unifies all of Athens. For even if such a thing exists (which we have found reason to doubt), and even if the envoys in their persons in some sense (which we have been unable to pinpoint) represent "Athens," the situation in which they find themselves does not allow for the unfettered uttering of a single, preformed position. These anonymous but particular Athenians engage in political speech as a mode of interaction, not simply as an instrument of articulation. They must choose their arguments according to what other speakers say and according to what they think the audience will accept. Unlike the passive herald who visits Delos, more like those who rise to speak in the Athenian assembly, the envoys become political actors in their own right, shaping and being shaped by the complexities and particularities of the moment.

VI. THE ATHENIANS AND THEIR ENVOYS

Thucydides shows us Athenian political actors engaging in two distinct strands of discussion about justice and, more broadly, about its role in the interactions of Greek cities. The Athenians, through their particular sort of deliberation, consider in assembly the Athenian way of dealing with allies and enemies; at the same time, Athenians appear outside Athens, making arguments about the traditional way of Greek cities and Athens' place in it. We should remember, of course, the difficulty involved in thinking about either as a strand of discussion, in finding links between what appear most immediately as particular rhetorical moments during which speakers make particular rhetorical moves designed to win favor with the silent demos; any echoes across such moments—say from Pericles to Cleon on the empire as a tyranny—appear clearer in hindsight than they can in the midst of political action. Finding links across these two "strands"—links necessary to any argument, say, about the impact of either set of envoys' arguments on Athenian politics—proves difficult for reasons that flow from the ambiguous status of the envoys and the sorts of arguments they make. I turn now, first, to highlight these difficulties by considering the challenges of political judgment that the envoys pose to other cities, and, second, to think about what bearing all of this might have on democratic politics in Athens.

I have already pointed toward the challenges that the ambiguous status of the envoys poses for other cities. Consider, again, the questions facing the Spartans in book 1 after they have heard the Corinthian and Athenian speeches. Certainly they might ask after the accuracy of the Corinthian and Athenian claims. Has Athens really acted in a grasping, daring manner, as the Corinthians contend? Have the Athenians, as the envoys claim, really practiced a certain sort of justice? At least potentially,[30] the answers to these questions surely bear on whether or not Sparta should go to war. But the Spartans might easily wonder, too, whether the envoys truly reveal an Athenian position on justice, empire, and war. Simply to assume, as Dionysius says all men do, that the envoys reflect opinion in Athens seems naive and potentially dangerous. Again, the envoys do not speak in an "official" capacity for Athens here. The Spartans could—and should, we might say—ask whether these particular Athenians' words bear on what the Athenians will do in the event of war. Do "the Athenians" really think they have justice on their side? If not, if the envoys' words stand simply as so much rhetoric, how will Athens act? If so, might the Athenians not prove even more self-righteous, obstinate, and unyielding as enemies?

The status of the envoys who speak at Melos and thus the implications of their claims for the immediate future ought to appear more clearly to the Melians. In this instance, after all, the envoys come as official representatives of the Athenian commanders whose forces are nearby, ready to act, their intentions fairly clear. The Melians have less reason to question whether the envoys' harsh words reflect the thinking of Cleomedes and Teisias. Certainly the envoys make it clear what will happen should the Melians not heed their words and surrender immediately: the Athenian forces at hand will destroy the city.[31] But, especially with the advantage of

---

30. Thucydides, of course, does not provide us with any clear evidence that the Spartans ask themselves any of the questions I have suggested. Again, I am interested here in trying to uncover the questions that the envoys and their words seem to pose to the Spartans. We can in this way, I think, draw on a close examination of the particulars of the context of inter-city relations—as they appear to the political actors themselves—to explore the difficulties and possibilities of political judgment as they emerge in the *History*. I mean here, then, to complicate the portrait of political judgment that I drew in Chapter 3 in the context of Athenian "domestic politics."

31. Barring, of course, some outside intervention. Even if they have little reason to question the envoys' words as reflections of the Athenian commanders' attention, the Melians still must determine whether the envoys are correct—as they turn out to be—in predicting that Sparta will not intervene.

hindsight, we might expect the Melians, too, to look a bit deeper into the future, to the possibility that they will eventually have to surrender to the Athenians.[32] If that comes to pass (as, of course, it does in the end), the Melians will surely find themselves at the mercy not of the Athenian army but of those Athenians who sit silently in decision at Athens (as, of course, they do in the end). With that possibility in mind, the Melians might perhaps ask questions of a familiar sort: What is the relation—if any—between what these envoys from the Athenian commanders say and what "the Athenians" think about Melos? If these particular Athenians represent their city in some sense, how will what they say about justice and empire translate into Athenian action? From the envoys' words, what can we Melians expect the Athenian demos to do with us should we be defeated?

Let us pause for a moment to think more directly about the issue of "representation" involved in such questions about the status of the envoys. Our own contemporary political experience focuses our attention on "representatives" who stand in for their constituents in the political processes of a larger whole. Most commonly, discussions of such representation revolve around the issue of whether or how representatives reflect the views of constituents, whether in fact we can hear the voice of the part in the whole. Thus our basic civics and government texts ask such questions as these: Do or should representatives act as mere "delegates," mere mouthpieces? Or do or should they act as "trustees," using their own judgment for the good of the whole? Clearly, insofar as Athens appears as one part of a broader Greek whole, some broadly analogous questions arise with respect to the envoys. Again, part of what the Spartans and Melians must ask involves whether the envoys, in the context of discussing what Greeks do, in searching for what "Greek" means, simply reflect general Athenian thinking or exercise their own political judgment. Yet clearly, too, the position of the envoys raises some more fundamental questions. The "part" that the envoys represent stands in its own right as a "whole," as a city that makes decisions and takes actions. Better to say that that city only potentially exists as a whole; its unity at most exists simultaneously with its basic plurality. The Melians, and earlier the Spartans, thus can (potentially, again) ask not simply after the role played by the representatives, but, more basically, after the status of the represented—especially since the latter may soon enough hold the Melians' fate in their hands. Beyond

---

32. Perhaps, too, we can consider it likely that the Melians remember what happened to Mitylene only two years before.

the question of whether the envoys faithfully represent "Athens," then, there stands the question of whether such an entity exists at all, whether one can find and know the unity of Athens among the plurality of Athenians.

In this context, whatever Athenian "representatives" say, it remains unclear just what "Athens" might emerge if and when the demos gathers on the Pnyx. But the particular sorts of arguments that both sets of envoys make poses an additional difficulty. Broadly speaking, the envoys, by virtue of the rhetorical context in which they find themselves, cast their arguments in a different idiom than do would-be advisers in the Athenian assembly. As we have seen, the former make arguments about human nature and the common Greek *tropos* or *nomos*, whereas the latter appropriately speak more particularly about common Athenian practice, about the Athenian *tropos*. Drawing conclusions about the Athenians and what they may do from what the envoys say thus often involves a certain sort of translation from one idiom to another, from general arguments about relations among Greek cities to the particular decisions the Athenian demos might make in the future. In this context, consider once more the crux of the argument made by the envoys at Melos: "According to our understanding, divinity, it would seem, and mankind, as has always been obvious, are under an innate compulsion [*physeos anagkaias*] to rule whenever empowered" (5.105.2). The Athenians, like the gods and the Spartans, will rule if they can. In the situation at hand, this means, according to the envoys, that Athenian forces will compel the surrender of the Melians if the latter will not willingly capitulate and that neither Spartans nor the gods will stop them. But if the Melians want to divine from this argument just what fate might befall them should they lose, just what the Athenian demos might do with them, they face a basic question to which the words of the envoys offer no clear answers. In the context of Athenian imperial practice, what form will the Athenian "rule" take? Nothing the envoys say eliminates the possibility that, should the Athenian assembly "determine their fate," as it does, the Melians will face death and enslavement, as they in the event do (5.116.3–4). But by the same token, nothing the envoys say ensures or requires or logically necessitates such a harsh sentence. The Melians cannot unproblematically know from the envoys' speech, cast in the broad idiom of human nature and Greek practice, what fate future Athenian decisions hold for them.[33] This uncertainty flows from the unclear

33. Orwin, *Humanity of Thucydides*, 113, makes a similar point from a slightly different angle, arguing that because the envoys' words do not require any particular treatment of the captured Melians, we cannot hold them responsible for the massacre; or, as he puts it: "as for

status of the envoys, from the fact that they speak in a rhetorical context different from that in which the Melians' fate will ultimately be decided, and from the consequent need to translate from one context to another.[34]

What, though, have all these challenges of political judgment, faced by Greek cities dealing with Athenian envoys, to do with Athenian politics? We might note, first, that Athens practices a form of democratic politics that makes it more difficult to answer questions about the status of the envoys and to translate their words into forecasts of Athenian action. No doubt, a speech by Spartan envoys would pose similar questions, similar challenges about what "Sparta" means, about whether something identifiable as "Sparta" even exists. Thucydides gives us no indication that any city remains free from the uncertainty of collective identity. But that uncertainty seems especially prominent in Athens; indeed, I have argued in earlier chapters that it stands at the center of Athenian democratic politics. Surely, then, the Spartans, the Melians—indeed, anyone who listens to an Athenian or a group of Athenians—must be particularly wary, as must readers of the *History*, when drawing conclusions regarding democratic politics in Athens, about what will result from the complicated interactions of silent demos and speakers in the Athenian assembly.

Of more interest for my purposes is that the envoys and their words pose to the Athenians at home, in the assembly, challenges analogous to those faced by their Spartan and Melian audiences. Insofar as the envoys do not "officially" or straightforwardly represent Athens, the Athenians surely must (or ought to or at least could) ask just what their relation to "Athens" might be. Who are these Athenians who appear at Sparta? Have our fellow citizens spoken for us to the Melians? Since we did not charge them with this specific mission, should we take them as our "representatives" or not? Moreover, neither set of envoys, whatever their status, in any way dictates Athenian action. As we have seen, the envoys at Sparta defend past Athenian actions as in accord with Greek practice and try to show the power of their home city, but they do not somehow reveal what

---

the 'cold calculation' of the envoys themselves, we must not assume that it vindicates the massacre." Orwin thus here seems to recognize the danger of equating the envoys with "the Athenians" and takes this point as speaking against the notion that the envoys reflect the "decline of Athens." I should want to say that this recognition undermines *any* attempt (including Orwin's own; see Section I above) to take the envoys as representative of "Athenian" thinking.

34. The Spartans face similar problems in translating the arguments made by the envoys about common Greek practice and Athens's relation to it into any sort of tentative conclusions about what Athenian practice may be in the future. I have hinted at these difficulties earlier in the section. For the remainder of this chapter, I focus mostly on the episode of Melos.

the Athenians will do in the future. The Athenians at home still face the basic decision of how to act on the Greek stage. So, too, with the envoys at Melos: nothing the envoys say can explain or account for the fact that the Athenian demos determines to pass a harsh sentence on the Melian captives. Rather, what the envoys have said at Melos, along with what the Athenian forces have done, helps define the context in which the Athenians make this decision, partially constituting the problem of political judgment that the Athenians face. Might not we imagine the Athenians pondering what they have heard about the dialogue on Melos,[35] thinking about what these envoys who seem to have spoken in their place have said about Athenian practice and inter-Greek relations?

Here begins to emerge, I think, the manner in which issues of justice and "foreign policy" complicate Athenian democratic politics. Given my argument, we should be wary of concluding, with Cornford or Orwin, that "Athenian" passions evinced or "Athenian" ideas enunciated by the envoys enter into and prove destructive of Athenian democratic politics. Rather, as I suggested in passing at the close of section I, the questions the envoys pose to the Athenians symbolize the more general challenges the city faces by its situation as a "unit of action" in the context of Greek affairs. Like speakers who discuss aspects of the Athenian way of life in the Athenian assembly, the envoys present accounts of "Athens," both to other Greeks and, in the sense discussed in the last paragraph, to the Athenians themselves. These envoys' accounts, though, differ from those offered in the Athenian assembly precisely because they are situated and themselves situate Athens in the midst of Greek affairs. Like the envoys themselves, the "Athens" these accounts describe stands at a certain distance from the silent Athenians at home. Insofar as issues of justice and foreign policy draw particular Athenians outside their protective walls to act in the city's name, the discussion of "Athens" thus moves beyond the confines of the Athenian assembly. The presence of the envoys reminds us that Athenian politics involves more than the endless but comparatively comfortable discussion among Athenians of the Athenian way of life. Precisely because the Athenians find themselves in the midst of the flux of Greek affairs, they confront images of Athens and of Athenian action spoken in other contexts. Such images depict an Athenian unity; yet at the same

---

35. Not, of course, that Thucydides gives any indication that the words of the envoys reached Athens. He leaves us, rather, once more to ponder possible links and, I think, to reflect on what sorts of things the Athenians might have considered in any debate on the fate of the Melians. I return momentarily to the fact that Thucydides records no such debate.

time, because they are particular images offered by particular Athenians, they exacerbate Athenian plurality. The actions of Athenians in the Greek world result both in questions for the demos and speakers to consider through their brand of democratic politics, and in arguments that, rather than revealing "Athens," provide, at least potentially, more fodder for that process of deliberation through political speech which we considered in the Chapters 3 and 4.

Indeed, the appearance of the envoys and their description of Athens seems to highlight the need for careful deliberation in the Athenian assembly. Particularly at Melos, the envoys' words raise and leave unanswered crucial questions about Athens and the Athenian way of dealing with the weaker cities of Greece.[36] Consider the contrast with Mitylene. In Chapter 2, I traced Athenian action, up to and including the initial sentence on the Mitylenians, as sudden and silent wishing and doing. At no point prior to the clash between Cleon and Diodotus do the Athenians appear to be deliberating the meaning of their actions on Lesbos. The Mitylene Debate appears rather suddenly as the consequence of some sort of moment of awareness; something about the first day's debate and its outcome apparently prompts at least some Athenians to ask some important and difficult questions: What sort of city should Athens be? Can Athenians really act as harshly as we did yesterday? As I noted at the end of Chapter 2, so far as Thucydides shows us, nothing of the sort happens in Athens over Melos.

That silence thus reigns in the Athenian assembly renders more problematic any account of Melos as a moment of decline in Athenian thinking from Mitylene. We do not for Melos have even the (ultimately unclear) guide to Athenian thinking that the speeches of Cleon and Diodotus provide in the case of Mitylene. Precisely because it comes from a handful of particular Athenians in a particular rhetorical context on an island far out in the Aegean, the speech of the envoys on Melos provides no substitute for a debate in Athens, however indecisive the latter might be as a reflection of "Athens." By the same token, we would have difficulty arguing, as Cornford and Orwin do, that Melos reflects a way of Athenian thinking

---

36. This is not to take away from the importance of the envoys at book 1. Arguably, insofar as the Spartans base their decision to go to war in part on what they hear about Athens from those envoys, the Athenians at home in a sense lose a measure of control—or fail to assert control—over the most fundamental issue: whether to engage in a costly war. Many of the points I make about the troublesome ambiguity of Melos apply to the beginnings of the war. In effect, we might argue that the Athenians deliberate directly on the possibility of war only after the Spartans have essentially decided the issue—say, with Pericles' first speech at the end of book 1.

or acting that returns with a vengeance to wreck Athenian domestic politics. The example of Melos reminds us, rather, that in dealing with other Greek cities, particular Athenians create—and at times themselves offer—understandings of Athens that they might, but do not always, consider through their brand of deliberation. More immediately, by no means can we conclude that the Athenians would have spared the Melians had they only stopped and thought for a moment. Nor, for that matter, can we say that the Athenians would themselves have settled on answers to the sorts of questions that Athenian actions raise. Given what we have seen in previous chapters, any debate about Melos in the Athenian assembly would have ended in an Athenian action open to various interpretations by the Athenians and others. Perhaps at this point the most we can say is that the Melians suffer and that, especially given the arguments of the Athenian envoys, their fate raises vitally important issues that the Athenians seem not to consider. Any further conclusions about the consequences for Athenian action of silence in the Athenian assembly must await a more complete account of the mode of sudden, unified action that takes the place of any deliberation in the affair of Melos and at many other points. I offer such an account in the next chapter.

6

Athenian Silence and the Fate of Plataea

I. INTRODUCTION

In the summer of the fifth year of the Peloponnesian War, the remaining inhabitants of the small Boeotian city of Plataea, at the end of a lengthy siege and after the heroic escape of a number of their fellows, give themselves over to the mercy of the Peloponnesian allies. Though they allow the captives a lengthy speech, the five Spartans who subsequently sit in judgment in the end put a simple question to each: Have you done anything for Sparta in the current war? Long and loyal allies of the Athenians, some of whom surrender with them, none of the Plataeans can (or will) answer in the affirmative. The Spartans execute the men of Plataea—"they made no exceptions," Thucydides says—and they enslave the women (3.68).

That Thucydides records this sham trial almost immediately after he presents the decision of the Athenian assembly to spare the majority of the Mitylenians seems obviously to invite some sort of comparison. By themselves, the sentences imposed on the smaller cities by Athens and Sparta present a striking contrast. Thucydides appears intentionally to heighten that contrast not only by placing the fall of Mitylene and the fall of Plataea in such close proximity, but also, more generally, by structuring his narratives of the two affairs similarly. Thucydides' accounts of the two episodes follow a common pattern. As in the matter of Mitylene (which I discussed at length in Chapter 2), Thucydides presents the affair of Plataea as developing episodically, by fits and starts. In both cases, interludes on other matters separate the beginning of the siege from a period of renewed hostilities and increased deprivations for the besieged. Also, another set of intervals precedes the respective surrenders and (again in both instances) the paired speeches that yield decisions on the captives' fates. Finally, Thucydides brings the two matters to a close with "rounding off sentences."[1] On Mitylene: "This was how things turned out regarding Lesbos" (3.50). On Plataea: "Such was the fate of Plataea, in the ninety-third year after it became the ally of Athens" (3.68).

All of this perhaps suggests that Plataea stands as something of a Spartan or Peloponnesian Mitylene. Taken side by side, these two episodes can be taken to show how the great Greek powers dealt with smaller cities as the war, which all parties initially thought would be short, dragged on through its fifth year with no end in sight. For Cogan, for example, Mitylene and Plataea together illustrate the "ideological" phase of the war, with Melos marking the turn to a "belief in a total war," at least among the Athenians.[2] But we can easily enough point to other possible progressions in which Mitylene and Plataea appear as sequential rather than parallel elements. Consider, first, the development of sentences imposed over the series Mitylene–Plataea–Melos. The Athenians spare the majority of the Mitylenians; the Spartans kill or enslave all the Plataeans; the Athenians kill or enslave all the Melians. Then, too, we can note the differing role of justice in the Athenian speeches on Mitylene and Melos. Cleon and Diodotus take the meaning and applicability of justice as central issues for consideration; the Athenian envoys at Melos, on the other hand, from the start rule out any appeal to justice, any such "fine words." Somewhere in between, the Plataeans do their best to raise the issue of justice; whereas the Spartans, as we have seen, succeed in framing the debate in terms of expediency. Finally, that the Spartans, though they do allow lengthier speeches, in the end pose to the Plataeans a short, blunt question seems to mark the transition from Diodotus' defense of deliberation to the terse dialogue form at Melos. In these progressions in punishments imposed, in the place allowed for justice, and in the role of deliberation and debate, Plataea stands as something of a mediating term. Words and actions there foreshadow—and perhaps help account for—Athenian words and actions at Melos and point to continuing changes in the manner in which Greek cities interact with one another.

At the close of the previous chapter we saw how difficult it is even to compare Athenian words and deeds at Mitylene and Melos. To say, for example, that justice has less of a place in Athenian discourse at Melos than in

1. I here draw on Connor, *Thucydides*, who discusses the similarities between Thucydides' descriptions of Mitylene and Plataea on pages 148–49 and presents them schematically in appendix 5, pp. 255–56.
2. Cogan, *The Human Thing*, 65–73 (on Mitylene and Plataea) and 161 (on Melos). See also Connor, *Thucydides*, 157, on the narrative differences in Thucydides' account of, on the one hand, Mitylene and Plataea and on the other, Melos.

the Mitylene Debate involves taking the Athenian envoys as spokesmen for Athens—something I argued against at some length in the previous chapter. On a slightly different note, to argue that speech and deliberation decline in Greek affairs from Mitylene to Melos is to overlook the fact that Cleon and Diodotus discuss speech and deliberation as aspects of the Athenian way of democratic political life, while at Melos, the role of speech and speeches stands as an issue regarding how Greek cities relate to one another. Adding Plataea to the mix surely complicates matters further. Most obviously, Plataeans, Thebans, and Spartans speak of Greek affairs at Plataea, but no Athenians do. Beyond the difficulties we have traced in saying that the Athenians think any one thing at any one time, can we hope or should we even try to include Plataea in any tracing of changes in Athenian thinking on punishment, justice, and speech if no Athenians—not even ambiguously representative envoys—speak on such matters? More broadly, can we find a way to articulate the sorts of progressions in Athenian and Greek affairs that the juxtaposition of Mitylene and Plataea and Melos seems to suggest while remaining attentive to the particularities of the key terms of those progressions?

Such questions arise in any attempt fully to grasp the implications for Athenian democracy of Athens' immersion in the world of Greek affairs; and to do so, furthermore, while paying heed to the multiple perspectives of Thucydides' account. We can work toward answers to these questions or at least begin to see whether or not such answers are possible or desirable, if we first go beyond thinking about Plataea simply as a Peloponnesian affair, a counterpart to the matter of Mitylene. In fact, the Athenians concern themselves with events at Plataea from the very start. They respond quickly to the initial Theban attack by, among other things, dispatching Athenian hoplites (2.6). Later, they encourage the Plataeans to hold out against newly arrived Spartan forces and promise aid to their besieged allies (2.73). There follow, finally, two important nonactions by the Athenians. They apparently fail to send the promised help at the crucial moment (3.20); and they make no move to intervene as the Spartans determine the fate of the captured Plataeans (3.52–68). Throughout, Thucydides reports no Athenian assembly; the silence of contending voices and the silent presence of the demos here merge into the complete silence of *hoi Athenaioi*. We hear no Athenian speeches inside or outside Athens, save the words of a lone Athenian herald.[3] But we should not take such Athenian

3. And those words, again, appear in indirect discourse. See my discussion of the Athenian herald at Delos in Chapter 5.

silence as an indication of the irrelevance of Athenian action for events at Plataea. Plataea does mark a moment (or a series of moments) of Athenian action, but as we will see, the Athenians consistently act in that sudden mode I sketched in Chapter 2 in the context of the early stages of the revolt on Lesbos. With the backdrop of the arguments presented in the intervening chapters, I want in this chapter to think more carefully and in some detail about this Athenian mode of action and its consequences at Plataea. From this beginning, I return once again to consider what we can say about justice and Athenian "foreign policy" from Mitylene to Plataea to Melos and what lessons we might in turn draw about democratic politics in Athens.

II. THE PLATAEAN SURPRISE

Plataea moves to center stage in the opening chapters of book 2. A Theban attack on the small city definitively ends the thirty-year truce, "flagrantly breaking" the existing treaty between the major powers in Greece (2.7.1). So, Thucydides says, "begins the war between the Athenians and the Peloponnesians and the allies on both sides" (2.1). Neither the narrative nor the speeches to this point have done anything to foreshadow this attack. Not that the outbreak of war itself comes as a surprise. Despite Archidamus' reservations, the Spartans have apparently determined to fight sooner rather than later (1.87–88; 1.125). They have sent several last-minute demands to Athens (1.126; 1.139), but the Athenians have rejected these ultimatums in the wake of Pericles' first speech (1.140–46). War thus seems a certainty by the closing chapters of book I. Still, one might expect open and general hostilities to develop more directly out of the tense situations at Potidaea or around Corcyra and Epidamnus, situations on which the *History* has dwelt at some length. Thucydides has mentioned Plataea only once to this point, in a passing reference to the site of the decisive battle of the Persian Wars (1.130). The "actual warfare" of the great war thus begins with what seems a peripheral skirmish, one that apparently springs from longheld but rather local hatreds. As Connor suggests, that the Thebans strike in the middle of the night makes Plataea a "double surprise" for the reader.[4]

---

4. Connor, *Thucydides*, 53, writes: "A sudden night attack at a place to which little attention has been paid encourages the reader to react like a contemporary with surprise at the unexpected form taken by the outbreak of the war." Connor moves from this thought to a more general argument about the theme of unexpected complications that he finds throughout book 2. As becomes clear below, I want to move in a slightly different direction.

By way of beginning to think of the manner in which Plataea constitutes a moment of action for the Athenians, I want here more specifically to consider the sense in which events at Plataea might be said to "surprise" not only the reader but also Thucydides' Athenians and how their (re)action appears in this context of the unexpected.

Clearly, the Athenians do not foresee the Theban attack on their long-time ally. The simple fact that they do nothing until the arrival in Athens of a Plataean messenger bearing news of the attack suggests that much. The Plataeans only send that messenger after they have successfully stemmed the initial Theban assault. At this early moment, they already display that courage and ingenuity that will mark their later attempts at escape and their long defiance of the Peloponnesians. The Thebans enter the city unopposed through gates opened by the Plataean Naucleides and quickly frighten the stunned inhabitants to the point of surrender. As terms are negotiated, though, the Plataeans perceive "that the Thebans [are] not numerous," and determine to resist (2.3). Gathering together by digging tunnels from one house to the next, falling in behind improvised barricades in the streets, attacking from the house tops and barring the gates to prevent escape, they rout the attackers, taking a host of prisoners.

A combination of inclement weather, a rising river and a harsh rebuke from the secure Plataeans stalls the Theban reserve force outside the walls. The situation having been at least temporarily stabilized, the Plataeans send their messenger to the Athenians, whose threefold response follows immediately (2.6). First, the Athenians "instantly" apprehend all Thebans in Attica. Second, they send a herald (*keryka*) to Plataea, asking that the Theban prisoners not be harmed. Finally, they send food to Plataea and leave a garrison of Athenian hoplites there. All of these actions Thucydides describes without recording or mentioning any discussion or deliberation or disagreement among the Athenians. We should remain wary of concluding that the Athenians act without some sort of prior political interaction. But Thucydides does nothing to describe this interaction. As a result, and as in the early stages of the rebellion on Mitylene, the Athenians seem to react to developments at Plataea in a silent, sudden and unified mode of action. What can we say about this mode of action in this case?

First, the fact that the surprised Athenians do not engage in deliberation about what they have at stake in Plataea need not mean that they act recklessly or without good reason. If Thucydides records no moment of consideration involving speakers and demos, we can nonetheless easily point to "considerations" that might seem to account for their action, might seem to reveal it as sensible. Perhaps, for example, the Athenians' long alliance with the Plataeans simply dictates their course of action here. More generally, perhaps a shared understanding of the war—which, we have said, everyone expected—and of proper Athenian strategy guides the initial response. Along these lines, perhaps the powerful Pericles has prepared the Athenians for precisely this sort of situation. The speech in which he lays out his defensive strategy (1.140–45) does immediately precede the attack on Plataea.

But we face some familiar problems with all these possibilities. As we have seen in book 1 and will see again, for example, as the Athenians consider whether to sail to Sicily at the beginning of book 6, any treaty or alliance admits of multiple and varying interpretations.[5] And so surely the Athenians still face the basic question of whether or not their alliance with Plataea in any way requires them to act in this instance. Then, too, given the ongoing juxtaposition of silence and speech, we have found it difficult to speak in a conclusive or authoritative way of any shared understanding prevailing in Athens, guiding Athenian action. Though Thucydides directly mentions no division at this moment, surely we cannot entirely rule out the possibility that different Athenians have different understandings of the attack on Plataea, the coming of war, and the proper way to proceed.

As for Pericles, in his first speech he says nothing directly about how the Athenians should treat independent allies like the Plataeans. He generally admonishes his fellow citizens "against yielding to the Peloponnesians," but says this in the context of specific Spartan demands for the Athenians to renounce or reverse particular actions they have already taken (1.140). He argues that Athenian advantages in money and at sea outweigh the Spartan advantage in hoplite warfare, but, naturally, he does not speculate about how this might bear on the defense of a landlocked Boeotian ally (1.141–42). Finally, he declares that the Athenians should not attempt to expand their empire, but says little or nothing about whether or how or which existing allies they ought to protect (1.144). Indeed, he says that the Athenians should not lament over houses and land, but willingly abandon the Attic countryside; this would include the land between Athens and Boeotia (1.143). Surely such a strategy lessens the importance of defending

5. Thus the Corcyreans and Corinthians present different accounts of the 30 Years Truce to the Athenians in book 1. (See my discussion of their speeches in Chapter 2.) As the Athenians consider their planned expedition to Sicily at the opening of book 6, the Egestaians remind them "of the alliance formed with the Leontines in the time of Laches" (6.6). In the debate that follows, Nicias questions the importance of this alliance with "barbarians" (6.11), while Alcibiades claims that the Athenians have "an obligation to support" their "allies" in Sicily (6.18).

a border city like Plataea, a city that in other circumstances might serve as a protective outpost of sorts. Following this line of thinking, might not some Athenian argue that Pericles' strategy, rather than dictating an active defense of the Plataeans, suggests sacrificing them?

The point is that on Thucydides' telling, no one in Athens makes such an argument about Plataea, or any other argument, for that matter. The reader—and surely, too, other Greeks—can search for the reasons behind Athens's response to the Theban attack, but the Athenians themselves, so far as Thucydides tells us, do not. This has the effect of rendering the meaning of Athenian actions at once more transparent than if we had witnessed some sort of Athenian deliberation and, at the same time, rather more opaque. On the one hand, we do not find Athenian speakers offering to the silent demos multiple accounts of potential Athenian action, as we do, for example, in the Mitylene Debate. The Athenians, again, appear to react to developments at Plataea as one, with no dispute or dissension. Their actions, in this sense, seem simpler, more straightforward, easier to understand than does the sparing of the Mitylenians in the wake of the arguments of Cleon and Diodotus. No competing accounts of the situation and of what should be done about it ring in our ears; we do not experience so directly that disharmony of democracy that Thucydides' portrays elsewhere. Surely, in this sense, Athenian politics appears more decisive at this moment.

On the other hand, the absence of *any* debate, of *any* Athenian account of the situation, leaves us unable to say, beyond the barest descriptions of their actions, just what the Athenians have done here. Thus a moment ago we found it impossible to determine, because Thucydides gives us no indication, precisely what the Athenians' apparent support for Plataea means in the context of the war strategy advanced by Pericles (if it in fact has anything at all to do with that strategy). As a more particular example of this ambiguity of Athenian actions, consider the immediate dispatching of a herald to Plataea. By this means, Thucydides tells us, the Athenians send "instructions" to their allies "not to take drastic action concerning the Thebans they were holding until they [the Athenians] had made their own plans [*bouleusōsi*] about them" (2.6). Clearly, the Athenians do not dispatch the herald rashly or recklessly, but with some purpose. But we cannot from what Thucydides says fully know that purpose. More important, in the absence of any contending Athenian voices, the Athenians themselves seem not to have fully thought through what they are doing. On this score, we should note carefully that in the herald's message, the process of deliberation—marked again, by a form of *boleuō*[6]—remains in the future. The Athenians act quickly, decisively, and purposively here, but the full meaning of this particular action has not yet been debated, much less decided, in Athens itself. Its meaning surely must, then, remain rather mysterious to others—the reader, the Plataeans, the Thebans—as well.[7]

We saw a similar, rather paradoxical combination of clarity and opacity in the Athenians' execution of the Melians. Thus we found ourselves wondering at the end of the previous chapter about the meaning of that gruesomely simple act and its implications for Athens' approach to justice, particularly in light of the harsh arguments of the envoys who speak at Melos. After the initial Athenian reaction to events at Plataea, a number of important questions remain similarly unanswered for the Athenians, for the Greeks affected by their action and for we readers. Do the Athenians think that what they have done will prove sufficient? Or have they merely taken the first steps in their support for the Plataeans? Do they mean to supplement the initial hoplite force or to intervene in other ways to check the Thebans' aggression? What will happen if the Spartans become involved, as they surely will? Have the Athenians by their initial response committed to a defense of Plataea that will quite likely prove long and difficult? Why should they defend this seemingly unimportant ally? Will Athens defend other allies with similar vigor? Undoubtedly, the press of events and the shortness of time hinder any attempt fully to confront such issues in democratic Athens. In the heat of the moment, a certain single-minded response no doubt serves the Athenians' wish to do something, and to do it quickly—perhaps, in fact, serves better than a potentially lengthy debate before the assembled demos would have. As events in Boeotia unfold, though, we will want to think more carefully about the consequences of this sudden and silent mode of action and at the way in which it leaves Athenian actions rather indecipherable.

III. A BROKEN ATHENIAN PROMISE?

Before recording its ultimate fall, Thucydides twice returns to narrate events at Plataea. He describes the Spartan attack on the city in the summer of

---

6. This, again, being the Greek verb that Thucydides uses to introduce the Mitylene Debate as a moment of deliberation. See my discussion of this usage in Chapter 1.

7. In fact, just what the Athenians, having "taken counsel," would have done with the Theban prisoners remains forever unknown. The herald arrives only after the Plataeans have executed their prisoners—a deed that figures in the eventual trial and execution of the Plataeans themselves. See Section IV below.

the third year of the war (2.71–78) and the spectacular escape attempt made by the beleaguered Plataeans in the winter of the fourth year (3.20–24). Together, these two episodes provide a detailed and fascinating portrait of siege warfare in fifth-century Greece. In describing the beginnings of the siege, Thucydides dwells on the engineering work done by the Spartans. After encircling Plataea with walls, they begin to erect a massive mound from which to assail the city. Thucydides tells us about "the wood and stones and earth and anything else" heaped together to form this mound. He describes the round-the-clock work schedule employed by the Peloponnesians, notes that they cut the timber for supports for the mound on Mt. Cithaeron, and details the design of these "lattice-work" structures (2.75).

The Plataeans, as they counter the Peloponnesians' every move, garner even more of Thucydides' attention. Already constructing a counterwall to match the mound rising before them, the Plataeans think of "a new expedient," opening a hole in their own walls opposite the mound so that they might chip away at its base. This plan thwarted, they dig a mine under the mound so that it keeps "settling down into the hollow space." And so the valiant resistance goes on, until the Spartans, in the face of Plataean ingenuity and determination (2.76)—not to mention Plataean good fortune, as when a sudden thunderstorm douses Peloponnesian arson (2.77)—finally reconcile themselves to a lengthy siege.

Even after that siege has lasted more than a year and a half, the weary, hungry Plataeans find the energy to launch an intricately plotted escape. Thucydides again describes every detail. He carefully mentions the names of the soothsayer and the Plataean general who together suggest the plan (3.20.2). He relates at some length the method the Plataeans employ in calculating the right height for the ladders they will use to surmount the Peloponnesians' walls, several of them counting the number of bricks in those walls so that, "although some miscounted, most hit on the right number" (3.20.3). He notes that the Plataeans who are to scale the walls wear only one sandal, to keep from slipping in the winter mud while making as little noise as possible (3.22). He tells us the specific route followed by those who manage to escape: for "six or seven stades," they "stayed together along the road to Thebes, with the shrine of Androkrates on their right," thinking this the last direction the Peloponnesians would expect them to travel; they then "turned and took the road toward the mountains to Erythrai and Hysiai" (3.24).

All these details work to focus attention on the determination, the resiliency, and the calm intelligence of the Plataeans. Even the most callous reader cannot help but admire their resistance in the face of Spartan power or feel at least some regret over the end that many of them meet at the hands of their captors.[8] At the same time, the forthright actions of the Plataeans in defending their city overshadow the role played by the Athenians. Though that role consequently seems to become increasingly passive, it remains crucial. When Archidamus confronts them with the alternative between surrender and a Spartan attack, the Plataeans send to their powerful ally for advice. Thucydides puts the Athenian response in the mouths of the returning Plataean envoys: "Men of Plataea, the Athenians claim that never in the past, from the time that we became allies, have they allowed you to be wronged by anyone, nor will they allow it now, and they command you by the oaths your fathers swore to commit no act against the alliance" (2.73.3). The Plataeans, of course, do determine to reject surrender and to resist the Peloponnesian assault. Later, Thucydides describes the situation at Plataea just before the launching of the escape attempt: "the Plataeans, still besieged by the Peloponnesians and the Boetians, were suffering from insufficient provisions, and there was no hope of rescue by the Athenians nor was any other salvation in sight, they made plans with the Athenians besieged along with them . . . that they should all leave the city" (3.20.1). Against the bravery of the Plataeans, Athenian actions here seem passive and faint hearted at best, treacherous and cruel at worst. The Athenians not only make a promise of assistance that they fail to keep, but also order the poor Plataeans to continue what amounts to a hopeless fight on the basis of that promise.

What the Athenians do (or do not do) at these crucial moments in the matter of Plataea clearly raises two questions. First, why do the Athenians at the outset of the Spartan attack in the third summer of the war insist that the Plataeans fight and that they will help? Second, why do they fail to provide that help, or—more accurately, as we will see—why by the fourth year of the war do the Plataeans see no possibility of Athenian help? These questions have rarely received more than passing comment. On the first, Donald Kagan, who considers the issue more carefully than most, writes that "we may be sure that the Athenians gave no such answer while Pericles

---

8. Thinking of Thucydides' description both of this escape attempt and of the Plataeans' initial resistance to the Theban assault, Pouncey, *The Necessities of War*, 18, argues that "such passages show the power of *akribeia*," the "accuracy" that Thucydides claims for his work. "The density of the details," Pouncey continues, "slows the pace of the narrative down, so that the reader is literally arrested in his stride and must consider what is involved." In the case of Plataea, "our sympathy is enlisted for the small band trapped inside the walls by the armies and the politics of far greater forces."

was in control. The response must reflect the momentary ascendancy [in Athens] of the war party, taking advantage of Athenian emotions of loyalty to the little state that had sent help to the men of Marathon and anger at the sophistry and hypocrisy of the Spartans. The promise [of assistance] was honestly intended."[9] Setting aside for a moment Kagan's conjecture about the "war party" in Athens, two motives he ascribes to the Athenians at first thought seem entirely reasonable. The Athenians might well feel a sense of loyalty, even duty, to a city with whom they have been allied for nearly one hundred years. Their first actions on hearing of the initial Theban attack on Plataea can be read to suggest as much. The Athenians at that point reacted quickly, apparently without dissent, ready at a moment's notice to come to the aid of their threatened ally. The rounding up of Thebans in Attica, the sending of food and forces to Plataea, the dispatch of a message that, in its attempt to influence the handling of the Theban captives, envisions Athenian involvement in Plataea's defense, all of these surely can be seen as an expression of a sort of solidarity. Particularly against this backdrop, neither we nor the Plataeans should be surprised that the Athenians again move decisively to support their small ally. The Athenians act in the heat of the moment, but, despite their silence, we can from this point of view understand their action—both in manner and substance—as consistent with their earlier response to events at Plataea.

Then, too, the Spartans do, as Kagan suggests, take a provocative tone in "offering" the Plataeans a chance to surrender. Having forgone an invasion of Attica, the Spartans nonetheless clearly have Athens in mind when they arrive at Plataea. Before the invaders can begin to lay waste to the surrounding countryside, the Plataeans through envoys remind the Spartan King Archidamus of the promises made by another Spartan. In the wake of the decisive victory over the Persians at Plataea in 479, Pausanias had called the Greeks together and made them bear witness to the restoration of the independence of the Plataeans. As the Plataean envoys tell it, "no one would ever march against them unjustly, nor to enslave them" as, so they say, the Spartans do now (2.71). Archidamus replies that he and his army have come precisely to keep that promise, ready to liberate the Plataeans, who like so many of the Greeks "are now subject to the Athenians" (2.72). If they wish to save their city, their land, and themselves, the Plataeans can either join in this crusade of freedom or remain neutral; they must not cling to the Athenians. From the outset of their clash

---

9. Kagan, *The Archidamian War*, 105.

with Athens, the Spartans have declared this goal of liberating Greece. And more than once charges of aggression and oppression have been leveled against the Athenians. The anonymous envoys at Sparta in book I, after all, found themselves defending the Athenians' imperial practices against the charges of the Corinthians. The rehashing of these charges, coupled with the Spartan mangling—at least from the Athenian point of view—of the history of the Persian wars, might well prove explosive in Athens. The words of Archidamus could easily move the Athenians to a determined expression of support for a stand at Plataea, assuming those words were reported to the Athenians by the Plataean envoys sent to gather Athens's instructions.

This latter assumption, though seemingly minor, nonetheless points to a central difficulty with the sort of arguments Kagan makes and that I have been tracing just now. In fact, though we can speculate about the role of thoughts of loyalty or momentary and intense Athenian disgust with the Spartans' "sophistry," we can, ultimately, only speculate. Thucydides' account of these new developments at Plataea offers no indication of such motives or considerations; neither he nor any of his Athenians say that Athens was moved by a sense of duty or that they exploded in anger at the Spartans. Nor, for that matter, can we find direct support here for Kagan's broader claim about the role of the Athenian "war party." The text gives no indication of division, no hint of the clash of rival "parties" over how to respond to the Plataeans' questions. Thucydides records no arguments addressed to the Athenian demos by rival speakers. Indeed, he now moves us farther away from the assembly. Instead of recording Athenian actions directly, he here offers the report of a Plataean herald returning from Athens. That Thucydides thus has us view Athenian action from a greater distance only heightens the sense of Athenian single-mindedness, of a sort of action that is unified and nondeliberative. As a result, and perhaps even more than in the initial stages of the affair of Plataea, the meaning of these new and apparently transparent Athenian actions remains irreducibly uncertain. The Athenians move quickly to order matters in southern Boeotia according to their wishes, without any careful consideration of those wishes or their implications.

The residual uncertainty about the Athenians' precise intentions that results from this silence in the Athenian assembly leaves the reader wondering, but presents a more serious problem for the Plataeans, who must act. As the herald reports it, the Athenian promise seems firm and sincere. But important questions remain. For one thing, the Athenian message promises help but gives absolutely no details about what such help will involve. What do the Athenians mean when they say they "will assist you with all their might?" Will more Athenian hoplites soon arrive in Plataea? Will the Athenians launch some grand naval expedition to divert the Peloponnesians' attention from Boeotia? Or do the Athenians perhaps intend to provide chiefly moral support, or to use their political "might" in Greece to influence the actions of others, instead of involving their own forces directly? And in any event, how durable will Athens's commitment to Plataea prove to be? If the battle with the Spartans turns into a long siege (as it does), will the Athenians continue to defend Plataea? Just how long can they be expected to expend effort and resources on a small ally? Might not some suspicious Plataean argue that the Athenian promise sounds too good to be true, that the Athenians haven't really thought through what they are saying, that when push comes to shove they may not be around?

Thucydides reports no Plataean consideration of such questions. The Plataeans thus seem not to have asked them directly or, perhaps, to have answered them only indirectly. They have little choice but to decide one way or another about the Spartan ultimatum. And they need to decide quickly, for Archidamus and his army are at the gates. In this context, the Plataeans must make what they can of the situation, try to glean from the herald's words as much as possible about Athens' intentions and what the Athenians may do in the future, and either surrender or fight. They choose the latter, seemingly taking seriously the Athenians' promise of support, however vague. Let us, then, ask ourselves why the Athenians do not keep that promise. Thucydides never reports Athenian deliberation or an Athenian decision on the matter. Nowhere does he point to a moment when any Athenian or "the Athenians" as one say that Athens will not or should not come to Plataea's aid. In the passage already cited, he says simply that the Plataeans "began to be distressed" by lack of food "and since there was no hope of aid from Athens nor any other means in sight," they determined to attempt an escape (3.20).

Now Kagan says that "the promise of aid was honestly intended, but it could not be kept."[10] This implies—and I think Kagan means it to imply—that the Athenian promise eventually came hard up against some sort of reality. Given the unfolding of the war, the Athenians really had no decision to make; they simply "could not" aid the Plataeans. From our distant historical perspective, we can identify a number of more or less objective

---

10. Ibid.

factors that would indeed seem to make the promise difficult if not impossible for Athens to fulfill. Most generally, to raise the siege at Plataea would mean engaging directly with Spartan forces in, as Kagan says, a "great battle of hoplite armies." Such a battle would violate the basic precepts of early Athenian or at any rate Periclean strategy and would in any event play to Spartan strength and likely prove quite costly. More specifically, at the crucial moment when the Plataeans determine to go it alone, the Athenians have other problems (namely Mitylene) on their hands. Prosecuting the siege on Lesbos stretches Athens' resources to the limit. In the paragraph immediately preceding his account of the Plataean escape attempt, Thucydides notes that the Athenians now for the first time "taxed themselves" and sent Lysicles to collect additional money from the allies (3.19). The Athenians, perhaps, simply "could not" afford the expenses associated with saving the Plataeans.

But Thucydides' understanding of the "broken" promise does not, I think, reduce to an explanation based on these material factors. He places the assertion that "there was no hope of aid from Athens" in the context of the Plataeans' understanding of their dire situation. Thus the fact that the Plataeans' food supply started to run out matters because they "began to be distressed" by shortages. When Thucydides says there were no "other means of safety in sight," he surely means us to understand that the Plataeans saw this to be the case and acted accordingly. And so it would seem that the importance of there being no hope of Athenian action lies precisely in the Plataeans' basing their own plans on their perception of this fact, on their reading of the silence of the Athenians. Indeed, in some sense we never know whether it is a fact or not—precisely because the Athenians never decide one way or another, never say that they will not come to the rescue, never directly indicate that there is no hope. Instead, we see the Plataeans making a fateful decision to act on their own in the face of what they apparently take to be clear indications that the Athenians have left them all alone. They undoubtedly base this decision in part on their understanding of the material factors just discussed. They, too, have seen Athens eschew sustained land warfare with Spartan armies, and they too "know" that the Athenians have found themselves in rather dire financial straits.

Beyond that, I would suggest, the Plataeans might well have concluded that the Athenians' concerns simply have turned elsewhere. In Chapter 2, I traced the development of the revolt on Mitylene and the Athenians' reaction to it. The escape of the Plataeans, I argued, marked a sort of interlude in this part of Thucydides' narrative, something of a sideshow providing a break in the main action, which at this point was taking place on Lesbos. The Athenians have devoted a good portion of their military and financial resources to Mitylene; not only that, but it seems possible and reasonable to think that, like the reader, they have begun to devote an increasing share of their attention to Mitylene as well. The Plataeans' lack of hope of help from Athens may thus follow from their reading of Athens' mode of acting. They perhaps see in the Athenians an inability to redirect their focus, even momentarily, to a small, insignificant, beleaguered ally. Now clearly the Plataeans may be wrong about all of this. Perhaps, if only they would call out for help, the Athenians, despite being in dire financial straits, despite an apparent reluctance to engage the Spartans on land, might come to their aid. Perhaps the Plataeans have, in a sense, misread Athens' single-mindedness, taken single-mindedness of purpose in one area for a single-minded inability to see other problems. Perhaps they should continue with the siege instead of allowing an escape attempt to weaken their defenses. Since they do determine on such an attempt, we do not know how Athens would have reacted to one last, desperate Plataean plea.

In this way, the question of the Athenians' responsibility for the fate of Plataea—and, more basically, any attempt to understand what the Athenians do here, what role Athenian actions play in the fall of Plataea—becomes considerably more complex than we might at first think. We cannot simply say that the Athenians desert the Plataeans, for in a sense they never do. Rather, the Plataeans decide to act on the assumption that Athens will not keep its promise to protect them, just as they had before apparently acted on the assumption that the promise was genuine. Though we can certainly argue about the soundness of their judgment, we can hardly fault the Plataeans for determining to act. From their perspective and in the face of the Spartan siege, Athens must have become something of a distant cipher. The Athenians seem to have acted decisively to indicate their support for Plataea, but they have never themselves thought through, much less made clear to the Plataeans, the reasons for that support or its implications or its depth. Indeed, we might say that the Plataeans, in trying to understand the meaning of Athens' words and deeds, have even less to go on than the Spartans in book 1 or the Melians in book 5. The latter can at least ponder the arguments of the anonymous envoys, who after all remain Athenians, whatever their relation to "Athens" might be. The Plataeans have only the barest "instructions" from their allies; and now the otherwise silent Athenians appear to have directed their attention elsewhere. The Plataeans altogether reasonably gamble that they have a better chance of survival if they go it alone than if they wait for the Athenians to act, even though the Athenians could conceivably act to help them at any time. Such are the dilemmas of dealing with a silent, unified Athens.

IV. ATHENS AND THE TRIAL OF THE PLATAEANS

Only in the narrowest sense can we say that Athens takes no part in the ultimate trial of the Plataeans. Certainly, Spartans serve as the judges, and only the Thebans and Plataeans speak. No Athenian herald or envoy delivers an official Athenian protest; we hear no expressions of outrage or regret from speakers in the Athenian assembly. But there are Athenians present at the trial; Thucydides says that about twenty-five members of the garrison sent from Athens after the initial Theban attack share the fate of the surrendered Plataeans (3.68.5). And, perhaps more important, both the Thebans and the Plataeans make "Athens" present through the arguments they make to the Spartan judges. Their exchange to some extent amounts to a debate over the Athenian role in Boeotian affairs past and present. Here I want to consider three central and interrelated issues that emerge in the course of the two speeches Thucydides here records: Why did Plataea ally itself with Athens in the first place? What manner of alliance followed? And how did the Plataeans come to their current desperate situation? Taken together, the contrasting answers offered to these questions highlight the ambiguous status of the Plataeans as "independent allies" of Athens and encapsulate the tensions inherent in the Athenians' place in the Plataean affair.

The Plataeans speak first, having begged permission to offer more than an answer of "yes" or "no" to the question, "Have you done anything for Sparta lately?" They move quickly to a major theme of their defense, Plataea's part in "past events of the highest importance" (3.55). As "the only Boeotians to join the attack for Hellenic freedom" during the Persian Wars, they say, "we stood by" the Spartans (3.54). Sparta should bear the blame for the enmity that later arose between the two cities, for it pushed Plataea away, into Athenian arms: "when we asked for an alliance at the time the Thebans were pressing us hard, you sent us away and told us to turn to the Athenians because they were nearby, whereas you lived far away" (3.55). The Plataeans in this way raise and address the central issue of the roots of their relationship with the Athenians: they became Athens' ally only after distinguishing themselves independently in the Persian Wars and then only out of necessity, fearful of their powerful neighbors, rejected by the other great power in Greece. All of this they mean not only to exonerate themselves but also to disparage the Thebans' willing submission to the Persians.

The Thebans naturally dispute such a characterization, offering their own account of their "Medism," and, more to the point here, of Plataea's "Atticism."[11] While a small faction seized control and handed an unwilling Thebes over to the Persians, the Plataeans stood against the Persians only because Athens did. The Plataeans cannot "expect to benefit from your good behavior when this was at the behest of others" (3.64). Then, too, their claim that they allied with Athens only from necessity and only in the aftermath of the war stands refuted: "you *chose* the Athenians," the Thebans say, "share the risks with them" (3.64; emphasis added).

These different accounts of the beginnings of the Athenian–Plataean alliance suggest, in turn, the different ways in which the Plataeans and Thebans depict the nature of that alliance in the years preceding the current war. The dispute here centers on the presence of an Athenian hand in Plataean actions. For the Thebans, Plataean and Athenian actions remain strictly separable, linked only by the choices made by the smaller city. Just as the Plataeans freely sought to ally themselves with Athens, so they have freely and openly continued to do Athens's bidding. If the Plataeans truly acted only out of the compulsions of necessity, out of fear of the Thebans, then they should only have sought Athens' help. Instead they have "assisted in the enslavement" of other Greeks (3.64). The Plataeans willingly "went along with the Athenians when they took the unjust road," so they must bear the burden of their complicity.

All of this comes in response to the Plataean claim that the same sorts of necessities that forced them into Athenian arms dictated their subsequent actions. Indeed, they say, beyond a concern for their own safety, a basic sense of honor kept them following Athens' lead. The Athenians protected them, brought them into the alliance, and even gave them "a share of their citizenship"; turning away from Athens would mark the Plataeans not only as fools but as ingrates as well. "It was," they claim, "right to follow their orders readily" (3.65). These reasons account for the Plataeans' "decision" to continue to do the Athenians' bidding, a constrained decision for which no one should blame them: "And wherever

---

11. Cogan, *Human Thing*, again, argues that this charge of "Atticism" marks a step in the ideologization of the war. See my discussion of this argument in Section I of this chapter.

the leadership on either side takes its allies, the followers are not to blame if some wrong was done, but those who direct them on an improper course" (3.65). "Following" here does not reflect a free and open choice. Whatever the apparent role of the Plataeans, the actions the Thebans will point to as evidence of aggression always remain more Athenian than Plataean.

These contrasting accounts of alliance with Athens as on the one hand a continuing free choice, and on the other hand a surrendering of independence, suggest, finally, two quite disparate understandings of the situation at hand. Having called on their glorious deeds in the Persian Wars, the Plataeans might well argue that their similarly brave and determined resistance during the just ended siege entitles them to renewed respect. Such an appeal might justify some sort of Spartan mercy. But the Plataeans instead set out to contrast their bold actions then with their utter inability to act independently now: "We Plataeans, ardent for Hellas beyond our power, have been thrust aside by all, deserted and unprotected; none of our former allies will help, and Lacedaemonians, we fear that you, our only hope, may not be relied on" (3.57). A small, helpless city, Plataea can only transfer its hopes from one great power to another; it must ultimately bear the dictates of whichever city looms before it. By now we can easily foresee the gist of the Theban retort. The Plataeans willingly followed Athens, willingly resisted, willingly fought the Peloponnesian allies. And so: "Their isolation now is also of their own making; for by their own choice they rejected the better allies" (3.67). Independent Greek cities must be held accountable for their actions and their choices; whatever they say, the Plataeans have always remained independent from Athens.

We can take these summary comments as indications of two very different but defensible ways of interpreting recent events at Plataea and, more particularly, Athens' role in those events. To put the point differently, we can find in Athens' actions in Boeotia support for both the Plataean and Theban perspectives. Thus, from one angle, the Plataeans indeed appear as subordinates dutifully following the wishes of the Athenians. We have seen how, as soon as they stem the initial Theban assault, they immediately dispatch a message to the Athenians, and how the latter, as the superior ally should, dispatch a herald with "instructions" for their subordinates (2.6). We have seen, too, that the Plataeans, when considering Archidamus' conditions for surrender, seek Athenian "permission" or "consent." Again the Athenians reply in kind, promising aid and "commanding" or "adjuring" the Plataeans to fight on (2.73). Finally, as I have suggested in the previous section, we can read the Plataeans' decision to attempt escape as that of dutiful allies who—reluctantly, only as a last resort—determine that their benefactor has deserted them, that they must finally take matters into their own ill-suited hands. Throughout, the alliance between Athens and Plataea appears from this point of view as the Plataeans describe it to the Spartans, as one of command and obedience, so long as the commanding city's attention holds.

From the Theban point of view, on the other hand, we can see the Plataeans making their own decisions at every turn, decisions that belie their claims of innocent submission to Athens. Indeed, the Thebans can point to a sequence of early Plataean actions apparently taken independently of the Athenians. The Plataeans, the Thebans point out, responded to the initial Theban appearance by "gladly coming up and making an agreement" (3.66) but later "attacked in violation of [that] agreement" and "lawlessly slaughtered" their victims (3.66). All of this took place, of course, before the arrival of the herald bearing Athens' "instructions." The Plataeans certainly seem to have acted independently of the Athenians. Indeed, by killing the captured Thebans, they acted in a way that proved contradictory to Athenian wishes. Surely we should not consider them hapless extensions of Athens itself. As for the Plataeans' later sending to Athens for permission to surrender, this, too, marks another "choosing" of Athens. If the pitiful Plataeans depend so on the whims of greater cities, would we not expect them to agree to Archidamus' terms, to turn themselves over to the power that immediately confronts them? In this sense, precisely by sending to Athens for permission, the Plataeans show their stubborn, determined independence even in the presence of overwhelming Spartan power. And soon enough, they show their independence from Athenian control even more directly by taking matters into their own hands, attempting a foolhardy escape when they might yet have surrendered peacefully. In all of this, Plataean actions remain central, Athenian wishes peripheral and largely impotent. The Plataeans act not as vassals of Athens or any other city, but as Greeks making their own decisions, fighting their own fights, taking help where they can get it, and striking out on their own when they think they must.

The contrast between these two perspectives on the relative roles of Plataean and Athenian actions in events in southern Boeotia brings us back to some familiar difficulties. We find in the debate two accounts describing and assigning responsibility for what has already happened at Plataea and what will soon happen to the remaining Plataeans. Put simply, if the Plataeans read matters correctly and Athenian actions dominate their own, then the fault for their fate falls largely at Athens' feet. If, on the other hand, the truth of the matter is somehow closer to the Theban perspective, then the Athenians can enjoy a certain exoneration; the Plataeans have brought about their own ruin. We should not overlook a certain irony here: the Athenians' long-time allies find themselves playing the part of Athens' sternest critic. In trying to save themselves, the Plataeans in effect charge the Athenians—as the Peloponnesian allies have been doing since before the war—with robbing fellow Greeks of their independence. While the standard argument of the Peloponnesian allies has them fighting a war of liberation against the tyrant Athens, the Thebans now claim that the Plataeans have always been free to do as they please, free to choose Sparta over Athens, freer than the Thebans themselves were in "meddling." By the end of the Plataean affair, the Athenians' erstwhile enemies have, in this sense, become their momentary defenders, their ardent allies their sternest critics.[12]

V. CONCLUSION

That the Spartan judges decide to adhere to their original plan, putting the bare question of expediency to the Plataeans, that no Plataean answers that question to suit the judges, that all the Plataean captives meet death or slavery at the hands of the Peloponnesians, none of this fully or unproblematically affirms the perspective of either the Thebans or the Plataeans. Mingled with an undeniable admiration for the determined Plataeans and a corresponding disgust with the Athenians must be the disturbing possibility that the Thebans are to some extent right. Might not the Plataeans have placed less hope in Athens, breaking with their inattentive ally earlier in order to save themselves? Ultimately, as so often in Thucydides, we can find no comfortable, certain answer to such a question. We find no definitive account of the role of Athenian action in the affair of Plataea; an irreducible uncertainty remains.

Such uncertainty follows first, of course, from the way in which silence undermines any authoritative understanding of political speech and political action—something I have traced in various contexts in previous chapters. But in the case of Plataea we can also, I think, say that the Athenians

---

12. Thus adding a certain ironic twist to the Corinthians' claim in their speech at Sparta that "friends critique, enemies accuse." I discuss this passage at some length in Chapter 2.

contribute to, or open or widen the space for, such uncertainty. After their initial (deceptively) straightforward actions, the Athenians move increasingly into the background. The absence on their part of any consideration or clarification of their own actions, their willingness to do without deliberation, becomes more pronounced. Accordingly, the space for the Plataeans to draw their own conclusions about Athens—and the necessity of their doing so—grows. We said earlier that the collective silence of all Athenians leaves the Plataeans to make guesses about what Athens will do and to gamble on the basis of such guesses.[13] Now we might say that by failing to consider the meaning and implications of their actions, the Athenians do more than place such a practical burden on other cities. They also, in the end, lose—or better, forfeit—whatever control they might have exercised over what their action or inaction will mean in the broader context of Greek affairs. The war goes on, politics go on, and the Thebans and Plataeans step into the breach with their own accounts of "Athens."

Against this backdrop of a growing and rather ominous silence in the Athenian assembly, let me return to the possibility, which I discussed at the outset of this chapter, of our detecting some sort of progression in Athenian politics over the series Mitylene—Plataea—Melos. As at Mitylene and Melos, the Athenians in the affair of Plataea find themselves drawn into the world of Greek affairs and thus into a swirl of questions surrounding "foreign policy"—the treatment of allies and other weaker powers, the importance of justice, the demands of expediency, and the like. The ultimate ambiguity of the Athenian role, though, renders problematic any attempt to take Plataea as a sort of turning point in the Athenian way of responding to such issues. Consider, for example, the progression of punishments that I mentioned above. One might argue that the comparatively passive Athenian role in the slaughter of the Plataeans prepares the way for the more direct Athenian role in the slaughter of the Melians, marking a mediating stage in the sorts of punishments the Athenians will countenance. This, though, involves a particular reading of Athens's role, a reading in which the blood of the Plataeans, as it were, permanently stains the hands of the Athenians. As we have seen, Thucydides' account leaves at least some residual doubt about the guilt of the Athenians. The same sort of uncertainty must undermine any account of Plataea as a moment of

---

13. Here we might recall Aristotle's aside, discussed in Chapter 2, that those who engage in political rhetoric may make "guesses about the future." Surely had the Athenians said more about their actions in the affair of Plataea, any such guesses as the Plataeans and others make might have been less blind.

change in Athenian attitudes toward justice. Beyond the fact that we hear no Athenian arguments about the right course of action for Athens to take, the justice and injustice of Athens' role in Plataea—and of the fate of the Plataeans more generally—remains a subject of dispute. Consequently, we once more are unable to settle on any single account of Mitylene, Plataea, and Melos as links in a chain of development or as stages in some decline in the substance of Athenian attitudes or actions—in what the Athenians say and do about justice and other issues of "foreign policy."

Still, even taken as more or less discrete instances of Athenian action, these three episodes do prompt us to think about the differing ways in which the Athenians, through their brand of democratic politics, respond to the challenges created by acting in the Greek world. More particularly, we can address more completely Thucydides' juxtaposition of the two modes of action in which the Athenians engage, a juxtaposition that, as it appeared in the contrast between Mitylene and Melos, left us puzzled at the end of the previous chapter. We now have a clearer idea about what happens when the Athenians do not engage in deliberation of any sort, when we do not hear even the contending voices of elites trying to persuade the always silent Athenian demos. In the cases of both Plataea and Melos, the Athenians' silent, sudden mode of action results in a ceding of control over the meanings and implications of their actions. As we have just seen, the silence that emanates from the Athenian assembly on the matter of Plataea makes it both possible and necessary for other Greeks to create and act on their own understandings of Athenian action. Similarly, the Athenians' execution and enslavement of the Melians, brutally simple though it seems, leaves a host of questions unasked; as I suggested at the close of the last chapter, we can hardly help but wonder how things might have been had the Athenians paused to think matters through, as they did at Mitylene. As it stands, they in a sense give up the opportunity to try to say what they are doing. The reader, other Greeks, and indeed the Athenians themselves must remain uncertain as to just what Athens has done.

In Chapter 2, I tried to suggest some ways in which we might understand the sudden mode of Athenian action in the *History*. Drawing on Arendt, I thus suggested that the Athenians undergo a collective version of the "fundamental experience of instrumentality," and that they often fail to become aware of the consequences of their actions. It seems clear that at Melos and Plataea, the Athenians indeed remain unaware of what they are doing (or not doing). Here, though, I want to focus on the analogy

I explored in Chapter 2 with Aristotle's "actions taken on the spur of the moment." Such actions, Aristotle contends, "we describe as voluntary, but not as chosen" (*Ethics*, III.ii.2/1111b). Insofar as the Athenians cede control over the meaning of their deeds by not engaging in deliberation, we might indeed say that they do not fully choose their actions. They do not, that is, decide to engage in an action that they understand in a particular way. As they act (or fail to act) in the affairs of Melos and Plataea, they leave it to others—other Greeks, readers of the *History*—to determine just what they are doing. But such spur-of-the-moment actions, though not fully chosen, are, Aristotle says, still voluntary. Nothing forces the Athenians to slaughter the Melians or not to intervene in the defeat and trial of the Plataeans.

This juxtaposition with Aristotle can help us sort out the sense in which we can blame the Athenians for silent, sudden actions. Let me here borrow T. H. Irwin's interpretation of Aristotle on responsibility. Aristotle restricts responsibility, Irwin argues, to those cases where the act is voluntary and the actor is "capable of deciding effectively."[14] The Athenians voluntarily act with regard to both Melos and Plataea. And we know that they are capable of deciding effectively. We have seen them—in, for example, the case of Mitylene—deliberate on what to do. In the cases of Plataea and Melos, though, they fail to exercise this capacity to choose. As we have seen, the precise meaning of Athenian action in these episodes remains open to interpretation; as a result, we have difficulty saying exactly what role the Athenians play and in what sense they are at fault. Perhaps we can, though, say that because they do not pursue a fuller awareness of their actions, because they do not deliberate, *hoi Athenaioi* forfeit an opportunity to shape the course of events, to try to control their impact on Greek affairs more fully.

Not that Thucydides presents the sort of deliberation he records as a panacea. We saw in Chapters 3 and 4 that no amount of speech giving in the Athenian assembly produces either full awareness of or firm control over Athenian action and its meaning. And we saw that while we can try to speak of and parcel out responsibility among Athenians in the wake of deliberative action, such efforts prove inconclusive. What separates Mitylene from Melos and Plataea is not some sort of certainty about Athenian action, but rather the attempt made by the Athenians to peer into what Diodotus calls "the dim and distant future" in order to, in Pericles words, "learn enough" prior to acting. We cannot say that, had the Athenians only

---

14. Irwin, "Reason and Responsibility in Aristotle," 132.

paused to deliberate, the Melians or the Plataeans would have been spared. And had they paused to deliberate, there would no doubt still be room for argument about just what the Athenians chose to do and why and how it mattered. What we do know is that, though they might have, the Athenians do not stop to think, and the Melians die; and that, though they might have, they do not stop to think, and the Plataeans die. Thucydides, as always, shows us what has happened and points us toward the necessity of thinking for ourselves.

Conclusion:
Thucydides for Democrats?

Thucydides' description of his work as a "possession for all time" and his assertion that the future will in some sense resemble the past (1.22) have long tempted readers to find more or less direct parallels between the *History* and their own time. In these concluding pages, I succumb to this temptation, briefly considering what the reading of the *History* I have offered here might have to tell us about American democratic politics in the first years of the twenty-first century. I do so with the caveat that finding contemporary relevance in the *History* is not so straightforward as it may first appear. The complexity of the *History* in fact allows for the exploration of historical parallels on various levels: comparisons of leading figures in the *History* with contemporary political actors; analyses of particular contemporary events in the context of purportedly similar happenings in Thucydides; warnings about the broad course of affairs as analogous to one or another narrative arc found in the *History*. What is more, the interpretive openness of the *History* invites the possibility that different readers may use the same passages to draw very different lessons.

Along these lines, consider two widely disparate understandings of the way in which Thucydides' account of the Athenian expedition to Sicily resonates with the American experience in Iraq. Observing the run-up to the Iraq invasion in October 2002, Lewis Lapham found rereading the clash between Nicias and Alcibiades to be like "reading the front page of that morning's *New York Times*." Lapham drew a particular parallel between Nicias and "several senior Republican statesman," including the former National Security Adviser Brent Scrowcroft, who tried in their way to warn the Bush administration of the dangers of the impending war. "They employed a modern vocabulary," Lapham wrote, "but the substance of their advice they could have borrowed from the speech that Thucydides assigns to Nicias." For opponents of the Iraq War, the broader lesson to be drawn from Athens' misadventures in Sicily concerns the disastrous consequences of diversionary and hubristic overreaching by a great power.[1]

Now consider, by way of contrast, the comparison drawn between Iraq and Sicily by the classicist Victor David Hanson, a staunch supporter of the war and of the Bush administration's foreign policy more generally. Hanson sees in Iraq not the failure of democracy to heed its tragic warners, but the failure of democracy to persevere in the face of adversity. He in fact rejects the basic juxtaposition of Iraq and Sicily, noting that Syracuse, Athens' main adversary on the island, "was democratic, larger than Athens and theretofore mostly neutral during the Peloponnesian War." And so "a more historically apt analogy" to the expedition to Sicily "would be if the United States had attacked India in the midst of its war against al-Qaeda." In 2005 the real lesson of Sicily for the United States was that "the great gamble might have worked had those back home put aside their squabbling and supported the expedition fully."[2]

In part, these diverging readings reflect the complexity of Thucydides' account of the Athenian decision to invade Sicily and the consequences of that decision. As we saw at the end of Chapter 4, that account seems to highlight both the folly of the initial decision and the fecklessness of the Athenians once the fleet sailed. Whether one emphasizes folly or fecklessness, though, also reflects a broader sense of the general message of the *History*. Does Thucydides counsel a hardheaded realism that advocates the persistent pursuit of the city's interest, even in the face of setbacks? Or does he offer a tragic realist warning of the dangers of, in Ned Lebow's words, "running red lights and ruling the world?"[3] Behind the very different answers given to these questions by those who would draw on Thucydides in supporting or opposing the Bush administration's war in Iraq looms a shared concern with the question of leadership. In their own ways, both Lapham and Hanson seem to long for Periclean leadership, either to restrain democracy's aggressive impulses or to hold the demos steady so that we might, in a now-abandoned presidential phrase, "stay the course."[4]

---

1. See J. Peter Euben, "Thucydides in the Desert." I have here drawn on Euben's excellent discussion of the uses of Thucydides in the debate about Iraq, particularly by Victor David Hanson.
2. Hanson, "Old Is New Warfare." See also Hanson, "Do We Have Enough Troops in Iraq?"
3. Lebow, *The Tragic Vision of Politics*.
4. On similar lines, see Kagan's reference to Pericles' claim of personal constancy amidst the Athenians' faltering support for his strategy. Kagan suggests that, like Pericles, he has held firm while many, many others have wavered in the face of adversity. Kagan, "On Iraq, Short Memories."

CONCLUSION: THUCYDIDES FOR DEMOCRATS? 183

Any attempt to grapple with the relevance of Thucydides to our contemporary situation perhaps inevitably leads in this way toward the relationship of leaders and people or advisers and demos. My aim in closing, as it has been throughout this book, is to consider what Thucydides has to tell us about democracy at war beyond a call for stabilizing or restraining leadership. Before I risk lurching further toward a juxtaposition of Pericles and George W. Bush, though, let me quickly review two other attempts to understand how American democracy has played out in the matter of Iraq and the "war on terror."

In the opening chapter of *Why Deliberative Democracy?* Amy Gutmann and Dennis Thompson measure the 2002–3 debate about the Iraq War against the standards of deliberative democracy. They conclude, not surprisingly, that "the debate did not represent the kind of discussion deliberative democrats hope for."[5] Perhaps more surprising is Gutmann and Thompson's suggestion that the war rhetoric of the Bush administration did in some ways approach their basic standards. Deliberative democracy, they write, holds first and foremost to a "reason-giving requirement," and at a fundamental level Bush "and his advisors recognized the need to justify the decision" to invade Iraq. Deliberative democracy further requires that the reasons given should be publicly "accessible," and so must be neither held privately in the decision maker's mind nor incomprehensible to ordinary citizens. Along these lines, Bush administration officials, again, made public appeals for their position; Bush "did not rest his argument on any special instructions from his heavenly ally"; and references to secret intelligence, while troubling, were not particularly egregious in the context of the modern state.[6] Then, too, the debate produced a "binding decision," something at which deliberation aims: "Once [Bush] decided, deliberation about the question of whether to go to war ceased."[7]

Gutmann and Thompson hardly mean to offer the Iraq War debate as a model of deliberative democracy. Indeed, they aim most simply to show that the principles of deliberative democracy appear "even in a less than friendly environment." And the most admirable aspect of the Iraq debate for Gutmann and Thompson is that, as deliberative democracy demands, it has proven "dynamic." While the decision to go to war was binding for a time, debate soon resumed about both the continued course of the war and the claims originally made to justify it. In this sense, the mere fact

5. Gutmann and Thompson, *Why Deliberative Democracy?* 2.
6. Ibid., 4.
7. Ibid., 6.

that the Bush administration felt it necessary to state its reasons publicly made possible the criticisms that followed: "The imperfect deliberation that preceded the war prepared the ground for the less imperfect deliberation that followed."[8]

The theory of deliberative democracy thus offers us resources and standards for evaluating public discourse. As the arguments of the preceding chapters would suggest, my main concern with the sort of analysis Gutmann and Thompson offer in their brief discussion of the Iraq War debate is its almost exclusive focus on the rhetoric of elites. As we judge the deliberative worth of elite rhetoric on both sides of the war, what becomes of the role of the mass of ordinary citizens? Gutmann and Thompson themselves acknowledge this concern with deliberative democracy understood as a way of thinking about representative government. Here "citizens become mere spectators; they participate in the deliberation only vicariously."[9] Ought we to understand the role of ordinary citizens during the Iraq War and, more broadly, the "war on terror" to be that of spectators silently observing elite debate?

Noam Chomsky recently suggested just this sort of approach. Chomsky reminds us of the dreary vision of "spectator democracy" conjured up by Walter Lippman in the first half of the twentieth century.[10] In *The Phantom Public*, Lippman offered the following (in)famous description of the silent ordinary citizen of mass democracy:

> The private citizen has come to feel rather like a deaf spectator in the back row, who ought to keep his mind on the mystery off there, but cannot quite manage to stay awake. He knows he is somehow affected by what is going on. Rules and regulations continually, taxes annually, and wars occasionally remind him that he is being swept along by great drifts of circumstance.... As a private person, he does not know for certain what is going on, or who is doing it, or where he is being carried. He lives in a world in which he cannot see, does not understand, and is unable to direct."[11]

For Lippman, this assessment of the ordinary citizen as a passive and detached spectator points toward the necessity of an elite corps of policy

8. Ibid., 2.
9. Ibid., 30.
10. Chomsky, *Media Control*.
11. Lippman, *The Phantom Public*, 3.

experts advising political leaders, who in turn manipulate potent political symbols as they compete with one another for the support or at least acquiescence of the public. The political role of the ordinary citizen, by contrast, consists chiefly in watching and, from time to time, choosing among a limited set of contending elites. Chomsky's purpose in recalling Lippman is to expose the continued role of this view of "spectator democracy" in justifying the use of propaganda to "engineer consent" by misleading ordinary citizens about all sorts of government adventures and misadventures up to and including the "war on terror." Lippman's vision and Chomsky's critique remind us of the more worrisome potential ramifications when silence prevails among the demos in mass democracy. Beyond the basic injustice of denying an equal political voice to many, the silence of ordinary citizens can enable the domineering machinations of political elites, even if those machinations might be cast as entailing elite "deliberation." Mass democracy, then, remains democratic in name alone, with disastrous results.

Thucydides, on my reading, points to an alternative to thinking about mass democratic politics as a matter of finding proper leaders or as a manipulative spectacle of elite deliberation carried out before a silent and passive audience. In the Introduction, I suggested that Thucydides' account of the Periclean transformation of Athenian politics showed some affinity with contemporary theories that see democracy as a disruption in any attempt to impose form on politics. I focused in particular on Sheldon Wolin's account of "fugitive democracy" as the revolutionary, if rare, "activation" of the demos. I also made reference to Jacques Rancière's understanding of the demos as possessing, albeit only rarely deploying, "the power of the Two of division," which interrupts the unity of the One or of the mob. What I have called moments of deliberative action similarly suggest the potentially disruptive nature of democracy, destabilizing both Athenian political identity generally and, in particular, claims to special position or influence made by would-be Athenian political elites. If, as I argued in Chapter 2, we take Thucydides' decision to record speeches for only a handful of Athenian assemblies as carrying substantive theoretical import, then we see that moments of truly destabilizing politics are indeed, as Wolin and Rancière suggest, few and far between. The debates over the fate of Mitylene and over the Athenian expedition to Sicily stand out as moments in which the disruptive nature of democracy bursts forth from the narrative of events, reminding us of the power of the demos and the inherent openness of action and identity in democracy. On this way of thinking, the task of the democratic theorist is not to argue over the merits of particular modes of leadership or to evaluate the rhetoric of elites against standards of deliberation or even to diagnose the dangers of spectator democracy. The task, which will be particularly crucial in times of war, is to search for signs of the revolutionary, if momentary, activation of the demos.

If Thucydides' account dovetails with the arguments of Wolin and Rancière, it suggests a somewhat paradoxical twist on those readings: the periodic destabilization that democracy brings in the *History*, again, appears as a consequence not of the vocal, active intervention of the demos, but rather of the very silence of its presence. This, in turn, suggests a different perspective on Pericles' imposition of *tou tropou andros arche*, the transformation of Athenian politics with which I opened the Introduction. On Thucydides' telling, "rule by the first man" does not result from the silencing or "deactivation" of the demos per se. I would suggest instead that Pericles' "free control" follows, on Thucydides' account, precisely from his ability to break the silence of the demos in a particular way. Thucydides thus credits Pericles first with correctly seeing the inclinations or attitudes or state of mind—"unreasonably afraid," "arrogantly confident"—of the demos and then with "leading" rather than "being led." In a sense, Pericles first makes the silence of the demos speak to him and then comes to speak for it. Periclean "rule," that is, marks the coming together of demos and dominant elite in a single voice.

This, in turn, suggests a particular angle of approach to the critique of contemporary mass democracy. Consider, for example, some aspects of political discourse in the United States after the attacks of September 11, 2001. Much has been written about the effective stifling of dissent in that period. Put in the terms I have been using here, for some time after 9/11 the relative silence of contending voices allowed the dominance of a particular strand of patriotic, warlike rhetoric. This rhetoric flowed especially from the Bush administration and its political surrogates and played a central role in that administration's subsequent drive for war with Iraq. The conventional wisdom of empirical political science points toward a deceptively simple explanation for this phenomenon. Under what is known as the "rally 'round the flag effect," U.S. presidents routinely enjoy surges of popular support following moments of national or international crisis. Chomsky and others are surely correct, too, to alert us to both the historical roots of nationalistic propaganda and its continued use by political elites abetted by a compliant mainstream media. The redeployment of such propaganda by an overwhelmingly popular U.S. president surely goes far in accounting for the relative absence of competing accounts of the proper response to 9/11 and, more generally, of the place of the United States in the world.

The reading of Thucydides I have developed here, though, would have us critique more directly the role played in these political developments by the mass of silent citizens—or, more precisely, by the interaction of the silent presence of the demos with elite rhetoric. Consider in this context one of the most quoted lines of Bush's first term in office. Standing atop the rubble of the World Trade Center towers on September 14, 2001, Bush through a bullhorn told an assembled group of rescue workers: "I can hear you, the rest of the world can hear you and the people who knocked these buildings down will hear all of us soon." The remark was (apparently) an improvised response to some in the audience who said they could not hear Bush over the shouts of "U.S.A., U.S.A., U.S.A." But whether utterly spontaneous or not, we might take note of two rhetorical maneuvers that Bush was attempting here. First, he moved from "you" as a reference to the specific crowd before him to "all of us," surely meaning all Americans. Second, he moved from claiming to hear the crowd to a promise to make others hear all Americans. In short, in this brief statement to a group of police officers, firefighters, and paramedics, Bush was claiming to hear and then was promising, in essence, to speak for "all of us" or, if you will, for the silent American demos, which he promised through his actions to make present to the world.[12]

Fundamental institutional and cultural differences aside, the relationship Bush was claiming here with the silent mass of ordinary American citizens was basically analogous to Pericles' relationship with the Athenian demos.[13] This is emphatically *not* to raise Bush to some lofty pedestal of Periclean statesmanship. It is rather to suggest that, besides resting on his surging popularity in the days after 9/11 and the vast flow of positive

---

12. Insofar as it claims to speak for the ordinary citizen and draws on a sense of national identity shaped by an Other that is depicted as a threat to the nation's survival, we might well see Bush's rhetoric as basically populist in character. Here we might say that a Thucydidean sense of the importance of the silence of the demos in the dynamics of mass democracy might add a useful wrinkle to recent thinking about populism, which aims to understand the elite mobilization of the masses. See the essays collected in Panizza, *Populism and the Mirror of Democracy*, especially the contributions by Laclau, Mouffe, and Arditi. See also Canovan, "Populism for Political Theorists?"

13. Here, too, consider Nixon's deployment of the idea of a "silent majority" of Americans who might support his policy in Vietnam, and the frequent claims of various elites to speak for the forgotten American middle class. Nixon first used the term "silent majority" in a White House address on November 3, 1969.

rhetoric from government and media outlets in those days, Bush's political position here hinged on his temporarily successful attempt to let the silence of the American demos speak. What is more, as with Pericles, Bush's success depended in considerable part on central claims about American unity and American identity. Over time, the relationship between the American populace and Bush (or, if one prefers not to focus on a single individual, the Bush administration, or, for that matter, the collectivity of the American political elite, among whom during this period there were distressingly few dissenters) would, of course, fray. There are again any number of explanations ready to hand: the simple passage of time since the "rally event" of 9/11; the reemergence of at least some contending elite voices; and what Guttmann and Thompson see as renewed deliberation over the increasingly undeniable fiasco in Iraq. Again here, though, a Thucydidean sense of the significance of silence in democracy points in another direction. We might say that the character of ordinary citizens' silence eventually changed. In place of a kind of collective silence to which a single elite might successfully give voice, the silence of the demos came again to render it, if not unknowable, at least less clearly knowable. Here witness the renewed struggle among elites in 2006 and 2007 to find the proper rhetorical pitch for discussing the very matters that must have seemed so clear to the president with the bullhorn on September 14.[14]

Ultimately, I mean neither to offer any sort of comprehensive analysis of contemporary American political discourse (as will surely be obvious from the brevity of my remarks) nor (as may be less obvious from the tone of my remarks) to offer a parting partisan screed. Instead, I aim in a more concrete way to suggest the sorts of questions posed by a Thucydidean perspective on mass politics in a nominally democratic polity. There emerges from that perspective a peculiar task if we wish to reinvigorate democracy in the context of contemporary mass politics, as a way to build resistance among ordinary citizens either to particular policies or to elite power more

---

14. The political pundit Joe Klein (of *Primary Colors* fame) recently published a new book bemoaning the state of contemporary American politics and, in particular, of contemporary political rhetoric, which he claims has become altogether mundane and predictable. Klein points longingly toward the Aeschylus-quoting speech of Robert Kennedy in Indianapolis in which the senator announced to a crowd the assassination of Martin Luther King Jr. Klein argues that Kennedy's rhetoric soared in part because he did not know how those silently gathered before him would react. By contrast, he sees contemporary rhetoric as resting on the resolution of the people's silence through public-opinion polling and focus groups. While I mean to make a deeper point about the destabilization of elite rhetoric and control, Klein does here gesture toward the way in which silence may render the demos unknowable to elites. Klein, *Politics Lost*.

generally. Thucydides' account suggests that, absent the reemergence of the sort of "fugitive democracy" that might overwhelm the elite-dominated form of contemporary politics and lead to more fundamental democratic change, some hope is perhaps to be found in ensuring that the demos maintains a proper sort of silence. Note well here that silence does not mean quiet acquiescence of the sort that, as I argued in Chapter 1, allows for the imposition of oligarchy at Athens. Nor would a proper kind of silence turn the ordinary citizen into the kind of spectator that Lippman envisions. As the critique of Chomsky makes clear, the silence of the detached spectator can all too easily be made to provide fodder for the propaganda of elites. As the temporary success of Pericles in reading and "leading" the demos makes clear, elites do not need modern public opinion polling to take advantage of this sort of silence. By contrast, the silence of the demos that emerges in Pericles' third speech, in the Mitylene Debate, and in the assembly that considers the expedition to Sicily renders the mass of ordinary citizens unknown and, in a sense, unknowable to would-be "leaders." If we are not to have a more fully participatory democracy in which all citizens might vocally engage, this kind of mysterious silence may well provide a key to democratic resistance to elite domination.

Thucydides provides us with little guidance on how to encourage the kind of democratic silence that avoids the pitfalls both of Periclean leadership and of quiet oligarchy.[15] In part, this is because of how he treats the demos as a collective force in Athenian politics and because of his relative lack of interest in the political lives of individual ordinary citizens. It is also a result of his obvious concern over the destabilizing tendencies of democracy and silence in the city. At one level, those concerns seem straightforward and familiar. Consider again Thucydides' comments on the fate of the Sicily expedition, which he sets in the context of his analysis of post-Periclean democracy:

> Many mistakes were made, since a great city ruling an empire was involved, especially the expedition to Sicily, which was a mistake not so much of judgment about those they were attacking as because the senders did not subsequently make decisions advantageous for the participants, but by engaging in personal attacks

---

15. I have recently turned to Aristophanes' comedies for help in thinking through the possible ways in which the silent ordinary citizen of mass democracy might resist elite domination of democratic politics. Zumbrunnen, "Elite Domination and the Ordinary Citizen"; "Fantasy, Irony, and Economic Justice in Aristophanes' *Assemblywomen* and *Wealth*."

over the leading position among the common people they both reduced the vigor of the armed forces and for the first time fell into confusion in the administration of the city. (2.65)

At the simplest level here, Thucydides is pointing toward a basic concern about the tendency of elites to chase after what he calls "the people's pleasure" and so of democratic politics to produce frequent and frequently disastrous changes of course. In a cruder version, this concern finds expression elsewhere in the *History* in Cleon's demagogic worry that "democracy is incapable of governing others" because of its "intemperance." In our time, this concern appears in Hanson's concern with domestic "squabbling over Iraq," and even more polemically in the charge that some politicians, pushed by what they wrongly perceive as a wobbly demos, would "cut and run" from military adventures abroad. Worried about the fate of his home city, Thucydides is not above such rudimentary concerns regarding the supposed inability of democracy to defend itself.

But as the arguments of Chapters 5 and 6 suggest, his concerns about the instability wrought by democracy work as well at a much deeper level than the mutability of "foreign policy" in democracy. These deeper concerns flow from his broader thematization of silence as an aspect of the interplay of action and identity. In the context of deliberation as the consideration of rival elite claims about the city and its proper course, the silent presence of the demos destabilizes elite attempts to exert control, thus at once making democracy more than merely nominal and rendering the meaning of the city's course deeply uncertain. More often, as we have seen, Thucydides presents Athens as acting absent this sort of deliberation, with the silence of the demos expanding to engulf all of *hoi Athenaioi*, absent the sort of vocal contention worthy of recording in the *History*. Here, I have argued, the city forfeits all attempts to control the meaning of its actions in the world, any attempt to say who *hoi Athenaioi* are. As a result, others step into the void: those claiming to represent Athens abroad, allies seeking assistance, enemies casting blame. The Athenians, meanwhile, remain a cipher—to others and, one supposes, to themselves. With the case of Plataea in particular in mind, we might say that they in a sense act collectively in the manner of Lippman's ordinary citizen, vaguely aware that events affect them, uncertain how to control them, detached, but ultimately in a way responsible for what occurs. The result is a radical destabilization of the city's understanding of itself and its place in the world, a destabilization that follows not from too much speech, but from too little.

Thucydides, ultimately, finds the "moderate"—and quiet—"blending" of the few and the many under the Government of the 5000 a necessary political expedient for the city, seeing it as providing a temporary stability that allows the city a moment of respite and recovery. We need not agree with that judgment, or with Thucydides' more general concerns about the destabilizing tendencies of democracy, to appreciate the *History*'s portrayal of democracy as a delicate balance of speech and silence. On my reading, the *History* itself embodies a similar sort of balance. We can only appreciate the full complexity of Thucydides' "speech"—his authorial comments, the words he puts in the mouths of his speakers, the structure he gives to his narrative—if we are attentive to the various silences he also allows the *History* to reflect. As I suggested in the Introduction, the play of silence in the *History* gives it an interpretive flexibility that allows and encourages readers—silent though they themselves may be—to question the claims made on the surface of the text. In this sense, we might think of the *History* as itself a fundamentally democratic text, enacting a dynamic relationship between an author trying to craft meaning from the complex world around him and readers alive to the ways in which that world always overwhelms any attempt at interpretive control. Put differently, the *History*, as a "possession for all time" (1.22), encourages among its readers a kind of engagement and criticality that we might hope for among all citizens, even those who remain silent.

BIBLIOGRAPHY

TRANSLATIONS OF THUCYDIDES

Thucydides. *History of the Peloponnesian War* (4 vols.). With an English translation by Charles Forster Smith. Cambridge, Mass.: Harvard University Press, 1991. (Loeb Classical Library; first published in 1919.)
———. *The Peloponnesian War.* Translated with an introduction and notes by Steven Lattimore. Indianapolis: Hackett, 1998.
———. *The Peloponnesian War: A New Translation, Backgrounds and Contexts, Interpretations.* Translated by Walter Blanco, edited by Walter Blanco and Jennifer Tolbert Roberts. New York: W. W. Norton, 1998.
———. *The Peloponnesian War: The Complete Hobbes Translation.* With notes and introduction by David Grene. Chicago: University of Chicago Press, 1989.
———. *The Peloponnesian War: The Crawley Translation.* Revised with an introduction by T. E. Wick. New York: The Modern Library (distributed by McGraw-Hill), 1982.

OTHER SOURCES

Adcock, F. E. *Thucydides and His History.* Cambridge: Cambridge University Press, 1963.
Aeschylus. *Prometheus Bound and Other Plays.* Translated by Philip Vellacott. New York: Penguin Books, 1961.
Ahrensdorf, Peter J. "Thucydides' Realistic Critique of Realism." *Polity* 30 (1997): 231–65.
Arendt, Hannah. *Between Past and Future: Eight Exercises in Political Thought.* New York: Penguin Books, 1968.
———. *The Human Condition.* Chicago: University of Chicago Press, 1953.
Aristotle. *The Ethics of Aristotle.* Translated by J. A. K. Thompson. London: George Allen and Unwin, 1953.
———. *The Nicomachean Ethics.* Translated by H. Rackham. Cambridge, Mass.: Harvard University Press, 1962.
———. *The Nicomachean Ethics.* Translated by David Ross. Oxford: Oxford University Press, 1980.

———. *Nicomachean Ethics*. Translated by T. Irwin. Indianapolis: Hackett, 1985.
———. *The Politics*. Edited by Stephen Everson. Cambridge: Cambridge University Press, 1988.
———. *The Rhetoric and the Poetics of Aristotle*. Introduction by Edward P. J. Corbett. New York: Modern Library, 1984.
Ball, Terence. "The Formation of Character: Mill's 'Ethology' Reconsidered." *Polity* 33 (2000): 25–48.
———. "When Words Lose Their Meaning." *Ethics* 96 (1986): 620–31.
Barber, Benjamin R. *Strong Democracy: Participatory Politics for a New Age*. Berkeley and Los Angeles: University of California Press, 1984.
Bickford, Susan. "Beyond Friendship: Aristotle on Conflict, Deliberation, and Attention." *Journal of Politics* 58 (1996): 398–421.
———. *The Dissonance of Democracy: Listening, Conflict, and Citizenship*. Ithaca: Cornell University Press, 1996.
Bluhm, William. "Causal Theory in Thucydides' Peloponnesian War." *Political Studies* 10 (1962): 15–35.
Botwinick, Aryeh, and William E. Connolly, eds. *Democracy and Vision: Sheldon Wolin and the Vicissitudes of the Political*. Princeton: Princeton University Press, 2001.
Bury, J. B. *The Ancient Greek Historians*. New York: Macmillan, 1909.
Canovan, Margaret. *Hannah Arendt: A Reinterpretation of Her Political Thought*. Cambridge: Cambridge University Press, 1992.
———. "Populism for Political Theorists?" *Journal of Political Ideologies* 9, no. 3 (2004): 241–52.
Carter, L. B. *The Quiet Athenian*. New York: Oxford University Press, 1986.
Chomsky, Noam. *Media Control: The Spectacular Achievements of Propaganda*, 2nd ed. New York: Seven Stories Press, 2002.
Cochrane, Charles Norris. *Thucydides and the Science of History*. London: Oxford University Press, 1929.
Cogan, Marc. *The Human Thing: The Speeches and Principles of Thucydides' History*. Chicago: University of Chicago Press, 1981.
Connolly, William. *Identity/Difference: Democratic Negotiations of Political Paradox*. Ithaca: Cornell University Press, 1991.
Connor, W. Robert. "A Post Modernist Thucydides?" *Classical Journal* 72 (1977): 289–99.
———. *Thucydides*. Princeton: Princeton University Press, 1984.
Cornford, Francis M. *Thucydides Mythistoricus*. London: Edward Arnold, 1907.
Dahl, Robert. *A Preface to Economic Democracy*. Berkeley and Los Angeles: University of California Press, 1985.
———. *Who Governs? Democracy and Power in an American City*. New Haven: Yale University Press, 1961.
Dietz, Mary G. "'The Slow Boring of Hard Boards': Methodical Thinking and the Work of Politics." *American Political Science Review* 88 (1994): 873–86.
Dionysius of Halicarnassus. *On Thucydides*. Translated and with commentary by W. Kendrick Pritchett. Berkeley and Los Angeles: University of California Press, 1975.
Disch, Lisa. *Hannah Arendt and the Limits of Philosophy*. Ithaca: Cornell University Press, 1996.
Donnelly, Jack. *Realism and International Relations*. Cambridge: Cambridge University Press, 2000.

Dover, K. J. *Aristophanic Comedy.* Berkeley and Los Angeles: University of California Press, 1972.
Doyle, Michael W. "Thucydidean Realism." *Review of International Studies* 16 (1990): 223–37.
Edmunds, Lowell. *Chance and Intelligence in Thucydides.* Cambridge, Mass.: Harvard University Press, 1975.
Euben, J. Peter. "Thucydides in the Desert." Paper presented at the 2006 Annual Meeting of the American Political Science Association, Philadelphia.
———. *The Tragedy of Political Theory: The Road Not Taken.* Princeton: Princeton University Press, 1990.
Farrar, Cynthia. *The Origins of Democratic Thinking: The Invention of Politics in Classical Athens.* Cambridge: Cambridge University Press, 1993.
Finley, J. H. *Three Essays on Thucydides.* Cambridge, Mass.: Harvard University Press, 1967.
———. *Thucydides.* Cambridge, Mass.: Harvard University Press, 1942.
Finley, M. I. *Politics in the Ancient World.* Cambridge: Cambridge University Press, 1983.
Fishkin, James. *Democracy and Deliberation.* New Haven: Yale University Press, 1971.
Forde, Steven. *The Ambition to Rule: Alcibiades and the Politics of Imperialism in Thucydides.* Ithaca: Cornell University Press, 1989.
———. "Thucydides on the Causes of Athenian Imperialism." *American Political Science Review* 80 (1986): 433–48.
Friere, Paulo. *Cultural Action for Freedom.* New York: Penguin, 1972.
Fuss, Peter. "Hannah Arendt's Conception of Political Community." In *Hannah Arendt: The Recovery of the Public World.* Edited by Melvyn A. Hill. New York: St. Martin's Press, 1979.
Gaventa, John. *Power and Powerlessness: Quiescence and Rebellion in an Appalachian Valley.* Urbana: University of Illinois Press, 1980.
Gomme, A. W., K. J. Dover, and A. Andrewes. *A Historical Commentary on Thucydides.* Oxford: Clarendon Press, 1945–72.
Grene, David. *Greek Political Theory.* Chicago: University of Chicago Press, 1965.
Gustafson, Lowell S. "Thucydides and Pluralism." In *Thucydides' Theory of International Relations: A Lasting Possession.* Edited by Lowell S. Gustafson. Baton Rouge: Louisiana State University Press, 2000.
Gutmann, Amy, and Dennis Thompson. *Democracy and Disagreement.* Cambridge, Mass.: Belknap Press of Harvard University Press, 1996.
———. *Why Deliberative Democracy?* Princeton: Princeton University Press, 2004.
Habermas, Jürgen. "Three Normative Models of Democracy." In *Democracy and Difference: Contesting the Boundaries of the Political.* Edited by Seyla Benhabib. Princeton: Princeton University Press, 1996.
Hahnel, Robin. *Economic Justice and Democracy.* New York: Routledge, 2005.
Hansen, Phillip. *Hannah Arendt: Politics, History, and Citizenship.* Stanford: Stanford University Press, 1993.
Hanson, Victor David. "Do We Have Enough Troops in Iraq?" *Commentary,* June 2004, 28–32.
Hardt, Michael, and Antonio Negri. *Multitiude: War and Democracy in the Age of Empire.* New York: Penguin Books, 2005.
———. "Old Is New Warfare: Iraq Conflict Shares Uncanny Likenesses with the Peloponnesian War." *National Post,* November 5, 2005.

Hayward, Clarissa Rile. *De-Facing Power*. Cambridge: Cambridge University Press, 2000.
Herodotus. *The Persian Wars*. Translated by George Rawlinson. New York: Modern Library, 1942.
Hobbes, Thomas. "On the Life and History of Thucydides." In *The Peloponnesian War: The Complete Hobbes Translation*. With notes and introduction by David Grene. Chicago: University of Chicago Press, 1989.
Honig, Bonnie. *Political Theory and the Displacement of Politics*. Ithaca: Cornell University Press, 1993.
———. "Toward an Agonistic Feminism: Hannah Arendt and the Politics of Identity." In *Feminist Interpretations of Hannah Arendt*. Edited by Bonnie Honig. University Park: Pennsylvania State University Press, 1995.
Hornblower, Simon. *Thucydides*. Baltimore: Johns Hopkins University Press, 1987.
Hunter, Virginia. *Thucydides: The Artful Reporter*. Toronto: Hakkert, 1973.
Irwin, T. H. "Reason and Responsibility in Aristotle." In *Essays on Aristotle's Ethics*. Edited by Amélie Oksenberg Rorty, 117–57. Berkeley and Los Angeles: University of California Press, 1980.
Jaeger, Werner. *Paideia: The Ideals of Greek Culture*, vol. 1, 2nd ed. Translated by Gilbert Highet. New York: Oxford University Press, 1945.
Jansson, Per. "Identity-Defining Practices in Thucydides' *History of the Peloponnesian War*." *European Journal of International Relations* 3 (1997): 147–65.
Johnson, Laurie M. *Thucydides, Hobbes, and the Interpretation of Realism*. DeKalb: Northern Illinois University Press, 1993.
Jones, A. H. M. *Athenian Democracy*. Oxford: Basil Blackwell and Mott, 1957.
Kagan, Donald. *The Archidamian. War*. Ithaca: Cornell University Press, 1974.
———. *The Peace of Nicias and the Sicilian Expedition*. Ithaca: Cornell University Press, 1981.
Kagan, Robert. "On Iraq, Short Memories." *Washington Post*, September 12, 2005, A19.
Kennedy, George. *The Art of Persuasion in Ancient Greece*. Princeton: Princeton University Press, 1963.
Keohane, Robert O. "Realism and the Study of World Politics." In *Neorealism and Its Critics*. Edited by Robert O. Keohane. New York: Columbia University Press, 1986.
Klein, Joe. *Politics Lost: How American Democracy Was Trivialized by People Who Think You're Stupid*. New York: Doubleday, 2006.
Lebow, Richard Ned. "Thucydides the Constructivist." *American Political Science Review* 95 (2001): 547–60.
———. *The Tragic Vision of Politics: Ethics, Interests, and Orders*. Cambridge: Cambridge University Press, 2003.
Lippman, Walter. *The Phantom Public*. New York: Transaction Publishers, 1993.
Locke, John. *Second Treatise of Government*. Edited by C. B. Macpherson. Indianapolis: Hackett, 1980.
Loraux, Nicole. *The Invention of Athens: The Funeral Oration in the Classical City*. Translated by Alan Sheridan. Cambridge, Mass.: Harvard University Press, 1986.
Markell, Pachen. "The Rule of the People: Arendt, *Arche*, and Democracy." *American Political Science Review* 100, no. 1 (2006): 1–14.
Mill, John Stuart. *On Liberty and Other Writings*. Cambridge: Cambridge University Press, 1989.

———. *A System of Logic: Ratiocinative and Inductive.* London: Longmans, 1961.

Monoson, S. Sara, and Michael Loriaux. "The Illusion of Power and the Disruption of Moral Norms: Thucydides' Critique of Periclean Policy." *American Political Science Review* 92 (1998): 285–97.

Montiglio, Silvia. *Silence in the Land of Logos.* Princeton: Princeton University Press, 2000.

Morgenthau, Hans J. *Politics Among Nations,* 5th ed. New York: Alfred A. Knopf, 1978.

Mouffe, Chantal. "Democracy, Power, and the Political." In *Democracy and Difference.* Ed. Seyla Benhabib. Princeton: Princeton University Press, 1996.

Nietzsche, Friedrich. *Twilight of the Idols / The Anti-Christ.* Translated by R. J. Hollingdale; introduction by Michael Tanner. New York: Penguin Books, 1990.

Nussbaum, Martha C. *The Fragility of Goodness: Luck and Ethics in Greek Philosophy.* Cambridge: Cambridge University Press, 1986.

Ober, Josiah. *The Athenian Revolution: Essays on Ancient Greek Democracy and Political Theory.* Princeton: Princeton University Press, 1996.

———. *Political Dissent in Democratic Athens: Elite Critics of Popular Rule.* Princeton: Princeton University Press, 1998.

———. *Mass and Elite in Democratic Athens: Rhetoric, Ideology, and the Power of the People.* Princeton: Princeton University Press, 1989.

Orwin, Clifford. *The Humanity of Thucydides.* Princeton: Princeton University Press, 1994.

———. "The Just and the Advantageous in Thucydides: The Case of the Mytilenian Debate." *American Political Science Review* 78 (1984): 485–94.

Palmer, Michael. *Love of Glory and the Common Good: Aspects of the Political Thought of Thucydides.* Lanham, Md.: Rowman and Littlefield, 1992.

Panizza, Francisco, ed. *Populism and the Mirror of Democracy.* New York: Verso Books, 2005.

Parry, Adam. "Thucydides' Historical Perspective." *Yale Classical Studies* 22 (1973): 47–61.

Pateman, Carol. *Participation and Democracy.* Cambridge: Cambridge University Press, 1975.

Pitkin, Hanna Fenichel. *The Attack of the Blob: Hannah Arendt's Concept of the Social.* Chicago: University of Chicago Press, 1998.

Plato. *The Last Days of Socrates.* Translated and with an introduction by Hugh Tredennick. New York: Penguin Books, 1969.

———. *The Republic.* Translated by G. M. A. Grube. Revised by C. D. C. Reeve. Indianapolis: Hackett, 1992.

Polsby, Nelson. *Community Power and Political Theory.* New Haven: Yale University Press, 1963.

Pouncey, Peter. R. *The Necessities of War: A Study of Thucydides' Pessimism.* New York: Columbia University Press, 1980.

Price, Jonathan J. *Thucydides and Internal War.* Cambridge: Cambridge University Press, 2001.

Proctor, Dennis. *The Experience of Thucydides.* Warminster: Arts and Phillips, 1980.

Rancière, Jacques. *Hatred of Democracy.* Translated by Steve Corcoran. New York: Verso, 2006.

———. *On the Shores of Politics.* Translated by Liz Heron. New York: Verso Books, 1995.

———. "Ten Theses on Politics." *Theory and Event* 5, no. 3 (2001).

Reeve, C. D. C. "Thucydides on Human Nature." *Political Theory* 27 (1999): 435–46.
Romilly, Jacqueline de. *Thucydides and Athenian Imperialism.* Translated by Philip Thody. Oxford: Basil Blackwell, 1963.
Ruderman, Richard S. "Aristotle and the Recovery of Political Judgment." *American Political Science Review* 91 (1997): 409–20.
Salkever, Stephen. 1990. *Finding the Mean: Theory and Practice in Aristotelian Political Philosophy.* Princeton: Princeton University Press, 1990.
Saxonhouse, Arlene W. *Athenian Democracy: Modern Mythmakers and Ancient Theorists.* Notre Dame: University of Notre Dame Press, 1996.
Sinclair, Robert K. *Democracy and Participation in Athens.* Cambridge: Cambridge University Press, 1988.
Smith, Michael Joseph. *Realist Thought from Weber to Kissinger.* Baton Rouge: Louisiana State University Press, 1986.
Ste. Croix, G. E. M. de. "The Constitution of the Five Thousand," *Historia* 5 (1956): 1–23.
Strauss, Leo. *The City and Man.* Chicago: Rand McNally, 1964.
Stockton, David. *The Classical Athenian Democracy.* Oxford: Oxford University Press, 1990.
Vernant, Jeane-Pierre, and Pierre Vidal-Naquet. *Myth and Tragedy in Ancient Greece.* New York: Zone Books, 1988.
Villa, Dana R. *Arendt and Heidegger: The Fate of the Political.* Princeton: Princeton University Press, 1996.
———. *Politics, Philosophy, Terror: Essays on the Thought of Hannah Arendt.* Princeton: Princeton University Press, 1999.
Westlake, H. D. *Individuals in Thucydides.* Cambridge: Cambridge University Press, 1968.
White, James Boyd. *When Words Lose Their Meaning: Constitutions and Reconstitutions of Language, Character, and Community.* Chicago: University of Chicago Press, 1984.
Wiggins, David. "Deliberation and Practical Reason." In *Essays on Aristotle's Ethics.* Edited by Amélie Oksenberg Rorty. Berkeley and Los Angeles: University of California Press, 1980.
Wolin, Sheldon. "Fugitive Democracy." In *Democracy and Difference: Contesting the Boundaries of the Political.* Ed. Seyla Benhabib. Princeton: Princeton University Press, 1996.
———. "Norm and Form: The Constitutionalizing of Democracy." In J. Peter Euben, John R. Wallach, and Josiah Ober, eds. *Athenian Political Thought and the Reconstruction of American Democracy.* Ithaca: Cornell University Press, 1994.
Woodhead, A. Geoffrey. *Thucydides on the Nature of Power.* Cambridge, Mass.: Harvard University Press, 1970.
Yunis, Harvey. *Taming Democracy: Models of Political Rhetoric in Classical Athens.* Ithaca: Cornell University Press, 1996.
Zumbrunnen, John. "Courage in the Face of Reality: Nietzsche's Admiration for Thucydides." *Polity* 35, no. 2 (2002): 237–63.
———. "Elite Domination and the Ordinary Citizen: Aristophanes' *Archarnians* and *Knights*," *Political Theory* 23, no. 5 (2004): 656–77.
———. "Fantasy, Irony, and Economic Justice in Aristophanes' *Assemblywomen* and *Wealth*." *American Political Science Review* 100 (August 2006): 319–33.

INDEX

accuracy (*akribeia*), 48, 93
Aeschylus, 129–30
Alcibiades
   and Athenian stasis, 31–33, 37–38
   and debate on Athenian expedition to Sicily, 81–82, 114–24, 129
   on justice and the Athenian empire, 134–35
   and the U.S. war in Iraq, 181–82
Arendt, Hannah
   and character or identity, 75, 77–78, 83–84
   and instrumental thinking, 62–63, 66–67, 178
   and storytelling, 93
   understanding of human plurality, 60–61
Aristophanes, 47, 189n15
Aristotle
   on action taken "on the spur of the moment," 51–52
   on character, 75–76
   on deliberation, wish and choice, 51, 56–58
   on democracy, 127
   on rhetoric, 80, 88–90, 177n13
   on voluntary vs. involuntary action, 68–69, 179
Athenian empire
   Alcibiades on, 134–35
   Athenian envoys on, 141–48
   Cleon and Diodotus on, 135–38
   Pericles on, 133–34
   and trial of Plataeans, 173–74
"Athenian thesis," 78, 128–29, 137, 144

Bush, George W., 181–88

Character (*tropos*)
   as actions, not traits, 74–79
   Athenian, 71–94
   Athenian vs. Spartan, 34, 72–73 142–43
   as subject of deliberation, 60, 81–87, 95–96
   Thucydides' authorial comment on, 71–72, 91–94, 97
Chomsky, Noam, 184–85, 189
Cleverness (*dexiotes*), 110–11
Cleon
   and Athenian character, 79
   on Athenian democratic politics, 45–47, 95–96, 108–14, 190
   and debate on Sicily expedition, 116–21
   on justice and the Athenian empire, 135–38, 148, 158–59
   in Mitylene Debate, 5, 63–66, 81, 154, 163
   and Nicias, 115
consent, 9–10
constructivism, 13, 16–19, 29, 88–89
Corcyra, 1, 28–31, 40, 80, 146, 160
Corinth/Corinthians
   analysis of Athenian and Spartan character, 35, 71–72, 77–79, 80, 99
   on justice and the Athenian empire, 142–45, 149

deliberation
   Aristotle on, 51, 56–58
   and Athenian character (*tropos*), 85–87, 116
   Cleon's critique of, 45–46, 109, 136
   and "decline" of Athenian politics, 96–96, 124, 158–59, 179–80
   and Pericles and Themistocles, 104–5
   See also deliberative action

INDEX   199

deliberative action
  and Athenian character (*tropos*), 73, 79, 84, 96–97
  defined, 50, 125
  Mitylene Debate as, 57–62, 108
  Pericles' Funeral Oration as, 90
  Pericles' third speech as, 99
  See also deliberation
deliberative democracy, 6–7, 183–84, 188
Diodotus
  on Athenian democratic politics, 95–96, 108–14
  and debate on Sicily expedition, 116–21
  on justice and the Athenian empire, 135–38, 158–59
  in Mitylene Debate, 5, 46, 63–66, 83–87, 154, 163
Dionysius of Halicarnassus, 131, 149

envoys (*presbeis*)
  Athenians at Melos, 129–31, 139–41, 145–54, 159, 164
  Athenians at Sparta, 128–30, 139–45, 147–48, 152–53
  Plataeans at Athens, 166

Five Thousand, government of, in Athens, 2, 39–41, 191
Four Hundred, government of, in Athens, 37–41

herald (*kerykos*)
  Athenian at Delos, 139–40, 142, 148
  Athenian at Plataea, 159, 161, 163–64, 174–75
Herodotus, 129–30
Hippocratic medicine, 30, 79n1
Hobbes, Thomas, 1, 18–19, 49n8, 97

ignorance (*amathia*), 110–11
intelligence (*gnome*), 101, 104–5
Iraq, war in, 181–84, 186–90

justice
  Alcibiades on, 134–35
  and Athenian democratic politics, 125–32
  Athenian envoys on, 141–48
  changing role of in the *History*, 158, 177–79
  in Mitylene Debate, 58, 63, 135–38
  Pericles on, 133–34

knowledge of what is necessary (*ta deonta*), 104, 110

Lippman, Walter, 184–85, 189–90
Locke, John, 9

Melian Dialogue, 125–26, 129–31, 139–41, 145–50, 157–60, 177–79
Mill, John Stuart, 76n13
Mitylene/Mitylenians
  and Athenian action at Plataea, 157–60, 170–72, 177–79
  and Athenian responsibility, 67–69
  revolt against Athens, 51–56
  See also Mitylene Debate
Mitylene Debate, 185, 189,
  and Athenian democratic politics, 45–51, 63–66, 81–88, 108–14, 185, 189
  justice and the Athenian empire in, 135–38
  See also Mitylene/Mitylenians
mob (*ochlos*), 32–33, 36, 37–40
Nicias
  and Athenian character, 79, 174n21
  and debate on Athenian expedition to Sicily, 5, 81–82, 114–24, 135
  lack of political judgment, 97
  and the U.S. war in Iraq, 181–82
Nietzsche, Friedrich, 19–20, 49n8, 78n18, 90n52

oligarchy. *See* Five Thousand, government of in Athens; Four Hundred, government of in Athens

Pericles
  on Athenian democratic politics, 97–107
  and debate on Athenian expedition to Sicily, 116–17, 119–20
  eulogy of, 1–3, 32, 97–98, 115
  first speech in *History*, 5, 7, 100–101, 133, 162–63
  Funeral Oration, 4–7, 47, 68, 77, 81, 87–91
  and George W. Bush, 182–83, 185–91
  on justice and Athenian empire, 45, 132–35, 148
  and Mitylene Debate, 108–114, 119–20
  and Plataea, 166–67, 170
  third speech in *History*, 4, 6–7, 46, 98–107, 133, 136
Persian wars, 92n54, 143, 160, 167, 172–73
Plataea/Plataeans, 35, 54–55, 126, 157–180
Plato, 3n6, 19, 47, 78, 98, 127
plurality
  and Athenian "character," 79, 85
  and Athenian envoys, 125, 153–54

and deliberative action, 59–62, 95–96
and Mitylene debate, 83, 88, 90, 108, 138
and Pericles' Funeral Oration, 88, 90, 108
and Pericles' third speech in the *History*, 135
and representation, 150
and sudden action, 64–65

quiet (*hesychia*), 34–38

Rancière, Jacques, 3, 61, 185
realism, 13–16, 73, 79, 84n38, 182
representation, 138–140, 150–53
responsibility
    of Athenians for fate of Mitylene, 67–69
    of Athenians for fate of Plataea, 171–76, 179–80
    in debate on Athenian expedition to Sicily, 114–15
    Diodotus on, 111–12
    Pericles on, 99–101

Salamis, battle of, 76–77
Samos, Athenian forces on, 31, 37, 39
Sicily, Athenian debate regarding, 5, 114–24, 134–35, 181–83
silence. *See* silence of contending voices, silent presence of demos
silence of contending voices
    and Athenian response to revolt of Mitylene, 56
    and Athenian role in Plataea, 132, 159–60
    and constructivism, 18
    defined, 4–5
    and deliberation, 6–7
    and democratic equality, 6
    and Hobbes, 19
    and Pericles, 4–5, 88, 97, 102
    and "quiet" (*hesychia*), 36
    and realism, 14, 16
    and U.S. response to 9/11 attacks, 186
silent presence of demos
    and acquiescence or consent, 9–10
    and Athenian "character" (*tropos*), 85–88, 93
    and Athenian envoys, 125, 130, 132, 148
    and Athenian expedition to Sicily, 120–22
    and Athenian response to revolt of Mitylene, 56, 60–62, 73, 113–14, 117, 135
    and Athenian role in Plataea, 159–60, 176–80
    and constructivism, 18
    defined, 7, 12
    and Hobbes, 19
    and listening, 8–9
    and Pericles, 90, 102, 107, 185–86
    and "quiet" (*hesychia*), 36
    and realism, 19
    and Thucydides' silence, 93
    and U.S. response to 9/11 attacks, 186–91
Socrates. *See* Plato
Sparta/Spartans
    character, 71–72, 78–79
    conference at (Book I), 125–26, 138, 140–45, 147–49
    and Plataea, 35n19, 165–67, 172–76
stasis
    at Athens, 31–32, 36–41
    at Corcyra, 1, 28–31
sudden action
    and Arendt's "fundamental experience of instrumentality," 62–66, 84
    and Aristotle's action taken "on the spur of the moment," 51
    and Athenian envoys, 125
    and Athenian response to revolt of Mitylene, 51–56
    and Athenian role in Plataea, 160–61, 164, 178–80
    defined, 50
    and Melian Dialogue, 154–55

Thebes/Thebans, 160–61, 167, 172–76
Themistocles, 103–9

unity
    and Athenian "character," 79, 85
    and Athenian envoys, 125, 130–32, 153–54
    and deliberative action, 59–62, 95–96
    and Mitylene debate, 83, 90, 108, 138
    and Pericles' Funeral Oration, 90, 108
    and representation, 150
    and sudden action, 64–65, 161, 168, 172

"war on terror," 181–84, 186–90
Wolin, Sheldon, 2–3, 7, 24, 27, 61, 185

www.ingramcontent.com/pod-product-compliance
Lightning Source LLC
Chambersburg PA
CBHW031551300426
44111CB00006BA/264